THE AUSTRALIAN ARCHAEOLOGICAL INSTITUTE
AT ATHENS

NUMISMATIC ARCHAEOLOGY
ARCHAEOLOGICAL NUMISMATICS

Proceedings of an International Conference held to honour Dr. Mando Oeconomides in Athens 1995

Edited by

K.A. Sheedy

and

Ch. Papageorgiadou-Banis

OXBOW MONOGRAPH 75

First published in the United Kingdom in 1997. Reprinted in 2017 by
OXBOW BOOKS
The Old Music Hall, 106–108 Cowley Road, Oxford OX4 1JE

and in the United States by
OXBOW BOOKS
1950 Lawrence Road, Havertown, PA 19083

Paperback Edition: ISBN 978-1-90018-823-4
Digital Edition: ISBN 978-1-78570-769-8

A CIP record for this book is available from the British Library

For a complete list of Oxbow titles, please contact:

UNITED KINGDOM
Oxbow Books
Telephone (01865) 241249
Fax (01865) 794449
Email: oxbow@oxbowbooks.com
www.oxbowbooks.com

UNITED STATES OF AMERICA
Oxbow Books
Telephone (800) 791-9354
Fax (610) 853-9146
Email: queries@casemateacademic.com
www.casemateacademic.com/oxbow

Oxbow Books is part of the Casemate Group

CONTENTS

PREFACE

The fourteen papers in this volume were presented at an international conference, *Archaeological Numismatics/ Numismatic Archaeology*, held at the Akropolis Studies Centre on the 31st May and the 1st June 1995. The conference was jointly organised by a committee representing the Athens Numismatic Museum, the National Hellenic Research Foundation, the British School at Athens, and the Australian Archaeological Institute at Athens. The committee consisted of Dr I. Touratsoglou, Dr Ch. Papageorgiadou-Banis, Dr M.J. Price† (replaced by Dr R.A. Tomlinson) and Dr K.A. Sheedy.

The theme of the conference, as its title indicates, was the on-going relationship of numismatic research to the wider discipline of archaeology. This seemed highly appropriate given the importance of the research facilities in Athens for the study of coins as archaeological artefacts recovered from excavations and as archaeological evidence in an increasing range of field studies. The Athens Numismatic Museum has been, of course, the great repository for all important coin finds in Greece (as well as a museum for significant numismatic donations). Its staff are regularly asked to assist with the identification of coins found by Greek and foreign archaeologists. The conference theme was also prompted, however, by a growing awareness that the disciplines of archaeology and numismatics were, after a century or so of ready interaction which had seen both grow in strength, now undergoing a period of estrangement. Numismatic research is more and more becoming the domain of 'coin specialists'.

Dr Mando Oeconomides retired from the position of Director of the Athens Numismatic Museum in 1994. It would be fair to say that over the many years in which she had served as Director of this great museum she herself had become an institution not only in the world of numismatics but also within the archaeological community of Greece. The conference and this volume of papers are dedicated to Dr Oeconomides.

In 1994 Dr Martin Price, formerly Deputy Keeper of Coins and Medals at the British Museum, returned to Greece as the newly appointed Director of the British School at Athens. He had been Dr Oeconomides' first pupil, and was now established as one of the most distinguished numismatists in the world. Martin relished the opportunity to hold this conference, and was delighted with the fact that it would honour Dr Oeconomides. It was with great sadness that we learnt that Martin Price had passed away one month before the conference. His loss has been keenly felt by all.

The conference brought together some of Dr Oeconomides colleagues and former students who have worked with her in Athens. It could not hope to include the many numismatists and archaeologists who visited the museum while Dr Oeconomides was Director and who had sought access to the collection, as well as her assistance in studying material. Instead it was intended simply to bring together a number of friends and colleagues who were then in Athens or who could be persuaded to visit Greece at that time and speak to the conference on an archaeological theme.

This is the second volume of papers to be published by the Australian Archaeological Institute at Athens (in conjunction with Oxbow Books). The kindness of the Council and Director of the Institute in making available this avenue for publication as well as allowing the Institute's Deputy Director, Kenneth Sheedy, to devote time and resources to the project is gratefully acknowledged. The editors wish to thank Jan Casson Medhurst, Dr Martin Kreeb and Professor V. Mitsopoulos Leon for their assistance in the production of the book.

K.A. Sheedy
Ch. Papageorgiadou-Banis

On numismatics and archaeology

ΑΡΧΑΙΟΛΟΓΙΚΗ ΝΟΜΙΣΜΑΤΙΚΗ
ΝΟΜΙΣΜΑΤΙΚΗ ΑΡΧΑΙΟΛΟΓΙΑ

I. Touratsoglou

Προϊόντα μαζικής παραγωγής, τα νομίσματα, η πρωτογενής αυτή πηγή γνώσης του παρελθόντος, παρουσιάζουν πλεονεκτήματα απέναντι στα υπόλοιπα αντικείμενα της ανθρώπινης δραστηριότητας από την αρχαιότητα.

Παρά τη λακωνικότητα των επιμέρους στοιχείων που περιέχουν και το μικρό τους μέγεθος, αντιπαραθέτουν στα έργα της μεγάλης τέχνης — γλυπτική, ζωγραφική-, στις επιγραφές και τους παπύρους, στους κώδικες, στα δημιουργήματα του κεραμικού τροχού και της μεταλλοτεχνίας, την πολλαπλότητα, το απείρως επαναλαμβανόμενο και το πανταχού παρόν.

Με την αντοχή στό χρόνο εγγυώνται την επαλήθευση της πιστότητας της μεταγραφής των μηνυμάτων που μεταφέρουν και επιτρέπουν την επιβεβαίωση των πληροφοριών — εικονιστικών ή και λεκτικής συνθηματολογίας — πού κομίζουν, με την ιστορημένη στιγμή που εσωκλείουν, μεταδίδουν ως αυτόπτες μάρτυρες γεγονότα και συμβάντα άγνωστα πολλές φορές από άλλες πηγές, συμβάλλοντας παράλληλα σε μια σφαιρικότερη και αντικειμενικότερη κατανόηση του ιστορικού γίγνεσθαι.

Πέρα από τη συμμετοχή τους στην πληρέστερη διαγραφή της ιστορίας της καλλιτεχνικής δημιουργίας με την απεικόνιση ακόμη και χαμένων αριστουργημάτων, τα νομίσματα συνεισφέρουν στην κατανόηση της οικονομικής κατάστασης ενός κράτους και των κατά καιρούς διακυμάνσεών της, σαν άλλα μέσα μαζικής ενημέρωσης αλλά και επιβολής/διασποράς ειδήσεων, προσφέρονται για τη διάδοση πολιτικών μηνυμάτων, τη γνωστοποίηση πολιτειακών μεταβολών, μετακινήσεων στρατευμάτων και ατόμων για εμπορικές συναλλαγές.

Με τις παραστάσεις των όψεών τους αιχμαλωτίζουν το φθαρτό των χαρακτήρων, εξιδανικεύουν αλλά και απαθανατίζουν το εφήμερο. Μεταβάλλονται σε κήρυκες, σήματα λαλούντα ιδεών, ονομάτων, προϊόντων — της προκοπής και της παράδοσης κάθε τόπου.

Πινακοθήκη των μορφών επιφανών θνητών και των αθάνατων κυρίων του ουράνιου Πανθέου, συντροφεύουν τους ανθρώπους στην τελευταία τους κατοικία μαζί με άλλα κτερίσματα, τοποθετούνται στα θεμέλια οικιών και ναών ως αποτρόπαια και ταλισμανικά αντικείμενα, θάβονται σε μέρη απόκρυφα, αποταμίευση των κόπων απλών ιδιωτών, λεία κακοποιών, ή ως μισθοί στρατιωτικών αγημάτων. Ενταφιάζονται μαζί με τους κατόχους τους κάτω από ερείπια, μάρτυρες ακατάγραφων καταστροφών, ή ξεπλένονται στα συντρίμια κάποιου ξέστρατου σκάφους, στα βάθη της θάλασσας.

Με τη λάμψη τους στολίζουν την ανθρώπινη ματαιοδοξία σε γυναικείους, ως επί το πλείστον, λαιμούς και δάκτυλα και διακοσμούν πολυποίκιλτα σκεύη, πλούσιων εραστών του χρήματος και της τέχνης πολυαγαπημένα αποκτήματα. Γήινα όσο και θεϊκά, ταξιδεύουν με θεϊκή αιωνιότητα στα πέρατα του γήινου κόσμου. Σαν το φως, που θερμαίνει αλλά και τυφλώνει, τρυπώνουν παντού. Πιστά όσο και άπιστα, δε γνωρίζουν θεό. Και εξαγοράζουν συνειδήσεις, επιβραβεύουν την άμιλλα, προδίδουν λαούς, αποτιμούν την ελευθερία, δίνουν σάρκα και οστά στη δύναμη.

Τα νομίσματα που λατρεύτηκαν, που λατρεύονται, ως θεοί.

Έστω και με την πλαστική τους μορφή στην εποχή μας.

Προϊόντα μαζικής παραγωγής, τα νομίσματα, η πρωτογενής αυτή πηγή γνώσης του παρελθόντος, αυτοσκοπός στο στόχαστρο μιας κατεξοχήν επίπονης και λεπτολόγου έρευνας, που προϋποθέτει πλήθος παντοδαπών γνώσεων, ερμηνευτές πολύπειροι δυσερμήνευτων αρχαιογνωστικών καταστάσεων και δυσεπίλυτων αρχαιολογικών προβληματισμών, καλούνται να παίξουν τό ρόλο που τους καθόρισε η συμμετοχή τους ταυτόχρονα στό ευτελές και στο αιώνιο. Καλούνται να υποδυθούν την ειδοποιό διαφορά, τον καταλύτη, ανάμεσα στον ωραίο γρίφο της τέχνης και στον κονιορτό μιας ανώνυμης καθημερινότητας. Να συνταιριάσουν σε αρμονικό σύνολο κάτω από τη σκέπη της Ιστορίας τις διάφορες και διαφορετικές μεταξύ τους εκφάνσεις της ανθρώπινης μεγαλοσύνης και ταπεινότητας.

Μια αρχαιογνωσία περισσότερο πραγματιστική, περισσότερο δυναμική, περισσότερο αληθοφανής, μια αρχαιολογία λιγότερο τέχνης, αισθαντική, καταγραφή, λιγότερο ιστορία διαίσθησης, λιγότερο απαρίθμηση τυπολατρική σχημάτων και απρόσωπων ιστορικών γεγονότων σε παρατακτική φορά, μόνο η συντονισμένη, αλληλοελεγχόμενη και αλληλοεπιβεβαιούμενη αντιπαράθεση των αποτελεσμάτων της έρευνας — της τεκμηριωμένης έρευνας — των δραστηριοτήτων περισοτέρων της μιας τέχνης, μπορεί να εγγυηθεί καί να υποσχεθεί.

Για τη νομισματική, η αυτοελεγχόμενη έρευνα — με ελάχιστες

εξαιρέσεις υπερβασιών και ευφάνταστων θεωριών που εύκολα ανιχνεύονται ως απορριπτέες — αποτελεί πρακτική δοκιμασμένη και επιβαλλόμενη από το ίδιο το υλικό. Αποτελεί μέθοδο με αυστηρή εσωτερική νομοτέλεια, που διέπεται από τις αρχές της ταυτότητας και όχι της απλής ομοιότητας. Τους νόμους της σειραϊκής ομαδοποίησης, με ζεύγη και τρίδυμα παραγωγής σε συμπλεκτική κατά μήτρες φορά, γεγονός που επιτρέπει τη συγκρότηση σωμάτων αξιόπιστης πληροφόρησης.

Είτε πρόκειται για σύνταξη νομισματικών συνταγμάτων (corpora), είτε για εργασίες καταγραφής και σφυγμομέτρησης της νομισματικής κυκλοφορίας, ακόμη και για συνθέσεις με θέμα τη νομισματική εικονογραφία, η συλλογιστική προσέγγισης του αντικειμένου διέπεται από τίς ίδιες απαραβίαστες αρχές μιας καταξιωμένης δεοντολογίας αλυσσιδωτής αναστρεψιμότητας.

Με αυτή της την ιδιότητα, αυτή την αυτοπειθαρχία και αυτές τις δυνατότητες, η νομισματική καλείται να αναπτύξει πρωτοβουλίες δασκάλου και μαθητού. Δασκάλου αναφορικά με τη μεθοδολογία που χρησιμοποιεί για νά προσεγγίσει το αντικείμενό της από πολλαπλές, φαινομενικά ετερόκλητες, οπτικές γωνίες. Μαθητού, για να διδαχτεί από τα επιτεύγματα και τα πορίσματα άλλων αρχαιογνωστικών επιστημών, εφοδιασμένων με περισσότερα αποδεικτικά στοιχεία.

`Ολο και περισσότερο αποδεικνύεται η αποτελεσματικότητα των νομισματικών μαρτυριών — ιδιαίτερα στην περίπτωση έλλειψης επιγραφικής επιβεβαίωσης — στον εντοπισμό αρχαίων τόπων γνωστών μόνο από φιλολογικές πηγές ή και άγνωστων από αλλού (νομίσμα Δικαίας στη Θέρμη Θεσσαλονίκης, νόμισμα Αιγών στη Βεργίνα, νομίσματα Ζώνης στην αιγαιακή Μεσημβρία, νομίσματα Ακάνθου και Ουρανουπόλεως στην Ιερισσό).

Ολο και περισσότερο γίνεται κατανοητό, σχεδόν αυταπόδεικτο, ότι ο χρονολογημένος κατειργασμένος χρυσός και άργυρος, ο χρονολογημένος πηλός, κοντολογής τα κλειστά σύνθετα σύνολα, είναι αυτά που θα υφάνουν, κατατεταγμένα σε προσθετική διάταξη επικαλυπτομένων περιπτώσεων, πρώτα κατά την οριζόντια γεωγραφική παράθεση και στη συνέχεια κατά την κατακόρυφη χρονολογική κατηγοριοποίηση, το στέρεο εκείνο καμβά πάνω στον οποίο θα περάσουν τα υφάδια μιας γνώσης ταυτόχρονα επαγωγικής όσο και αναλυτικής.

Τα παραδείγματα δε λείπουν και για τις δυό όψεις ενός και του αυτού νομίσματος. Τα τελευταία δημοσιεύματα που πιστοποιούν τη σταδιακή άνοδο του αριθμού περιπτώσεων αγαστής συνεργασίας και ανταλλαγής πληροφοριών και προβληματισμών, πλεονάζουν στον τομέα της κεραμικής. Τα παραδείγματα αφορούν σε ουσιαστικές ανακατατάξεις της κεραμικής παραγωγής κυρίως των υστεροκλασικών και των μετακλασικών χρόνων με καίριες επιπτώσεις στην ορθή, πολυδιάστατη και διεπιστημονική ανάλυση των εμπλεκομένων στοιχείων και στην κατανόηση αιτίων και αιτιατών.

Η αναχρονολόγηση της πρώιμης ελληνιστικής κεραμικής του αττικού εργαστηρίου, για παράδειγμα, έργο πρωτίστως της ίδιας εκείνης αγγλοσαξωνικής σχολής, που στη δεκαετία του 1930 με τον Homer Thompson έθετε τις βάσεις για μια διαχρονική μελέτη της αθηναϊκής αγγειοπλαστικής κυρίως των μεταλεξάνδρειων χρόνων (κωδικοποιήθηκε κατά τον καλύτερο δυνατό τρόπο από τους Sparkes-Talcott), δεν θα είχε οπωσδήποτε επιχειρηθεί αν δεν είχαν τεθεί τα εύλογα όσο και ανατρεπτικά ερωτηματικά των νομισματικών ευρημάτων στο πτολεμαϊκό στρατόπεδο της Κορώνης, τόσο υποδειγματικά ανεσκαμμένο από την ομάδα των Vanderpool, McCredie και Steinberg, και δεν είχαν εκφραστεί οι σκεπτικισμοί των Jones, Graham και Sackett, πεπειραμένων και ευσυνείδητων ανασκαφέων της αγροικίας στη Βάρη της Αττικής.

Οι θεμελιακές εργασίες του John Kroll, επιστέγασμα των οποίων υπήρξε ο τελευταίος τόμος της σειράς *The Athenian Agora* (XXVI, *The Greek Coins*, 1994), δε συνέβαλαν μόνο στην αναθεώρηση των γνώσεών μας για την αθηναϊκή νομισματοκοπία, ιδιαίτερα αυτή των χαλκών εκδόσεων. Ανασκαφικά ευρήματα σε κλειστά ταφικά σύνολα ή οικιστικά στρώματα κεραμικής, τα νομίσματα αυτά από την αθηναϊκή Αγορά και τον Κεραμεικό, αποτέλεσαν τον αποφασιστικό εκείνο παράγοντα και το ασφαλές σημείο αναφοράς για τις εποικοδομητικές χρονολογικές αναθεωρήσεις της παραγωγής του αθηναϊκού κεραμικού τροχού στο δεύτερο μισό του 4ου αι.π.Χ. και στο πρώτο του 3ου, πρωτίστως από τη Susan Rotroff και στη συνέχεια από τους Ursula Knigge και W. Kowacskovics, Karin Braun, Schöne-Denkinger, Vogeikof και Stichel.

Παραλαμβάνοντας τη σκυτάλη, ενεργώντας ωστόσο ανεξάρτητα, ορισμένοι έλληνες μελετητές των πλούσιων και σε κεραμικά κτερίσματα παντός τύπου τάφων στη Μακεδονία, επιβεβαίωσαν, σε δημοσιευμένα και σε υπό δημοσίευση συγγράμματα, τα πορίσματα των ερευνών των "νοτίων" συναδέλφων τους: με την αποφασιστική συνδρομή των μεθοδικών και λεπτολόγων συμβολών μιας Margaret Thompson και των μνημειακών συνθέσεων ενός Georges Le Rider και ενός Martin Price, έργων τα οποία με περισσή οξυδέρκεια και επιστημονική πληρότητα διήλθαν τη νομισματοκοπία του Φιλίππου Β', του Αλεξάνδρου Γ' και του Φιλίππου Γ' του Αρριδαίου, οι Στέλλα Δρούγου, Πέτρος Θέμελης και Κατερίνα Ρωμιοπούλου μαζί με τόν Γιάννη Τουράτσογλου, και στο κατόπιν μερικώς οι Βικτώρια Αλλαμανή, Κατερίνα Τζαναβάρη και Μαρία Λιλιμπάκη, αξιοποίησαν τα νέα και πολλαπλά μηνύματα της αναθεωρημένης μακεδονικής νομισματικής — οπωσδήποτε περισσότερο "εύγλωττης" από εκείνη των Αθηνών — και αποτόλμησαν ακόμα και τη στενότερη χρονολόγηση εγχωρίων απομιμήσεων του αττικού Κεραμεικού και τοπικές δημιουργίες παραδοσιακών κατευθύνσεων.

Η πληθώρα εξάλλου των ταφικών νομισματικών 'θησαυρών' με νομίσματα από πολύτιμα μέταλλα, αλλά και άλλων με χαρακτήρα αποταμιευτικό στη Μακεδονία του τελευταίου τετάρτου του 4ου αι.π.Χ. και των αρχών του 3ου, ήρθε να προσδώσει, με τη σύγχρονη, ταυτόχρονη σχεδόν χρονολογία απόκρυψής τους, μια ξεχωριστή ιστορική διάσταση στα αρχαιολογικά κατάλοιπα από το χώρο, αποδίδοντας στους βετεράνους της ασιατικής εκστρατείας και στα πλούτη που αυτοί συναποκόμισαν, τη χλιδή και τη ματαιοδοξία των κατάγραφων Μακεδονικών τάφων, των ανακτορικών οικιών, των χρυσοποίκιλτων κοσμημάτων και των αργυρών αγγείων και σκευών συμποσίου στην Πέλλα, στη Βεργίνα, στο Δερβένι, στη Νικήσιανη, στο Δίο, κ α. Αναδεικνύοντας συνάμα και τον Κάσσανδρο σε ηγετική μορφή με προκαθορισμένες όσο και μεγαλόπνοες επιδιώξεις και στόχους στον τομέα της πολεοδομίας, της οχυρωματικής — γενικά μιας κατεξοχήν εσωστρεφούς δυναστικής πολιτικής, που αξιοποίησε κατά τον επιτυχέστερο τρόπο για το κράτος και τους πολίτες του τα εμβάσματα και τις εμπειρίες από τη μυθική Ανατολή. Την Ανατολή των Ιώνων και των Περσών.

Επεκτείνοντας τις εύστοχες παρατηρήσεις του Kamen Dimitrov για τους λόγους συγκρότησης των 'θησαυρών' νομισμάτων από πολύτιμα κυρίως μέταλλα που μαρτυρούνται στο θρακικό χώρο του τέλους του 4ου αι.π.Χ., και εκμεταλλευόμενος τίς πρωτοποριακές διαπιστώσεις του François de Callatäy για τη νομισματική κυκλοφορία στο θρακο-μακεδονικό χώρο την ίδια εποχή, ο Γιάννης Τουράτσογλου συνδυάζοντας τις έξοχες αναλύσεις των ταφικών συνόλων, πήλινων, κυρίως αργυρών μεταλλικών αγγείων, στην προ και μετα-λυσιμάχεια Θράκη, από τον Peter Alexandrescu, επιχείρησε την προσγραφή τόσο των νομισματικών 'θησαυρών', όσο και των πολυτίμων σκευών από τη χώρα του Σεύθη, στούς θράκες μισθοφόρους του Αλεξανδρου Γ' αναχρονολογώντας παράλληλα, με τα διδάγματα των Le Rider και Price, στα τέλη του 4ου αι.π.Χ., μεμονωμένα νομίσματα, κτερίσματα σε πλούσιους στό Maltepe/ Mezek και στη Gornjani. Η Άρτεμις Ωνάσσογλου, πάλι, χρησιμοποιώντας τα συμπεράσματα και τις διαπιστώσεις του Olivier Picard από τη μελέτη των ανασκαφικών νομισμάτων του Κωρυκείου Άντρου στον Παρνασσό — χαλκών στην πλειονότητά τους εκδόσεων πόλεων και εθνών της Κεντρικής Ελλάδος—, σταθεροποίησε τις χρονολογήσεις σειρών μελαμβαφών αγγείων του αττικού εργαστηρίου του 3ου αι.π.Χ., κτερισμάτων σε αδιατάρακτα ταφικά σύνολα στην Τριανταφυλλιά Λιβανατών Λοκρίδος. Το υλικό συνεξεταζόμενο και αντιπαραβαλλόμενο προς εκείνο από το ελληνιστικό νεκροταφείο της Μεδεώνος και προς εκείνο από τις πρόσφατες ανασκαφές στη Λαμία και την περιοχή της, ασφαλώς με τις νέες εκτιμήσεις θα αποτελέσει το καλύτερο υπόβαθρο για τη σφαιρική μελέτη της επείσακτης και εγχώριας κεραμικής του χώρου.

Ειναι ευτύχημα ότι οι παραπάνω περιπτώσεις δεν αποτελούν κόκκους άμμου στην κονίστρα της έρευνας, αφού ούτε στους πρώιμους μετακλασικούς χρόνους τελικά περιορίζονται, ούτε όμως και εξαντλούνται στον αριθμό που παρατέθηκε. Ο θεσμός των Επιστημονικών Συναντήσεων για την Ελληνιστική Κεραμική πού είδε το φώς της δημοσιότητας το 1989 στα Γιάννενα, με την ομόθυμη αποδοχή του από τη διεθνή επιστημονική κοινότητα συντελεί ώστε τα παραδείγματα, τουλάχιστον για τους μετά τον Αλέξανδρο Γ' χρόνους, να πολλαπλασιάζονται, με αριθμητική για την ώρα πρόοδο, καλύπτοντας ωστόσο ολόκληρο τον αρχαίο κόσμο.

Τόσο η Αρχαία Μακεδονία και η Θράκη με τον Βασίλη Πούλιο, τη Μαρία Τσιμπίδου, τη Βικτώρια Αλλαμανή, την Κατερίνα Τζαναβάρη, τη Στέλλα Δρούγου, τη Vera Bitrakova, τη Viktoria Sokolovska κ.ά., όσο και οι Κυκλάδες με τη Φωτεινή Ζαφειροπούλου και τον Κωνσταντίνο Τσάκο, η Ήπειρος με τη Γραβάνη, η Θεσσαλία με την Αργυρούλα Δουλγέρη-Ιντζεσίσογλου και άλλες περιοχές με άλλους, συνεισέφεραν στην αρτιότερη κατανόηση της εξέλιξης της κεραμικής στον ελλαδικό κορμό και στο νησιωτικό χώρο στα ύστερα ελληνιστικά χρόνια ώς και την άνοδο του Αυγούστου, εκμεταλλευόμενοι τα νομισματικά τεκμήρια των χρονολογημένων ενοτήτων.

Οπωσδήποτε, η έξοδος από τον εικοστό αιώνα θα έχει ήδη προσδώσει στον τομέα της αρχαίας κεραμικής — για να περιοριστεί κανείς σε αυτήν την τέχνη—, μιαν άλλη προοπτική αντιμετώπισης ορισμένων εγγενών προβλημάτων που την αφορούν, όπως εκείνο της χρονολόγησης, θα έχει καταγράψει άλλους κανόνες διακίνησης του εξαγωγικού εμπορεύσιμου υλικού, διαγραφής του χαρακτήρα των τοπικών εργαστηρίων, αναγνώρισης επιδράσεων. Και σε αυτό θα έχει τα μέγιστα συμβάλει η νομισματική με την αδιαφιλονείκητη ευελιξία και την αποτελεσματικότητα των μεθόδων της, την οικουμενικότητα των συμπερασμάτων της, τη συμμετοχή της στις διεργασίες πλειόνων της μιας επιστημών.

Η νομισματική που έχει ονόματα πολλά και υπόσταση μία.

Επιλεγμένη Βιβλιογραφία

Γενικά

Επιστημονική Συνάντηση για την Ελληνιστική Κεραμική: Α (Ιωάννινα 1989), Β (Ρόδος 1992), Γ (Αθήναι 1994)

Μακεδονία

ΑΕΜΘ [Το Αρχαιολογικό έργο στη Μακεδονία και Θράκη] Θεσσαλονίκη: 1 (1988), 2 (1991), 3 (1992), 4 (1993), 5 (1994)

Στ.Δρούγου, Ι. Τουράτσογλου, *Ελληνιστικοί Λαξευτοί Τάφοι Βεροίας* (Αθήναι 1980)

St. Drougou, J. Touratsoglou, "Hellenistische Keramik aus Makedonien: Chronologische Indizien", *AntK* 34, 1991, 13 κε

Δ. Λαζαρίδης, Κ. Ρωμιοπούλου, Ι. Τουράτσογλου, *Ο τύμβος της Νικήσιανης* (Αθήνα 1992)

I. Touratsoglou, "Baupolitik Kassanders", στο: *Basileia, Die Paläste der frühhellenistischen Könige* (Berlin 1996) 176-181

I. Touratsoglou, "Dated Gold: The Evidence from Hellenistic Macedonia", στο: *Art of the Greek Goldsmith* (London 1997, υπό εκτύπωση).

Αττική-Κεντρική Ελλάς

C. Vatin κ.ά., *Médéon de Phocide* V. *Tombes hellénistiques: Objets de métal-Monnaies* (Paris 1976)

E. Vanderpool, J.R. McCredie, A. Steinberg, Koroni; "A Ptolemaic Camp on the East Coast of Attica", *Hesperia* 31, 1962, 26-62.

G.R. Edwards, "Koroni: the Hellenistic Pottery", *Hesperia* 32, 1963, 109-111.

V.R. Grace, "Notes on the Amphoras from the Koroni Peninsula", *Hesperia* 32, 1963, 319-334.

E. Vanderpool, J.R. McCredie, A. Steinberg, Koroni, "The Date of the Camp and the Pottery", *Hesperia* 33, 1964, 69-75.

V.R. Grace, "Revisions in Early Hellenistic Chronology, *AM* 89, 1974, 193-200.

J.E. Jones, A.J. Graham, L.H. Sackett, "An Attic Country House below the Cave of Pan at Vari", *BSA* 68, 1973, 355-452, πίν.63-86

Susan I. Rotroff, "Athenian Hellenistic Pottery: Toward a firmer Chronology", *Akten des XIII. Internationalen Kongresses für klassische Archäologie* (Berlin 1988) 173-178, πίν.24-25

U. Knigge, *AA* 1980, 256-265.

U. Knigge, W. Kovacskovics, *AA* 1981, 385-389

Νομισματική

N. J. Price, *The Coinage of Alexander the Great and Philip III Arrhidaeus* (London 1991)

G. Le Rider, *Le monnayage d'argent et d'or de Philippe II* (Paris 1977)

O. Picard, L'Antre Corycien II, Chapitre VI: "Monnaies", *BCH Suppl.* IX, 281-306

COINS AND STRATIGRAPHY

S. I. Rotroff

Some numismatists are archaeologists, and some archaeologists are numismatists. Usually, however, the two species are quite distinct, and they regard coins in very differing lights. The numismatist sees iconography and die sequences, the rise and fall of great states, the payment of armies, economics, trade, and the marketplace. The archaeologist sees instead a tool, and he or she makes a simple demand but an insistent one: What is the date? Other issues might arise — an unusual concentration of coins might, for instance, suggest commercial activity in a certain area of the site. First and foremost, however, the digger — or whoever inherits the task of interpreting what the digger dug — wants dates.

It is the digger's perspective that I represent, for my experience with coins comes almost entirely from my work on Hellenistic pottery from the Athenian Agora and from Sardis. In the course of this work I have used the evidence provided by coins excavated long ago to try to establish the dates of the deposits in which that pottery was found. I have also, as an excavation supervisor, used coins to date the stratigraphic levels I was excavating. To me, as to many field archaeologists, a coin is an inscrutable lump of corroded metal in an envelope that, if we're lucky, has written on it an identification that can be translated into a date. The identification may be fifty years old; the handwriting of the numismatist responsible for it may be illegible; and the notations left by subsequent experts may be enigmatic. But since this unpromising morsel of bronze may be the only datable object in a stratum or deposit, it assumes an important place in the roster of archaeological evidence.

There are, however, a number of obstacles to the usefulness of coins for archaeological purposes: the kinds of coins archaeologists find; their preservation and conservation; the differing ways in which archaeologists and numismatists handle this material; and poor communication between archaeologists and numismatists.

Gold and silver coins — the coins that historically have received the greatest scholarly attention — are rare finds. The Agora excavations have been in progress for over sixty years. During that time excavators have recovered only three ancient gold coins and one of electrum in stratigraphic contexts: a Daric of Artaxerxes I, a Kyzikene stater, a posthumous stater of Alexander III, and a solidus of Arcadius.[1] Although these are beautiful and valuable objects, they are of minimal archaeological significance, for they were found in contexts hundreds, even thousands of years later than their own dates. The Kyzikene stater was found on a Byzantine floor, the Persian Daric comes from a late Roman context, and the solidus comes from a context of the 6th to 7th century after Christ. The coin of Alexander made up part of the fill under a Hellenistic stoa; the excavation notebooks are silent on the details of its discovery, but oral Agora history has it that the coin was found by a workman looking for snails after a heavy rain. Silver coins are more abundant. Close to 300 have been recorded (exclusive of coins from Turkish hoards) and sometimes they have chronological value. But the common, day-to-day finds are bronze coins; something in the region of 54,000 are currently held in the Agora collection, and many more have been found but have disintegrated or been discarded. This means first of all that coins are of minimal use as a chronological tool before the widespread introduction of bronze coinage.

A second problem is posed by the preservation and conservation of these bronze coins. Preservation varies from site to site. Because of adverse soil conditions, many coins recovered in the Athenian Agora have disintegrated to the point of illegibility. This is particularly true of coins from the earlier excavations, which were cleaned chemically with a solution of sodium hydroxide and zinc. This method removed all corrosion products, stripping the coin down to the surviving metal. In those days many coins simply melted during the cleaning process, and excavators were regularly advised to "test" coins by trying to break them. The conventional wisdom was that if they could be broken, they would not survive cleaning, and this was probably true, since only coins with little or no uncorroded metal could be broken easily. The results of these policies and treatments can be illustrated with statistics from a section of the Agora that was excavated in 1972. 64 of the 486 coins found in that season (about 13%) disintegrated in cleaning. I was the excavator, and I followed the

1 Coin inventory number Y-83 (Daric of Artaxerxes I); ΒΓ-68 (electrum Kyzikene stater, J. H. Kroll, *Agora* XXVI, *The Greek Coins* [Princeton 1993], 257, no. 866, pl. 29); ΜΣ-204 (Alexander III, *Agora* XXVI, 185, no. 487, pl. 23); BE-453 (Arcadius). There is a slightly larger number of much later gold coins, mostly from Turkish hoards.

"break and discard" rule, so more coins that would probably have disintegrated in cleaning never entered the record at all. This situation improved dramatically, however, in 1979, with the arrival of a trained conservator at the Agora. Since then coins have normally been cleaned mechanically under a binocular microscope. This procedure can recover and preserve the image even on a heavily corroded coin. On a recently cleaned coin from section BE, for instance, surface detail of the reverse is preserved in the corrosion products, malachite and cuprite, which would have dissolved if the coin had been treated chemically (*Pl. 1a*). Alan Walker was thus able to recognize this as an Athenian coin of Kroll's variety 99, with two owls on a thunderbolt, and dating ca. 130-90.[2] Statistics from the excavations in section BE, which began in 1980, attest to the success of this method, for only five of the nearly 1000 coins found there have disintegrated in cleaning.

Despite care and proper cleaning, however, a depressingly large number of excavation coins turns out to be illegible. Two-thirds of the coins from the recent excavations cited above could not be read. About half of those are completely illegible; the other half, though not identifiable, can be dated, usually just to a period (Greek, Hellenistic, Roman, or Byzantine) but occasionally to within a century. Although such dates might have some statistical use, they are of little or no value from the perspective of the field archaeologist, for the accompanying pottery can often provide a closer date. On the more positive side, about 30% of the coins from these recent excavations could be identified; but even identified coins do not always provide close and secure dates.

A cistern and well complex at the Agora, excavated by Stella Miller in 1968, provides a striking instance.[3] This feature, known as Menon's cistern from graffiti scratched on pottery found there, is located in the courtyard of a house outside the southwest corner of the Agora. The deposit includes a particularly large and rich collection of pottery and terracotta figurines clearly dating in the early Hellenistic period. When Menon's Cistern was excavated, the ceramic chronology of that period was in disarray. The canonical dating of the ceramics had been established by the work of Homer Thompson in the 1930's.[4] This chronology, however, had been challenged by discoveries at Koroni, a small site located on a high promontory near Porto Raphti, on the east coast of Attica, which had been

---

2 BE-1040; see *Agora* XXVI, 75.

3 S.G. Miller, "Menon's Cistern," *Hesperia* 43 (1974) 194-245.

4 H.A. Thompson, "Two Centuries of Hellenistic Pottery," *Hesperia* 3 (1934) 311-480.

investigated in a brief campaign in the summer of 1960.[5] Koroni appeared to be a single-period site with a short occupation, and excavators had recovered coins, stamped amphora handles, and pottery from its buildings. The coins had played a crucial role in the interpretation of the site, for a large collection of bronzes attributed to Ptolemy II placed the occupation in a short span of years in the 260's. Furthermore, the unusual concentration of Ptolemaic coins, otherwise rather rare in Athens, suggested that the site had been used as a military encampment by Egyptian forces during the Chremonidean war. This was all extremely satisfying — except for the fact that the canonical ceramic chronology placed the associated pottery some thirty to forty years earlier, around the turn from the 4th to the 3rd century.

It took some time, much debate, and considerable anguish before this conundrum was solved — by shifting the ceramic and amphora chronologies downward[6] — and even today there are scholars who are reluctant to abandon the older chronology. At the time when Menon's Cistern was dug the matter was still very much under debate. The pottery closely resembles that from Koroni. Stella Miller audaciously argued for the lowered chronology in her publication of the Agora material, but the support of numismatic dates would have strengthened her case immeasurably. As it happened, however, 68 of the 71 coins found in Menon's Cistern disintegrated during cleaning, and the four survivors could be identified only as "Greek."[7] If the coins had been cleaned with modern methods, this deposit might have done much to conclude a debate that was to continue for another decade and more.

Another obstacle that may confront the archaeologist attempting to use numismatic evidence is just the issue that prompted this meeting: the lack of cooperation and communication between archaeologists and numismatists. Almost everything there is to say about this has already been said in print, in an essay by A. Johnston and T.V. Buttrey entitled "Numismatic Site Find Procedures," published in *Sardis Monograph* 7.[8] It is the sort of essay no one reads; the archaeologists assume it was written for the numismatists, and the numismatists assume it is directed at the archae-

---

5 E. Vanderpool, J.R. McCredie, and A. Steinberg, "Koroni: A Ptolemaic Camp on the East Coast of Attica," *Hesperia* 31 (1962) 26-61.

6 G.R. Edwards, "Koroni: the Hellenistic Pottery," *Hesperia* 32 (1963) 109-11; V.R. Grace, "Notes on the Amphoras from the Koroni Peninsula," *Hesperia* 32 (1963) 319-34; *eadem*, "Revisions in Early Hellenistic Chronology," *AM* 89 (1974) 193-200.

7 K-1807 to K-1810.

8 T.V. Buttrey, A. Johnston, K.M. MacKenzie, and M.L. Bates, *Greek, Roman, and Islamic Coins from Sardis* (*SardisMon* 7, Cambridge, Mass./London 1981) xiv-xvii.

ologists. But it gives a very good set of instructions for how coins should be recorded, handled, and studied to the greatest advantage of all parties. Even with good intentions, however, things can go awry. Archaeologists studying material from old excavations are usually dependent on the identifications made at the time the coin was found. In the best of all possible worlds, these identification would always be made by an experienced numismatist. In fact, however, all kinds of people identify coins on excavations: numismatists, sometimes, but also graduate students, volunteers, or simply whoever is not too busy doing something else. The result is that in many cases one cannot be certain that an old identification is correct. To open the envelope and actually look at the coin is the counsel of desperation, usually accompanied by feelings of deep inadequacy, along with admiration and wonder that anyone ever saw anything on the wretched scrap of metal that has tumbled out. One would imagine, though, that this problem would largely disappear once the coins had been restudied by the experts and published. This, however, is not always the case. Scribbles and question marks on the coin envelopes may indicate that the coin is definitely *not* what it was originally thought to be, but they often do not say what the coin really *is*. The problem seems to be that numismatists deal in types and statistics, while archaeologists need to know about individual specimens. The final publication gives the types, sometimes with statistics about how many examples of each type were found, but generally without any inventory numbers to identify them. The answer, of course, is a concordance. Preparing such a list is one of the most boring tasks on the face of the planet, and it is no wonder that no one wants to spend any more time on it than is absolutely necessary. The job has become much easier, however, with the widespread use of the computer, and no excavation director should accept a manuscript on coins without such a list. If the editor balks at publishing it, as he or she quite reasonably might, someone must take responsibility for seeing that the list is kept up to date with changes in the manuscript so that the final list agrees with the published information about the coins. And the list must be accessible to those working on the excavation and with its records.

Given all this, how useful are coins, really, to the field archaeologist and the archaeological researcher who are pursuing questions of chronology? The answer is that in most cases, most excavation coins are not very useful in this pursuit. John Kroll, in his book on Greek coins from the Agora, notes that most of the coins in his study come from late fills, for which the coins themselves are not chronologically significant.[9] The laboriously and

---

9 *Agora* XXVI, 2.

successfully cleaned Hellenistic coin discussed above (*Pl. 1a*) is a good example, for it was found in a fill of the 5th or 6th century after Christ. There are situations, however, in which the numismatic evidence has been crucial in the correct reading of a site or a monument. I have already mentioned the case of Koroni. There both the dating of the coins and their unusual provenience — Ptolemaic Egypt — proved essential. Without the coins, neither the date nor the identification of the site as a Ptolemaic military camp could have been achieved.

At the Agora, too, coins have sometimes played a large role in dating and interpretation. One instance is the Square Peristyle, a large structure at the northeast corner of the Agora that probably served as a law court.[10] The close dating of the building is heavily dependent on the material in the fill that was brought in to level the floor at the time of the building's construction. This includes the famous anti-tyranny decree, which can be placed in 337/6 on the basis of an archon date.[11] The fresh surface of this inscription suggests that it did not stand for a long time and that it was buried shortly after it was taken down. Homer Thompson therefore argued that the building was built in the 20's or teens of the 4th century.[12] The pottery, like that from Menon's Cistern, falls in the controversial early Hellenistic period. Applying a high ceramic chronology would support a date of around 325; applying a low chronology suggested by the material from Koroni would support a lower date, close to 300. Over sixty coins had been found in the fill when it was excavated; all were either illegible or datable before ca. 325. But when Jack Kroll reexamined the coins in the 1970's he was able to identify a badly corroded and broken coin of Demetrios Poliorketes, dating it to 300-295 (*Pl.1 b-c*).[13] This single, miserable specimen, then, turns out to be unexpectedly important. It has proved decisive for the dating of a major Athenian building. It has lent support to a downward shift in early Hellenistic pottery chronology. It has also had an impact on the chronology of the Athenian coin types found

---

10 For the definitive publication see R.F. Townsend, *Agora* XXVII, *The East Side of the Agora: The Remains beneath the Stoa of Attalos* (Princeton 1995); for the date see especially 90, 143-53.

11 Agora inventory number I 6524 (B.D. Meritt, "Greek Inscriptions," *Hesperia* 21 [1952] 355-59, no. 5).

12 H.A. Thompson and R.E. Wycherley, *Agora* XIV, *The Agora of Athens: The History, Shape and Uses of an Ancient City Center* (Princeton 1972) 61; H.A. Thompson, "Athens Faces Adversity," *Hesperia* 50 (1981) 350. Other assessments of the fill put it later: "before ca. 300 B.C." (R.H. Howland, *Agora* IV, *Greek Lamps and Their Survivals* [Princeton 1958] 243, under O-R 7-9); "mostly of the third quarter of the 4th century and before but probably not sealed over until near the end of the century" (B.A. Sparkes and L. Talcott, *Agora* XII, *Black and Plain Pottery of the 6th, 5th and 4th Centuries B.C.* [Princeton 1970] 396, under O-R 7-10).

13 ΣΑ-377 (*Agora* XXVI, 188, 315. no. 504h).

with it in the building fill. This is a triumph; but it is important to remember that it is not at all impossible that this coin is intrusive in the fill.

That, however, is not a problem in a second instance, from quite a different point in the history of Athens. From the early 2nd century after Christ down to the late Roman period, the road from the Dipylon to the Agora was lined by stoas. I excavated part of one of the colonnades on the south side of the road in 1972.[14] After its construction in the early 2nd century after Christ the building underwent various modifications and suffered at least three destructions. The first of these could be attributed to the Herulians. This is no surprise, for the raid of the Herulii is well known to historians, and they left behind them massive debris, which has been identified at many places in the Agora. The stoa was eventually rebuilt, only to be destroyed again. This second destruction, however, is a little more surprising. Heavily burnt debris was uncovered in two rooms of the stoa, and the head of an Archaistic herm had been deliberately buried in a small pit against the west wall of one of these rooms (*Pl. 1d*).[15] A remarkably precise date is furnished by coins from this room. Issues of Theodosius I, Valentinian II, and Arcadius were found within the stratum of burnt debris (*Pl. 2-3*), and coins of Gratian (or colleague), Valentinian II, and Arcadius were recovered from the pit with the herm head (*Pl. 4 a-b*).[16] All were struck between 383 and 395, and the slight degree of wear shows that they had circulated for a while, but not for long. Leslie Shear, in his preliminary report, drew the conclusion that the destruction was the work of Alaric, who attacked the cities of Greece in A.D. 396. Historical sources give conflicting accounts of Alaric's activities in Athens, one claiming that he left the city untouched, others maintaining that he took Athens by conquest. While other 4th-century damage that may be attributed to Alaric has now been identified at the Agora, this little deposit remains the most unequivocal evidence of military action against Athens by the Visigoth lord.[17]

---

14 T.L. Shear, "The Athenian Agora: Excavations of 1972," *Hesperia* 42 (1973) 370-82.

15 *Ibid.*, 380.

16 In the burnt stratum: ΒΓ'-217 to ΒΓ'-230, including, as the latest ΒΓ'-217, ΒΓ'-218 (Theodosius I, dating A.D. 383-392), ΒΓ'-219, 229 (Valentinian II, dating 383-392), and ΒΓ'-230 (Arcadius, dating 383-395). With the herm head: ΒΓ'-199 to ΒΓ'-205. The latest are ΒΓ'-200 (Gratian or colleague, dating 378-383); ΒΓ'-201, ΒΓ'-202, ΒΓ'-203 (Valentinian II, one datable to A.D. 383, the others 383-392); ΒΓ'-204 (Arcadius, dating 383-395). The coins were identified by Agora numismatist John Kroll. (To correct a tiny error, the list of coins with the herm head does not include ΒΓ'-206, mistakenly cited by Shear [*ibid.*, 380, note 46]. Thus there were seven coins, not eight as stated by A. Frantz, *Agora* XXIV, *Late Antiquity: A.D. 267-700* [Princeton.1988] 54; the 2nd-century coin Frantz lists comes from a different context.)

17 *Agora* XXIV, 51-54.

Coins can be useful, though less dramatic, in the interpretation of fine stratigraphy, like house floors and road metal. The coins in such layers are likely to have been quickly trodden into the surfaces on which they were dropped. The attendant pottery is usually very fragmentary and often not diagnostic. Coins are far less useful, however, for dating the secondary, dumped deposits in which I usually deal. One of the unique features of the Athenian Agora is the many so-called "sealed" or "closed" deposits that have been discovered there. These are mostly wells and cisterns, sometimes containing material that accumulated while they were in use as water sources, but more frequently filled with secondary dumps. These deposits form the backbone of the Agora pottery chronology. The pottery thus dated is used in turn to help date excavated features and monuments, and therefore the interpretation of these "closed deposits" ultimately has an effect on the interpretation of the site as a whole. The deposits can rarely be associated with any known historical event, and the first step in evaluating their dates is the search for a *terminus post quem*, which usually takes the form of the latest datable object in the deposit. For the Hellenistic period there are only two kinds of objects that can provide that kind of a date: coins and the stamped handles of transport amphoras.

In general, the coins have been less useful than the amphora handles in developing deposit dates. My study of the pottery has involved over 200 different deposits. In 29 of them coins are the only datable objects,[18] but the coins in question are useful for dating in only 11 of these 29 deposits — just over one third. In the other 18 deposits the coins are much earlier than the ceramic material. There are 48 deposits that contain both coins and stamped amphora handles. In five instances the dates of the latest coins and stamps are about the same, but in 26 cases (well over half of the remaining 43 deposits) the stamped handles are significantly later than the coins. Coins have been most useful in the early Hellenistic period, when amphora handles cannot be dated with precision, and in the late Hellenistic period, after the Sullan sack, when coins often constitute the only evidence that material deriving primarily from the Sullan destruction was actually deposited some years later.

In conclusion, I would like to plead for greater and more careful communication between excavators and numismatists. The enormous project of excavating, recording, studying, and publishing an archaeological site requires a large team of people. Our colleagues in the sciences are accustomed to working as teams, but Classical archaeology is rooted in

18 For some of these deposits see S.I. Rotroff, *Agora* XXII, *Hellenistic Pottery: Athenian and Imported Moldmade Bowls* (Princeton 1982) 94-106.

the humanities, and humanists tend to be individualists. The concept of teamwork has been applied to the "dig" itself but is rarely extended in any meaningful sense to study, interpretation, and publication. There, each scholar goes his own way, with the predictable loss of insights and misuse of information. It is incumbent upon excavation directors, from whom leadership must come, to work to build meaningful cooperation among all the scholars at work on the publication of their sites. The benefits to be reaped are very great.

EXCAVATION COINS: THE USE AND MISUSE OF NUMISMATIC EVIDENCE IN ARCHAEOLOGY*

A. S. Walker

In 1882, the year when the American School of Classical Studies at Athens began, Percy Gardner, then Disney Professor of Archaeology at Cambridge and a member of the staff of the Coin Room of the British Museum, gave a series of twelve lectures during Lent term. In the following year, that of the inauguration of the British School at Athens, these lectures, accompanied by magnificent illustrations, were published under the title, *The Types of Greek Coins: An Archaeological Essay.*[1] This was the first major work to explicitly show the connection between Greek coins and classical archaeology, and was followed in 1887 by Gardner's epoch making study, written in collaboration with the eminent Swiss scholar Friedrich Imhoof-Blumer, *A Numismatic Commentary on Pausanias* (it initially appeared from 1885 to 1887 in the *Journal of Hellenic Studies*, of which Gardner was,

---

* Taking part in a conference in honor of Mando Oeconomidou is a particular pleasure for me since I can remember so many hours as her "guest" in the Numismatic Museum during my years in Athens. Sometimes things became unusually hectic there, or even Felliniesque, with numerous minions scurrying here and there on mysteriously urgent and inexplicable errands involving vast numbers of forms, each with a multitude of stamps; yet cups of coffee, infinite kindness, willing help and friendly advice were dispensed as well. I think I was able to amuse her then, and I hope I still can.

Abbreviations:
Agora = The Athenian Agora, Results of Excavations Conducted by the American School of Classical Studies at Athens, Princeton
XIV = H.A. Thompson and R.E. Wycherley, *The Agora of Athens: The History, Shape and Uses of an Ancient City Center*, 1972
XXVI = J.H. Kroll with contributions by A.S. Walker, *The Greek Coins*, 1993.

1 P. Gardner, *The Types of Greek Coins, an Archaeological Essay* (Cambridge 1883). Reprinted, with an introduction by Margaret Thompson, Chicago 1965.

coincidently, the first editor).[2] Still a standard work, *NCP* showed how contemporary or near contemporary coins could serve as a commentary on classical literary texts, as well as providing a store of illustrations of original ancient monuments long lost, in ruins or only existing in later copies.

These studies, and others like them written later, focused on those aspects of numismatics which contribute to our understanding of the classical world: coins can illuminate past events by their types, inscriptions, or the hoards in which they are found:[3] the representations on the coins can be related to ancient sculpture which either survives or is known from ancient literary sources;[4] trade routes can be followed utilizing findspots, and the copying of coinages well-known for their purity and value can show the extent over which those coins circulated (as Levantine and Arabian copies of the 5th century BC coinage of Athens, and Indian imitations of Roman gold and silver coins of the 1st through the 4th centuries);[5] the accurately datable ruler portraits which began to appear on coinage beginning in the late 5th century, and then spread throughout the Greek world, provide both contemporary images of known and unknown personages, and a useful set of comparanda for unidentified marble and bronze portrait sculpture;[6] the representations of buildings which commonly appear on the Roman Provincial coinage of cities of the

---

2 P. Gardner and F. Imhoof-Blumer, *A Numismatic Commentary of Pausanias.* (Cambridge 1887). Reprinted with additions by A.N. Oikonomides under the title, *Ancient Coins Illustrating Lost Masterpieces of Greek Art* (Chicago 1964).

3 C.M. Kraay, *Greek Coins and History, some current problems* (London 1969); L. Lacroix, *Monnaies et colonisation dans l'occident grec* (Brussels 1965); M.N. Tod, "Epigraphical Notes on Greek Coinage.," *NC* 1945, pp. 108-116, *NC* 1946, pp. 47-62, *NC* 1947, pp. 1-27, *NC* 1955, pp. 125-130, *NC* 1960, pp. 1-24; J.R. Melville Jones, *Testimonial Numaria — Greek and Latin Texts Concerning Ancient Greek Coinage. Volume 1: Texts and Translations.* London 1993 (Volume 2 is forthcoming); S.P. Noe, *Coin Hoards*, ANSNNM 1 (New York 1921); M. Thompson; O. Mørkholm, C.M. Kraay, *An Inventory of Greek Coin Hoards (IGCH)* New York 1973.

4 L. Lacroix, *Les réproductions de statues sur les monnaies grecques. La statuaire archaïque et classique. Bibliothéque de la Faculté de Philosophie et Lettres de l'Université de Liège.* CXVI (Liège 1949); Gardner and Imhoof-Blumer (supra n.2) ; P.W. Lehman, *Statues on Coins of Southern Italy and Sicily in the Classical Period* (New York 1946); M.D. Stansbury-O'Donnell, "Reflections of the Tyche of Antioch in Literary Sources and on Coins," in S.B. Matheson, *An Obsession with Fortune. Tyche in Greek and Roman Art Exhibition Catalogue. Yale University Art Gallery Bulletin* 1994, pp.51-63.

5 T.V. Buttrey,"Pharaonic Imitations of Athenian Tetradrachms," *Actes CIN* 1979 (Louvain-la-Neuve 1982) pp. 137-140; P.J. Turner, *Roman Coins from India. RNS SP* 22 (London 1989). A useful compendium of articles on coins and trade, among many, is A.K. Jha, editor, *Coinage, Trade and Economy. January 8th-11th, 1991. 3rd International Colloquium.* (Maharashtra 1991).

6 J. Babelon, *Le portrait dans l'Antiquité d'après les monnaies.* (Second Edition. Paris 1950); G.M.A. Richter, *The Portaits of the Greeks* (London 1965).

eastern Mediterranean area can be used to reconstruct or to identify the actual remains of those structures found in excavations;[7] religious predilictions, and sometimes, the games and rites celebrating them, can be illustrated through a city's choice of coin types;[8] etc.

Nevertheless, while these specialized studies show the breadth of reach in modern scientific numismatics, and all fall within the greater general field of classical archaeology, they are, perhaps, not really that immediately important to the classical archaeologist. In part this is because many of these topics can be studied through coins which have not been properly excavated; additionally, the topics themselves can be seen, in a narrow sense, as being peripheral to the excavator's interests. The numismatist may well be enthralled by an excavated coin which fills a gap within a pre-existing sequence of dies, or which answers an historical problem, or is particularly beautiful or rare, like the splendid Kyzikene electrum stater found in the Agora;[9] just as the Red Figure specialist will be when a mid-fifth century well produces a sherd from an amphora by the younger Epiktetos, the Kleophrades Painter, bearing a hitherto unknown mythological scene. The archaeologist, however, will be far more excited by an ugly, common coin, or even a vile Megarian bowl fragment, if it comes from an uncontaminated layer and, even more importantly, can provide a precise date for that layer.

Numismatists have long had another problem with archaeologists, and this is one of expectations. Archaeologists tend to be very exigent about chronology; some can even *taste* an architectural fragment and immediately say, "Hmm, ca. 435 BC, probably designed by Mnesikles." An impressive feat, until one realizes that they've said that while chewing on the Propylaea! Nevertheless, it was naturally expected that coins, which seem so obviously datable, would be a great help in clearing up all manner of chronological problems. But when an early numismatist would tell the site director that a coin in a foundation deposit could only be given dates like 430-322 *or later*, or 322-229, or 229-27, as was the case with Athenian bronze coins in 1931, the year in which the American excavations in the Agora began, the excavator would tend to dismiss numismatic evidence as unreliable and unimportant; or, in Margaret Thompson's words of thirty years ago, as "...a very unsubstantial chronological prop."[10]

---

7 M.J. Price and B.L. Trell, *Coins and Their Cities* (London 1977).

8 M. Bernhart. "Dionysos und seine Familie auf griechischen Münzen.," *JfNG* I, 1949 (entire number).

9 *Agora XXVI*, 866. Unfortunately, this coin was found in disturbed fill and has no real archaeological significance.

10 Gardner (supra. n.1) ix.

To be rather simplistic, the reason why coins were so unsubstantial a chronological prop is that numismatists had such unsubstantial grounds for dating them. While Roman coins often can be exactly dated, many Greek issues could only be dated relatively. In some cases precisely dated historical events known from literary sources, as the conquest or freeing of a city, decisive battles, or major political unheaveals, would be used as fixed points for the chronology of a city's or region's coinage. This was done on the assumption that such outside events always would have an affect on the coins of the state involved.[11] Then these coins, which apparently provided reasonably accurate dates, would be compared with coins from cities whose histories were more opaque, giving them, in turn, what seemed to be equally accurate dates, and so on *ad infinitum*. In fact, a considerable number of such identifications proved perfectly accurate. However, many supposed connections between coins and events have proven baseless: like the cessation of Larissa's coinage upon Philip II's takeover of Thessaly,[12] the coinage of Athens under Solon,[13] or the identification of an early 5th century silver coin of Syracuse as the famous Demareteion. Diodorus[14] recorded that the Carthaginians rewarded Queen Demarete with a crown of 100 talents of gold for her efforts on their behalf after the battle of Himera, and that from it she struck coins, which were known as Demareteia, valued at 10 drachms or 50 litrai. In 1830 the rare early dekadrachms of Syracuse were confidently identified as being these very coins, thus precisely dateable to 480/479, and this apparently valid equation had tremendous influence on all subsequent attempts at establishing a chronology for the coinage of Greek Sicily. Yet it instantly falls flat when one realizes the difficulty of striking a *silver* dekadrachm out of a *gold* crown.[15]

An even worse problem, from the archaeologist's point of view, was the fact that at that time most corpora or detailed studies of individual Greek mints focused primarily on artistically significant and intrinsically valuable coinages in gold or silver, rather than the more common, and less

---

11 Perfect examples of this form of reconstruction are: B.V. Head, *On the Chronological Sequence of the Coins of Ephesus* (London 1880); and, idem., *On the Chronological Sequence of the Coins of Boeotia* (London 1881).

12 T. Martin, *Sovereignty and Coinage in Classical Greece* (Princeton 1985).

13 The controvery over Solon, derived from *Ath. Pol.* 10, has raged almost endlessly, though with all hoard evidence now placing the earliest Athenian coinage no earlier than c. 550 the argument seems moot. Cf. Kraay, *Archaic and Classical Greek Coins* (London 1976) 55-63, and *Agora XXVI*, p. 5 and n. 6.

14 *Diod.* XI, 26, 3.

15 Kraay (supra n.3) 19-42.

prestigious, issues in copper or bronze.[16] Those last, of course, being the kind of coins archaeologists actually find.[17]

In fact, aside from the relative and absolute chronologies supplied by the contents of hoards, accurate dates for many Greek coins could only be given by securely datable foundation trenches, destruction levels or similar closed deposits revealed by careful excavation. Thus, even while archaeologists were complaining about the unreliability of numismatic evidence for dating, their own excavations were providing numismatists with the building blocks needed to construct a truly reliable chronology for the coins involved.[18]

So what should an archaeologist expect from an archaeological numismatist in Greece today? And vice versa? Every coin found poses a number of questions: What is it? How worn is it? What is its date? Can it be associated with other coins from the same find spot? Is it an intrusion? How should it be stored?

The first thing the numismatist should do when a coin appears is to determine whether it *is* a coin, since excavators commonly hand in such things as tack heads, buttons, seals, bottle caps and curiously-shaped rocks! While most of these objects should go to another specialist, the rocks can either be tossed through the nearest convenient window, or, more diplomatically, be returned to the excavator with the explanation that they are *monetaform lithic intrusions*.

---

16 For example, really detailed studies seldom touched on bronze coinage (as K. Regling, *Terina, BWPr* 66, 1906; C.T. Seltman, *The Temple Coins of Olympia* (Cambridge 1921); and E. Boehringer, *Die Münzen von syrakus* (Berlin 1929), and others only mentioned it in passing (as E.T. Newell, *The Coinages of Demetrius Poliorcetes* (London 1927)). Bronzes were included in the major collection catalogues, as those of the British Museum;, The Hunterian in Glasgow and McClean collection in the Fitzwilliam, as well as in some *Sylloges*, in major general surveys or area studies as the *Traité, AMNG, RG*; J.-N. Svoronos, *Numismatique de la Crète ancienne* (Macon 1890), etc.; in specialized studies containing *only* bronzes, as E. Rogers, *The Copper Coinage of Thessaly* (London 1932), or E. Gàbrici, *La monetazione del bronzo nella Sicilia antica* (Palermo 1927); or in a few complete mint studies, as J. Mavrogordato, *A Chronological Arrangement of the Coins of Chios* (London 1918). Actual die studies including bronze coinage only came much later, as H.A. Cahn, *Die Münzen der sizilischen Stadt Naxos* (Basel 1944).

17 Of the approximately 16,557 Greek coins found in the Agora, there were only 3 gold and 182 silver pieces, or 1.12% of the total found. *Agora XXVI* xviii-xxvi and 1 (the percentage given there is marginally erroneous).

18 F.S. Kleiner, "The Agora Excavations and Athenian Bronze Coinage, 200-86 B.C.," *Hesperia* 45 1976, pp. 1-40. The tremendous advances in research which took place in the sixty years after the publication of K.M. Edwards, *Corinth, Results of Excavations Conducted by the American School of Classical Studies at Athens, VI, Coins 1896-1929* (Cambridge, Mass. 1933) are brought out by *Agora XXVI*.

Assuming that it really *is* a coin, the numismatist ought to look at it soon after its discovery, before the cleaning process begins. Even in a "raw" state, it probably can be generally identified as one of the six basic coin types found on any Greek site: Greek,[19] Roman, Byzantine, Frankish/ Venetian, Turkish or modern. There is always a chance that it will disintegrate, and if it does, this will be the only identification the archaeologist will have.

Not surprisingly, once cleaned the coin will either be legible or illegible. While some illegible coins are completely worthless, others can be roughly identified, often by module, and, as we will see, the illegibility itself may have its uses. When it comes to legible coins, there are varying degrees in difficulty in their identification. Neither Roman Imperial nor Byzantine coins ought to pose any great problem, unless the "coin person" has the misfortune of never having seen a coin before (in early excavations epigraphers were often dragooned into identifying the coins since they bore inscriptions;[20] or an excavator's spouse might be given the choice of either washing sherds or being numismatist). Modern coins since 1821 are equally easy, especially since extremely convenient literature for collectors exists cataloguing them.[21] More specialized literature will be needed for European issues of 1500-1821, but such coins are not commonly found on Greek sites. The medieval Frankish coinage of Greece takes some getting used to, but it is well documented,[22] and if large numbers are found the numismatist will surely be able to call upon some of the members of the Hellenic Numismatic Society for aid in their identification, since they have developed a remarkable amount of expertise and interest in this subject.[23] Ottoman issues are usually best left to specialists. As for Greek coins, which are the ones of greatest interest to this conference, paraphrasing the late Eugene Vanderpool Senior, *a coin is easy to identify if you know what it is.*

---

19 By "Greek" coins I mean those struck in Archaic, Classical, Hellenistic and Roman times (to ca. AD 267) with inscriptions in Greek, as well as Roman colonial issues with Latin legends (as Corinth and Patrai, for example).

20 Gardner (supra n.1) vii.

21 For example, C.L. Krause and C. Mishler, *1995 Standard Catalog of World Coins* (22nd Edition. Iola, W1 1994).

22 D.M. Metcalf, *Coinage in South-Eastern Europe 820-1396 RNSSP* 11 (London 1979), pp. 234-267; Idem., "The currency of *deniers tournois* in Frankish Greece", *ABSAthens* LV (1960), pp. 38-59; Idem., "Frankish petty currency from the Areopagus at Athens", *Hesperia* XXXIV (1965), pp. 203-223; A.G. Malloy, I.F. Preston, A.J. Seltman, *Coins of the Crusader States 1098-1291* (New York 1994) 45-411.

23 The Hellenic Numismatic Society, Didotou 45, GR-106 80, Athens, Greece. Its president (1995), A.P. Tzamalis, has produced a number of detailed studies revealing issue sequences and suggesting possible mints, viz., A P. Tzamalis, Το Εύρημα της Ηλείας 1964, *NomKhron* 13, 1994, pp. 65-84 (Greek and English text).

If the ancient city being excavated had a mint, most coins found there will have been struck there; and if not, they will come from the major mints in the immediate area. For example, of the 16,557 identifiable Greek coins from the Agora, only 13% were non-Athenian (of which nearly 60% came from Central Greece, the Peloponnesos, and nearby Salamis and Megara); at Corinth, as of 1929, there were 1186 Greek coins: 752 Corinthian (63%), 106 from neighboring Sicyon (9%), and 328 from the rest of the Greek world (28%); at Troy 50% of the Greek issues were from the civic mint with a further 18% from Alexandria Troas.[24] The numismatist who has become familiar with the ancient coinage of the region of the excavation site will discover that the vast majority of the coins found pose little problem in identification. Useful sources for comparative material are local museums; local collectors with an interest in their region; illustrated catalogues or sylloges;[25] and, of course, the National Numismatic Museum in Athens. At an excavation in Greece, coins from the West, northern Thrace, Asia Minor and the East (a total of 2% of all the Greek coins in the Agora) will be unusual, unfamiliar, and much more troublesome; though if they are fully legible they will simply require a little more effort on the numismatist's part. Worst of all are partially legible coins which still can not be identified; neither the numismatist nor the excavator should be discouraged by this (the Agora has 158 pieces like that, most found in the 1930's, and every museum I have ever visited has a tray of similar material).

Sooner or later the numismatist may find out what they are while looking for something else; casts can be made and inflicted on the BM Coin Room (or the ANS, the BN, or the NNM in Athens); or a numismatic visitor will recognize them (all such visitors, whether scholars or collectors, should be compelled to view every excavation's "horrors box", especially if they are interested in coins from outside the region of the site). A very few partially legible coins are probably unknown varieties, and will simply remain unidentifiable until a more completely preserved specimen is found.

---

24 *Agora XXVI. xx-xxvi;* Edwards (supra n. 18) pp. 163-164 (these figures are now out of date and need to be modified to take over sixty years of continuing excavations into account - the basic proportions remain unchanged); A.R. Bellinger, *Troy. The Coins. Troy Supplementary Monographs 2* (Princeton 1961) 156-161.

25 For mainland Greece a number of catalogues are especially useful: *SNG* Copenhagen fasc. 11-17 (Thessaly-Illyricum — Argolis — Aegean Islands), Copenhagen 1943-1944, has long been standard (and there is now an extremely convenient single-volume reprint of these fascicles, West Milford NJ 1982); S.W. Grose, *Fitzwilliam Museum. Catalogue of the McClean Collection of Greek Coins.* Volume II: The Greek Mainland, The Aegean Islands, Crete (Cambridge 1926). Well-financed excavations might think of purchasing the record photographs of the British Museum coins, taken by tray, of the relevant areas.

Both the reason why a coin is illegible, and the degree of wear a coin displays are vital pieces of information.[26] A coin which is illegible or partially illegible due to corrosion may have originally been in nearly perfect condition prior to being dropped. If the numismatist is able to determine that fact from whatever small amount of the design remains, the coin may still be valuable for dating its context. On the contrary, coins which are illegible because of extreme wear have no chronological value at all: only their context can provide the date when they were used. In fact, wear is vital to determine the *date of deposition* for even the most precisely dated coin: a denarius struck in 144/5 in perfect condition may well have been dropped no later than 150, while a very worn example could still have been in use in the 240s. In the Agora during the 1st century AD exceptionally worn coins still circulated freely, even if several hundred years old;[27] this fact can be correlated with the city's economically straitened situation at that period,[28] and both implies that civic authorities saw no need to strike new coins for purely aesthetic reasons, and, perhaps, that in any event they lacked the resources to do so. Not only that, earlier coins were found and then reused in antiquity, perfect examples being the 1st and 2nd century Roman bronzes, long out of circulation, which were countermarked by the Ostrogoths for use in early 6th century Italy; and the Tetrarchic radiates overstruck by Leontius in 695/6.[29]

Normally, the date a numismatist gives a coin is the date when it was struck, and can be as exact as a specific month or part of a specific year, a span of several years, or many decades (if not generations). In general, the better studied any coin series is, the narrower the dates can be. However, when the archaeologist rushes up with a coin and demands to know its date, the canny numismatist should reply "what date would you like it to be?" If the excavator then proudly states that the coins come from an undisturbed well of the 6th century AD, and the pot specialist nods in agreement, the numismatist can, at least, get out of range before identifying all the coins as Frankish! Better still is when some of the coins confirm the excavator's theories, and others, previously more loosely dated, can be given more exact chronologies thanks to their new contexts.

26 A. Walker, "Worn and Corroded Coins; Their Importance for the Archaeologist", *JFA* 3 (1976), pp. 329-334.

27 *Agora XXVI* 91-92 discussing the floor packing of the Library of Pantainos (Agora deposit U 13:2a). Built in 98-102, some exceptionally worn, albeit still legible, coins found in the floor go back to the late 4th century BC.

28 J. Day, *An Economic History of Athens under Roman Domination* (New York 1942) 177-183.

29 P. Grierson and M. Blackburn, *Medieval European Coinage. I The Early Middle Ages (5th-10th centuries).* (Cambridge 1986) 28-31; G.D.R., "Three Overstrikes of Leontius", *NCirc* LXXIX, 1 (1971), p.7.

It should never be forgotten that a single coin can get almost anywhere: it can be moved around by water, by animals or can fall from one layer to another during excavation; and so the use of a single coin as a linchpin for dating an ancient monument is particularly risky. When one Roman coin turns up beneath an Archaic building it can be easily dismissed as a intrusion, but not if several do; and just because a 3rd century BC Athenian coin from under an 18th century house may be in far better condition than the more contemporary Turkish *para* of the 1720s with which it was found, it doesn't mean that we have to radically revise our ideas of architectural history. Coins do not move around by supernatural means, nor can we envision an ancient Athenian saying "I wonder what Homer Thompson will make of these", while carefully placing a group of Hadrianic Period VB bronzes in the foundation of the Stoa of Attalos! This is where context becomes extremely important: the numismatist must always remember to check through all the coins found in any specific area, rather than concentrating on them as individuals, since if this is done, closed assemblages may be revealed which had not been noted when found. Sometimes groups of coins are surely lost purses. The type of coin found in such purses usually accurately reflects the coins in general circulation at the time they were lost, as compared to hoards meant as savings, and can provide extremely important chronological fixed points for both the excavator and the numismatist.[30] Coins from roads or drains will not necessarily be as mixed as archaeologists might assume: drains are periodically cleaned, or have sections closed off, so deposits within them can be chronologically uniform; and groups of coins from along roadsides may indicate market booths or stalls selling souvenirs, as were likely along the Panathenaic Way. Also of potential importance is the presence of foreign coins in unusual numbers, such as the massive numbers of bronzes of Antigonus Gonatas in the Agora,[31] since they may be connected with known military or commercial movements, or be otherwise unattested.

As with all excavated objects, coins have to be stored in a way that makes their further study as convenient as possible. Yet, because coins were, and are, *money*, the excavation director may be worried about security

30 Three examples from the Agora are A14:2 (*Agora XXVI*.301), surely a lost purse of ca. 250 dropped into a cistern; P7:10, a dropped purse reflecting the coins in circulation ca. 200-250 (*Agora XXVI* 315); and the extraordinary N12:5, a lost purse found in the burnt debris of the Odeon. The date of the purse, ca. 150, can be explained by it having been lost during the roof repairs of the mid 2nd century, and remaining inaccessible within the roof until the building's destruction by the Herulians in 267 (*Agora XIV* 111-114, 208; A. Walker, *A Chronological Study of the Greek Imperial Coinage of Athens Based on the Collection of the Agora Excavations at Athens*. 1980 University of Pennsylvania, Ph.D. Dissertation (Ann Arbor 1980, pp.128-129).

31 *Agora XXVI* 69, 507-509.

and seek to take elaborate precautions over their storage. If instead of being kept in the excavation *apotheke* the coins are removed to a vault for safe keeping they will be very difficult to study; and if they are removed to a central storage depot out of the control of the site director, they will doubtless be misfiled and disappear into thin air as happened with so many coins from Kenchreai.[32] Frankly, unless the site has produced a magnificent hoard of gold, as the 1930 Corinth hoard of staters of Philip II and Alexander III now sensibly kept in the Numismatic Museum,[33] no special arrangements should be made. After all, most thieves are simply opportunists and if the coins are even vaguely difficult to get at, or to recognize, they will probably settle for something more attractive to the uncultivated eye, like Hellenistic pots (thieves with guns are more serious, and anyone seen skulking about with a chisel is merely an epigrapher). The safest thing to do is to keep the coins in archaeological order[34] in a locked cabinet similar to those used for the storage of all other small finds. The coins should be in opaque paper envelopes so that the casual viewer can not see inside (plastic liners can be used if the conservator insists). Under no circumstance should all the most attractive pieces found in the excavation be kept separately in a box carefully labeled *Good Coins*: that's just asking for trouble!

All coins from closed deposits or distinct levels should be kept for future study, whether legible or illegible; though there are some coins which simply do not need to be kept and should be discarded. These are coins which are illegible due to corrosion from surface or mixed fills, or unstratified levels. They serve no useful purpose except to clutter up space. This may sound like heresy to those excavators who insist that all coins, *save those that disintegrate*, be kept since they are sure that in the future machines will be developed which will enable the numismatist's identification of "Illegible late 4th century Roman" to be changed to the more precise "Unidentifiable copper based Roman issue of ca. 380-400 CE". Coins can be a vitally important tool for the archaeologist, as long as the numismatist uses them in an archaeological way and the archaeologist is willing to understand their limitations and peculiarities. We have come a long way since Gardner.

---

32 A. Walker, review of R.L. Hohlfelder, *Kenchreai, Eastern Port of Corinth, Results of Investigations by the University of Chicago and Indiana University for the American School of Classical Studies at Athens. III, The Coins* (Leiden 1978) in *NC* 1980, 217-219.

33 *IGCH* 77.

34 I.e., as found rather than in numismatic order by city and ruler.

Numismatics and the archaeological site

MONNAIES DE FOUILLES ET HISTOIRE GRECQUE: L'EXEMPLE DE THASOS

O. Picard

Dans cette réunion consacrée aux rapports entre numismatique et archéologie, je voudrais poser une question naïve que j'ai ressassée pendant les nombreuses heures passées au musée numismatique d'Athènes, à l'ombre de Mando, à identifier et classer les monnaies de fouille de Thasos: que peuvent nous apprendre les monnaies de fouille sur l'histoire et sur l'économie d'une cité? Je laisserai de côté les apports de la stratigraphie à la datation des monnaies et des niveaux archéologiques et d'autres questions plus archéologiques, comme les informations que nous fournissent les monnaies sur les périodes où un quartier d'habitation est occupé ou abandonné. Je ne toucherai pas non plus à la question pourtant capitale de la durée d'utilisation des monnaies; à cet égard, il faut attirer l'attention des archéologues sur un risque très grave de confusion: la date de la monnaie que le numismate cherche à établir et que le fouilleur lui emprunte pour dater un niveau archéologique, est celle de l'émission de la pièce, alors que ce niveau est contemporain de la perte de la monnaie, quelques années ou quelques décennies plus tard.[1] Je resterai aujourd'hui sur le terrain de l'interprétation historique.

Les fouilles de l'Ecole française à Thasos ont mis au jour plus de 20.000 monnaies, qui proviennent de secteurs très différents de la cité: lieux publics, comme l'agora et les rues; sanctuaires, tant païens que chrétiens; maisons occupées à différentes périodes de la vie de la cité antique. Cet ensemble est important, moins par le montant du nombre, qui s'accroîtra naturellement avec le développement des fouilles, que parce qu'il nous permet d'en tirer des informations fiables: il apparaît en effet que la composition du lot ne dépend plus désormais des aléas de la fouille, mais

---

1 La publication par Y. Grandjean, *Recherches sur l'habitat thasien*, *EtThas* XII (Paris 1988), des niveaux du quartier du Silène permet une étude précise de la longévité des petits bronzes, qui peut dépasser le siècle.

reflète, dans ses grandes masses, la proportion des différentes composantes des monnaies perdues par les Thasiens au cours des temps. Deux observations, faites sur des points précis, viennent conforter cette affirmation d'ordre général: j'avais écrit en 1979 que les trouvailles monétaires permettaient d'établir que la cité antique avait été détruite en 619, date des dernières bronzes d'Héraclius, et que le site avait alors été abandonné pour plusieurs siècles; depuis, l'étude des monnaies trouvées dans les fouilles de nos collègues grecs et l'exploration de niveaux de destruction de la fin de la cité ont sensiblement accru le nombre de pièces de cette période sans démentir mes conclusions.[2] Chr. Dunant et J. Pouilloux avaient dressé en 1956 une liste des monnaies étrangères mises au jour;[3] en trente ans, leur total a beaucoup augmenté, sans modifier pour autant la carte des provenances, à condition de s'en tenir à des régions, et non aux cités, dont le nombre continuera à s'accroître. Ce ne sont que des vérifications empiriques du postulat que je viens d'énoncer, et dont il serait intéressant de chercher à obtenir la validation par des méthodes statistiques: à partir du moment où la fouille d'un site archéologique a une extension suffisante pour donner une image représentative de l'occupation des lieux, l'ensemble des monnaies mises au jour constitue une masse critique — concept sur lequel il convient d'insister — qui fournit des informations fiables pour différentes études sur les formes d'occupation et les types d'échange sur ce site.

Que nous apprennent alors ces monnaies retrouvées? C'est ce que je voudrais analyser à propos de l'histoire et de la géographie antique.

Histoire du monnayage, histoire de la cité

Les monnaies mises au jour sont, pour une écrasante majorité, des monnaies de bronze, comme sur tous les chantiers. Moins de la moitié se situe avant l'ère chrétienne; parmi celles-ci, j'ai pu identifier quelque 850 monnaies de cités étrangères, parmi lesquelles, naturellement, les monnaies romaines, que je ne prends ici en compte que jusqu'au triomphe de l'antoninianus.

C'est que la grande coupure dans l'histoire monétaire de l'Antiquité ne se situe pas au moment de la réforme d'Auguste, quelles qu'en aient été

---

2 O. Picard, "Les trésors et la circulation monétaire à Thasos du IVe au VIIe siècle après J.-C.", *BCHSuppl* V. *Thasiaca* (Paris 1979) 411-454. Ch. Bakirtzis, "Τί συνέβη στη Θάσο στις αρχές του 7ου Μ.Χ. αί; Φίλια Επη εις Γ.Ε. Μυλωναν III. (Athènes 1989) 339-341.

3 J. Pouilloux - Chr. Dunant, *Recherches sur l'histoire et les cultes de Thasos* II, *EtThas*. V (Paris 1958) 10, avec la carte en vis-à-vis et annexe IV, 214-215, à partir des résultats compilés par A.-M. Bon.

les conséquences sur le monnayage des cités grecques, mais bien vers le milieu du IIIe siècle ap. J.-C., quand, parallèlement aux autres mutations qui s'opèrent alors, la monnaie impériale en voie de dépréciation, l'antoninianus, élimine toutes les autres espèces. Au contraire, la découverte dans des niveaux impériaux de monnaies hellénistiques du IIe et du Ier siècle, dont certaines ont été retrouvées dans un état d'extrême usure, montre que des bronzes hellénistiques continuent à circuler sous l'Empire (dans une proportion que je suis incapable d'estimer), et qu'il y a donc continuité d'une période à l'autre.

Le passage d'un système monétaire qui était resté, au moins dans la partie orientale de l'Empire et pour le monnayage de bronze,[4] un système décentralisé, alimenté presque exclusivement par la production locale, à un système centralisé, alimenté par quelques grands ateliers impériaux amène l'historien à modifier profondément les questions qu'il peut se poser devant un ensemble de monnaies de fouille. Dans l'Antiquité tardive, le nombre de monnaies retrouvées a toute chance d'être proportionnel au nombre de monnaies introduites sur le site et, à condition de raisonner sur des monnaies de valeur comparable, on est en droit de se demander si la variation du pourcentage des exemplaires d'une période donnée par rapport à l'ensemble ne correspond pas à des variations des petits échanges utilisant ce numéraire, donc à la variation d'une certaine forme d'activité économique. La méthode a été utilisée avec fruit par des spécialistes du haut Moyen-Age, notamment en Angleterre[5] et, à Thasos même, les résultats obtenus par J.-M. Saulnier sont encourageants.[6]

Or quelles que soient les précautions prises, la méthode est inapplicable pour les temps antérieurs: en effet, jusqu'à la réforme d'Auguste, l'ensemble des trouvailles est constitué dans une proportion écrasante, dépassant 90%,[7] par des bronzes de l'atelier de Thasos; par conséquent, le

---

4 On notera cependant que, dans la circulation des monnaies précieuses, en argent et en or, l'effacement du monnayage des cités devant les deniers et les aurei impériaux ne fait que porter à son terme l'évolution commencée au IVe s. av. J.-C. qui tendait à limiter de plus en plus le monnayage des cités aux espèces en bronze, les échanges en monnaies lourdes se faisant en "monnaie hellénique", le tétradrachme de poids attique: la composition des fortunes mobilières de Téos que fait connaître l'inscription des pirates, S. Sahin, *Epigraphica Anatolica* 23 (1994) 1-36, en donne un bon exermple.

5 Citons ici les recherches de Bischoff, *Mittelalterliche Schatzverzeichnisse* ou les études réunies par H. Clarke et E. Schia, *Coins and Archaeology, BAR Int.Series* 556 (Oxford 1989).

6 J.-M. Saulnier, *Monnaies byzantines à Thasos*, thèse inédite (Paris IV), à paraître dans les *EtThas*.

7 Il est impossible de donner un chiffre précis, à cause du nombre des pièces illisibles du fait de leur usure et surtout de leur oxydation, dont la plupart, il est vrai, sont vraisemblablement thasiennes.

nombre des exemplaires d'une période qui ont été retrouvés est fonction de la production des monnaies en cette période, donc de la politique monétaire de la cité. Même sous le Haut Empire, où les émissions thasiennes sont peu nombreuses et sont d'un volume très limité, à en juger par le nombre de coins utilisés, leur présence suffit à fausser complètement tout essai d'analyse statistique: du début de l'Empire jusqu'au milieu du IIIe siècle ap. J.-C., les fouilles ont mis au jour 334 AE, dont 128 de l'atelier de Thasos (38%), qui se répartissent entre 4 émissions entre le règne d'Hadrien et l'avènement de Caracalla, frappées avec 12 coins de droit et 17 de revers.[8] Quelle que soit la prospérité de Thasos sous les Antonins et les premiers Sévères, l'accroissement proportionnel des monnaies de ces années ne s'explique que par l'existence des émissions thasiennes. De la même manière, l'augmentation spectaculaire des monnaies venues de la côte thrace entre le règne d'Antonin le Pieux et 212 ne traduit aucun développement des échanges, mais enregistre simplement l'existence des émissions de Topiros(*Pl. 5a-b*).[9]

Il n'est donc pas douteux qu'à cette période, les enseignements à tirer des monnaies de fouilles concernent surtout la production monétaire locale. Comme les bronzes de Thasos ont peu circulé à l'extérieur, les monnaies de fouille sont indispensables pour établir le corpus des émissions de bronze. Leur richesse est telle qu'elle nous procure sans aucun doute des exemplaires de toutes les émissions et même de la grande majorité des coins utilisés par la cité. Soulignons au passage l'efficacité de cet effet de masse: il est possible de reconstruire dans son intégralité l'histoire monétaire de la cité, et donc de mettre en lumière les interruptions du monnayage de Thasos au IIIe siècle. Même négative, cette information est d'autant plus précieuse que les historiens antiques n'ont pratiquement transmis aucune information sur cette période et que les aléas de la conservation des inscriptions ne permettent pas de raisonner sur des absences. La mise en évidence d'un rythme sur la longue durée ne se limite pas à l'histoire de Thasos, mais vaut pour l'ensemble des monnaies, qu'elle conduit à diviser en trois périodes. Le Haut-Empire en constitue une, même si l'on peut y distinguer un premier moment allant jusqu'à la fin du règne de Trajan, et un deuxième, marqué par le développement croissant de la production, d'Hadrien aux Sévères et aux frappes du IIIe

8 Cf. O. Picard, "Thasos", *The Greek Renaissance in th Roman Empire*, S. Walker — A. Camareon eds, *Institute of Class. St., Bull. Suppl.* 55 (1989) 173-179.

9 O. Picard, "Thasos et la Thrace: l'apport des monnaies de bronze", *Settlement Life in Ancient Thrace, IIIrd International Symposium "Cabyle"* (Jambol 1994) 266-276.

siècle. D'autre part, l'étude des monnaies hellénistiques fait apparaître une distinction chronologique très nette entre deux périodes: les monnaies du IVe-IIIe siècle, du début du monnayage de bronze, qui, à Thasos, apparaît en 390, jusqu'à la fin de la prépondérance des grands royaumes, c'est-à-dire jusqu'au tournant des années 180-170; et celles de la basse période hellénistique, qui commencent par un indéniable renouveau avant de s'enfoncer dans la crise du Ier siècle.

En revanche, si complet et précis soit-il, ce tableau de la production ne permet aucune estimation de la variation des activités économiques. Ce n'est pas ici le lieu de s'interroger sur les raisons pour lesquelles une cité décide de frapper une monnaie de bronze et détermine le volume de ses émissions. L'exemple de Thasos, où le volume du monnayage diminue à une époque de grande prospérité et d'intense activité commerciale, vient s'ajouter à celui d'Erétrie pour me convaincre que la production monétaire n'est fonction ni de la richesse ni de l'importance des activités d'une cité.[10] En fait, fruit d'une décision politique, la monnaie nous renseignerait plutôt sur la *politeia* de la cité, à la fois ses institutions et les pratiques sociales qui structurent la vie de la communauté;[11] mais une analyse précise nous entraînerait trop loin du sujet d'aujourd'hui.

A défaut de fournir un critère pour l'activité économique, les monnaies de fouille peuvent apporter un éclairage nouveau sur un fait historique, par leur présence comme par leur absence. J'ai montré ailleurs comment celles-ci permettaient de résoudre par la négative la question de la garnison macédonienne dont certains historiens avaient supposé la présence, au moins intermittente, sur l'île avant sa conquête par Philippe V en 205. En effet les monnaies macédoniennes ne sont pas proportion plus grande au IIIe siècle qu'aux périodes où nous savons que la ville n'était pas occupée par les Macédoniens, entre 360 et 323, puis à la basse période hellénistique. La situation est donc différente de celle de villes comme Corinthe ou Erétrie, où la garnison macédonienne, dont le séjour est attesté par les

10 Sur l'absence de relation directe entre le volume du monnayage et l'activité économique d'une cité, cf. O. Picard, "Monnaies et commerce à Thasos", *Economie antique. Les échanges dans l'Antiquité: le rôle de l'Etat, Entretiens d'archéologie et d'histoire, Saint-Bertrand-de-Comminges* (Toulouse 1994) 31-45 et, pour Erétrie, "Chalcis revisité", *Le IVe siècle. Approches historiographiques, colloque de Nancy,* (Nancy 1996) 190-192.

11 La monnaie de bronze a joué un rôle croissant dans le paiement des salaires ou dans le fonctionnement de la vie religieuse des cités hellénistiques, qu'il serait utile d'étudier systématiquement: cf. pour le misthos à l'assemblée d'Iasos, Ph. Gauthier, "L'inscription d'Iasos relative à l'ekklésiastikon", *BCH* 114 (1990) 441-443.

sources littéraires, a laissé une trace archéologique manifeste sous la forme d'un lot très important de monnaies macédoniennes.[12]

Inversement, la présence d'un ensemble de cinq bronzes d'une émission très rare d'Amphipolis me paraît confirmer et enrichir nos informations sur la politique antimacédonienne de Thasos entre 360 et 338. Philippe II, dans sa *Lettre aux Athéniens,*[13] se plaint véhémentement de l'hostilité des Thasiens qui accueillent libéralement dans leur port des bateaux ennemis du roi, voire des pirates. J. Pouilloux avait pu utiliser l'épigraphie pour montrer que des Olynthiens s'étaient réfugiés dans l'île après la chute de leur cité.[14] Ces cinq bronzes d'Amphipolis, qui présentent des types nettement macédoniens, la tête d'Héraclès au droit et un lion ou un sanglier au revers,[15] forment masse, si je puis dire, à côté des onze bronzes aux types traditionnels de la tête d'Apollon et de la torche. En effet, si la chronologie de ceux-ci n'est pas établie avec une parfaite précision,[16] il n'en est pas moins certain qu'ils ont été frappés en beaucoup plus grand nombre et pendant beaucoup plus longtemps que les deux émissions ultérieures dont le volume était très réduit. Celles-ci datent apparemment de la période où la cité d'Amphipolis s'intègre de plus en plus au royaume de Macédoine, tout en gardant une assez large autonomie (*Pl. 5c*).[17] La transformation de la cité entraîne le départ en exil d'un certain nombre d'habitants: la découverte de cinq de ces pièces rarissimes à Thasos me paraît indiquer que certains s'y sont réfugiés.

Je serais tenté de chercher une explication analogue pour expliquer le grand nombre de bronzes des Thasiens du Continent retrouvés sur le site de Thasos: 41 pièces répartis entre trois ou quatre émissions, à comparer aux 48 spécimens de la colonie romaine de Philippes et surtout aux 5 bronzes de Néapolis (*Pl. 5d*).[18] Or ce monnayage a été frappé dans un contexte d'opposition violente aux Thasiens de l'île, au cours d'une *stasis* qui a affaibli les positions thasiennes sur le continent, entraînant une

12 O. Picard, "Thasos et la Macédoine au IVe et au IIIe siècle", *Comptes rendus Acad. Inscr.* (1985) 760-776. "Les monnaies", *in* P. Ducrey, I. Metzger et K. Reber, *Le Quartier de la maison aux mosaïques, Eretria* VIII (Lausanne, 1993) 149-157, pl. IV.

13 [Démosthène] 12,2.

14 J. Pouilloux, *Recherches sur l'histoire et les cultes de Thasos* I, *EtThas*. III (Paris, 1954) 317, 430.

15 O. Picard, "Deux émissions de bronze d'Amphipolis", *BCH* 118 (1994) 207-214.

16 C. Lorber, *Amphipolis. The civic Coinage in Silver and Gold* (Los Angeles, 1990), fait débuter le monnayage d'argent en 370, tout en supposant que la première émission d'oboles ait pu être plus ancienne et même remonter au Ve s.

17 Voir M. Hatzopoulos, *Actes de vente d'Amphipolis*, *Meletémata* 14 (Athènes 1991) 62-86.

18 Sur la rareté des monnaies de Néapolis à Thasos, cf. O. Picard, "Thasos et Néapolis", *Mnémé D. Lazaridis, Recherches franco-helléniques* I (Athènes 1990), 541-548.

attaque des Thraces: pour y résister, les Continentaux durent faire appel au roi de Macédoine,[19] puis se fondre dans l'ensemble des colons macédoniens que le roi installa dans sa nouvelle ville. Les monnaies des rebelles ne devaient pas être acceptées par la cité mère pendant la durée du conflit. Leur présence en aussi grand nombre à Thasos me paraît indiquer qu'un certain nombre des dissidents avait regagné l'île après la fondation de Philippes.

Un autre épisode important de l'histoire de Thasos, son rôle de base arrière des Républicains lors de la bataille de Philippes en 42, explique la venue d'une pièce inattendue en ce lieu (*Pl.5e*).[20] Il s'agit d'un bronze de 8g, ayant au Droit une tête masculine à dr. et au Revers un cavalier à dr., une palme sur l'épaule; le style est assez rude et les légendes du D. et du R. sont écrites en un alphabet qui n'est ni grec ni sémitique: c'est un as de la haute vallée de l'Ebre en Espagne, au nom de Kese, qui est frappé à partir du milieu du IIe siècle jusque dans la première moitié du Ier siècle av. J.-C.[21] Il faut y joindre deux des trois pièces d'argent de la République romaine trouvées dans les fouilles, un quinaire frappé par Caton en Afrique en 47/6 et un denier au type du Grand Pompée, frappé par Q. Nasidius en 44/3:[22] c'est le numéraire utilisé par le camp républicain face aux Césariens. Le bronze de Kese est percé, ce qui indique que les Thasiens ont refusé de l'accepter et l'ont saisi.

On voit toute la richesse de l'apport des monnaies de fouille à notre connaissance d'une cité. Dans le cas de villes moyennes ou petites auxquelles les historiens anciens n'avaient prêté que peu d'attention, le monnayage de bronze local, dont la fouille a fourni la masse la plus importante, constitue véritablement l'ossature de notre information sur l'histoire de la cité. L'information fournie par les monnaies étrangères est d'un autre ordre; il apparaît cependant que l'afflux ou, inversement, l'absence remarquable de certaines séries, par rapport à une moyenne que

---

19 Cf. O. Picard, "Les Thasiens du Continent et la fondation de Philippes", *Tranquillitas. Mélanges en l'honneur de Tran tam Tinh* (Québec 1994) 409-424. Sur le statut de Philippes, voir M. Hatzopoulos, *BCH* (1993) 321-324.

20 J. Pouilloux — Chr. Dunant, (supra n.3) 55-56. Une découverte épigraphique, publiée par J.-Y. Empereur — A. Simossi, *BCH* 118 (1994) 407-415, vient éclairer les raisons du choix malheureux de Thasos pour le camp anticésarien par ses liens anciens avec la famille du grand Pompée.

21 *SNG Copenhague*, n°296. M. Beltran-Lloris, *Arqueologia e Historia de las Ciudades antiguas del Cabezo de Alcala de Azaila (Teruel), Monografias arqueologicas* 19 (Saragosse 1976) 331-337. Sur les dates de ce monnayage très uniforme, voir M. Crawford, *Coinage and Money in the Roman Republic* (Londres 1985) 91-96, fig. 29.

22 M. Crawford, *Roman Republican Coinage* (Londres 1974) n°462,2 et 483,2; supra n.21, 251, sur des trésors liés à la guerre civile.

les autres émissions d'une cité ou les autres ateliers d'une région permettent d'estimer,[23] a une signification qu'il peut être difficile d'élucider, mais qui doit, en tout état de cause retenir l'attention de l'historien.

Géographie de la circulation, géographie des échanges

Apport à l'histoire, mais aussi apport à la géographie historique. Ici encore, la difficulté est d'apprécier exactement la nature de cet apport.

La première hypothèse qui vient à l'esprit est qu'à défaut de nous permettre de retracer l'évolution du commerce de la cité, les monnaies de fouille feraient au moins connaître ses partenaires commerciaux. Il faut renoncer à cet espoir. Le grand produit exporté par les Thasiens fut le vin, vendu dans des amphores que leur profil caractéristique et surtout le timbre qu'elles portent sur une anse au IVe et au IIIe siècle font aisément reconnaître. Le corpus en cours de préparation[24] permettra de dresser un jour une carte précise de leur diffusion, mais l'on peut d'ores et déjà affirmer que la zone de prédilection du commerce thasien se trouve en Mer Noire, dans les ports du Pont gauche et de la côte Nord. Or mon enquête archéologique m'a conduit à constater une double absence: les mêmes fouilles qui ont mis au jour tant d'anses d'amphores thasiennes à Panticapée ou à Olbia, à Histria ou à Messembria, n'ont pas donné de bronzes thasiens;[25] de même, les ports de la Mer Noire ne sont pas représentés parmi les trouvailles de Thasos, en dehors de deux monnaies de Panticapée du IVe-IIIe siècle et d'une du Royaume du Bosphore Cimmérien de l'époque impériale (*Pl. 5f*). La contradiction est si flagrante entre les indications des amphores et celle des monnaies qu'il faut bien se résoudre à renoncer à voir dans le mouvement des monnaies de bronze un indicateur du mouvement des bateaux transportant le vin thasien.[26]

La zone d'où proviennent nos monnaies étrangères se laisse assez bien délimiter. A l'Est, deux ports en marquent l'accès, Byzance au N-E et

---

23 C'est cette méthode qu'a appliquée G. Le Rider, *Suse sous les Séleucides et les Parthes* (Paris 1965) 302-306, quand il essaie d'interpréter le nombre particulièrement élevé de bronzes de Séleucie du Tigre trouvé à Suse pendant le règne d'Antiochos III. Cette étude monumentale illustre bien, par ailleurs, la différence qui existe entre la richesse de la documentation numismatique et la pauvreté de notre information historique.

24 Y. Garlan, *Vins et amphores de Thasos, Sites et Monuments* V (Paris 1988); "Nouvelles remarques sur la chronologie des timbres amphoriques de Thasos", *JSavants* (1993) 149-181.

25 C'est à tort que les bronzes contremarqués de Thasos étudiés par T. Gerassimov, *BIAB* 15 (1946), 65-67, sont indiquées comme trouvées à Apollonia du Pont, (supra n.3) 217, n°31. Je ne sais rien sur les 12 monnaies thasiennes que B. Filow, *AA* 26 (1911), 353, indique avoir été trouvées dans un bassin des thermes d'Aquae Calidae à 15 km au N-O de Burgas.

26 Cf. mes remarques dans "Monnaies et commerce à Thasos" (ci-dessus n.10).

Rhodes au S-E: au-delà de cette borne, je ne connais qu'une monnaie isolée de Tarse, du IIe siècle av. J.-C. (*Pl. 6a*), ainsi que quelques bronzes d'Alexandrie, trois de Ptolémée I et II et quatre de l'époque impériale (*Pl. 6b*). A l'Ouest, la situation est moins claire. Je rattacherais volontiers les monnaies isolées (représentées par un seul exemplaire par atelier) des Molosses, d'Argos Amphilochikos et des Etoliens à l'ensemble du Péloponnèse et de Grèce Continentale qui date du IVe-IIIe siècle; en revanche, les quatre bronzes de Dyrrachion et d'Apollonia d'Illyrie sont incontestablement des apports du trafic le long de la Via Egnatia dont l'odyssée du petit cochon d'Edesse constitue un témoin pittoresque.[27] Je vais revenir sur la limite Nord. Au Sud, on notera l'absence totale, à ce jour, de monnaies des Cyclades et de la Crète.

Ainsi délimitée, cette zone se divise très clairement en trois régions d'importance très inégale: la côte thrace et la Macédoine fournissent naturellement le nombre de pièces de beaucoup le plus important à toutes les périodes; à l'Ouest, seule la première période a donné un nombre significatif de monnaies, tandis que la côte d'Asie Mineure et les Détroits sont toujours restés en relation avec Thasos.

Avec près de 650 pièces le Nord fournit, de manière écrasante, le contingent le plus nombreux de monnaies étrangères. C'est, de toute évidence, le milieu géographique dans lequel baigne Thasos: il se compose de deux ensembles distincts, la Macédoine, dont on a trouvé un bronze dès le règne d'Amyntas II (*Pl. 6c*), et les cités grecques de la côte, de Potidée à Ainos, un ensemble géographique qui évoque le district thrace dans les listes du tribut athénien au Ve siècle; il faut y ajouter, en arrière plan, les monnayages thraces nettement moins abondants, mais présents depuis la fin du VIe siècle jusqu'au milieu du IIIe siècle ap. J.-C.[28] Les bronzes macédoniens les plus nombreux sont ceux aux types de Philippe (32 AE) et d'Alexandre (41 monnaies). Par la suite, on trouve surtout des pièces aux types du bouclier et du casque, ou au cavalier saluant. Philippe V se signale par 15 AE. Dans la deuxième et la troisième période, les monnaies royales sont relayées surtout par celles de Thessalonique (1 AE hellénistique et 20 d'époque impériale) et d'Amphipolis (17 AE pour chaque période). En Thrace, on trouve naturellement parmi les grands partenaires de Thasos Abdère (où, très curieusement, les fouilles sont loin de donner une proportion aussi élevée de monnaies thasiennes), avec quelque 130 pièces, et Maronée, avec environ 80 pièces. Malgré l'inter-

27 O. Picard, *Iliria* (1986), 137-144. Sur le fameux "Cochon d'Edesse", voir Ph. Petsas, *AAA* 2(1969) 186-189; G. Daux, *BCH* 94 (1970) 609-617.

28 Voir ci-dessus n.9.

ruption de son monnayage du IIIe au Ier siècle, Philippes-Crénidès atteint lui 90 exemplaires. Un peu plus loin vers l'Est, Ainos et Samothrace, avec respectivement 34 et 12 bronzes , tiennent encore une place respectable. Je ne donne pas le détail par période, car elles sont toutes représentées et je reviendrai ci-dessous sur la signification qu'il convient, me semble-t-il, d'attribuer à ces chiffres.

Revenons en Grèce. Je laisse de côté un tétartémorion éléen du IVe siècle, qui doit marquer le souvenir de la participation d'un Thasien aux fêtes olympiques. Les autres monnaies viennent de deux groupes hétérogènes d'ateliers. D'une part, des cités maritimes, le long de la route qui descend du Nord vers le golfe Saronique et Athènes: c'est le cas de Skiathos, de Péparéthos, des cités eubéennes (où les fouilles suisses ont trouvé un bronze thasien); avec 11 pièces, dont 4 aux types d'Eleusis, Athènes occupe sans contredit la première place (*Pl. 6d*), mais ce chiffre reste modeste à côté de ceux des ateliers de Macédoine ou de Thrace; ni Corinthe, ni Egine, ni Mégare ne sont présents. L'autre groupe est constitué de deux cités du Péloponnèse (Hermionè et Cleitor) et de peuples de Grèce Continentale: 1 AE étolien, 1 phocidien, 1 molosse; j'y rangerai aussi les 4 AE béotiens, les 4 locriens ainsi que les thessaliens. A la basse époque hellénistique, seuls les Thessaliens (avec les Ainianes) se maintiennent. Sous l'Empire, je ne compte plus qu'un seul AE thessalien. Bref on constate une quasi disparition des relations avec la Grèce. D'autre part la présence de bronzes "continentaux" au IVe et au IIIe siècle, qui est comparable à celle des cités maritimes, ne laisse pas d'être remarquable; je me demande s'il ne faut pas y voir le reflet de l'emploi de mercenaires.

L'image fournie par les monnaies venant de l'Est est bien différente. Soulignons d'abord l'importance, à toute période, des Détroits auxquels on ajoutera la Troade: le déclin apparent des bronzes de Chersonnèse de Thrace (au sens large, en y englobant les petites cités, comme Madytos ou Alopéconésos) à la basse période hellénistique, après une très forte présence au IVe siècle, s'explique simplement par le fléchissement du monnayage de ces cités à cette époque; le relais sera pris, avec éclat, par le monnayage d'Alexandrie de Troade sous l'Empire (*Pl. 6e-f*); à la même époque la Propontide occupe une place croissante. Plus au Sud, il faut souligner le contraste qui existe entre la côte Ouest et la côte Est de l'Egée: cette dernière fournit régulièrement, du IVe siècle av. J.-C. au IIIe après, des bronzes qui viennent aussi bien des grandes îles que des ports du continent. Avec 9 AE, Chios est la mieux représentée au IVe siècle. Ce sera le cas d'Ephèse, avec le même chiffre, sous l'Empire. Mais on note surtout un grand nombre de cités qui fournissent de 1 à 4 AE.

Voilà le tableau que les monnaies étrangères trouvées à Thasos permettent de dresser. Je me suis demandé quel type de document géographique se rapprochait le plus de cette liste des cités et de rois. A propos de la côte thrace, j'ai parlé du district thrace des listes du tribut athénien: or celles-ci se présentent clairement comme un *Périple*, celui que les stratèges accomplissaient chaque année pour aller percevoir le phoros. L'observation est valable pour la quasi-totalité des régions, à l'exception des deux cités à l'extrémité Ouest de la via Egnatia et des monnaies de Grèce Continentale et du Péloponnèse. En Asie Mineure, quatre cités de l'intérieur, Nakrasa (*Pl. 6g*), Apamée de Phrygie (*Pl. 6h*), Blaundos et Sardes, constituent certes des exceptions, bien qu'elles soient dans des vallées bien reliées à la côte; les autres monnaies nous font longer les côtes grecques depuis le canal eubéen[29] qui conduit aux grands ports du golfe Saronique (pourtant, eux, bien mal représentés, en dehors d'Athènes) jusqu'à la Propontide et à la côte Ouest de l'Asie Mineure, en passant, bien sûr, par la côte Nord de l'Egée, de Thessalonique ou de la Chalcidique à l'embouchure de l'Hèbros et surtout aux Détroits: c'est là que bat le coeur des échanges thasiens. La réalité qui se cache derrière la perte de ces menues monnaies, ce n'est donc pas le "grand" commerce thasien, l'exportation de vin vers la Mer Noire, mais l'activité sans doute beaucoup plus importante d'un cabotage qui faisait de Thasos une escale très vivante le long des côtes égéennes: ce dont les *Plaidoyers Civils* de Démosthène, ou les services rendus par un Dionysodôros fils de Pempidès, au temps de Mithridate[30] apportent quelques échos. Il me paraît significatif que le reflet que ces monnaies nous donnent de la fidélité des Thasiens à l'alliance athénienne entre 375 et 338, c'est l'asile offert aux bannis qui fuient l'avance de Philippe II dans la région et surtout l'importance des liens avec la Chersonnèse de Thrace. Je retiendrai aussi l'importance des liens avec l'Eolide et avec l'Ionie: une étude récente sur le développement de l'architecture thasienne à l'époque classique trouvait dans ces relations une source d'inspiration particulièrement féconde pour Thasos.[31] Cet accord remarquable entre deux formes apparemment très éloignées de l'archéologie, l'histoire de l'art et la numismatique, montre combien notre documentation monétaire restitue une réalité complexe, qui échappe complètement à l'historien des textes, mais qui constitue le socle de la réalité antique: c'est dans ce cadre géographique qu'il convient d'apprécier la politique menée par Thasos.

---

29 Voir O. Picard, *Chalcis et la Confédération eubéenne* (Paris 1979), 212-218.

30 Voir J. Pouilloux — Chr. Dunant (supra n.3) 21-35.

31 J. des Courtils, *Architectures thasiennes*, thèse (1992) à paraître dans les *EtThas*.

FUNDMÜNZEN AUS AIGEIRA I: LOKALE PRÄGUNGEN

Manfred Hainzmann

Im Zuge der bis 1988 — unter der Leitung von Prof. Wilhelm Alzinger — durchgeführten archäologischen Ausgrabungen auf dem Gelände des antiken Aigeira wurden an die 300 Münzen gefunden, deren Bearbeitung in den nächsten Monaten abgeschlossen sein wird. Wie erwartet, kamen auch einige (insgesamt 13) Münzen der örtlichen Prägestätte zutage. Sie sollen in diesem Tagungsband erstmals vorgestellt und besprochen werden.

Wie die meisten ihrer achaiischen Nachbarstädte (s. Karte), hat auch Aigeira, dessen klassische Schreibweise ΑΙΓΙΡΑ[1] lautet, wahrscheinlich in der ersten Hälfte des 4. Jh. v. Chr. mit der Produktion von Bronzemünzen begonnen. Bislang kennen wir vier verschiedene Typen (vgl. Tabelle 1), von denen wiederum drei (Fundmünzen Nr. 1, 3, 4) auf der Vorderseite eine Gottheit (Kopf bzw. Büste) zur Darstellung bringen. Während die Interpretation des ältesten Prägetyps als *Athena*-Kopf, gesichert ist, habe ich für die *Schleierbüste* und den *Asklepios* (Nr. 3 und 4) zuletzt eine neue Deutung vorgeschlagen.[2] Nach dem was uns Pausanias über die Denkmäler Aigeiras berichtet, zählten die Kultstatuen der Athene und des Zeus wohl zu den berühmtesten Kunstwerken dieser Stadt.[3] Und obwohl er auch Asklepios-Statuen erwähnt und der griechische Heilgott in Aigeira womöglich auch eine Kultstätte besessen haben wird, möchte ich in der

1 So das Ethnikon aller autonomen Prägungen und die epigraphischen Zeugnisse wie etwa in der Inschrift aus Oreos [*Bull.hell.* XV 414, 34]:[ΑΓ]ΑΘΑΡΧΩΙ ΔΗΜΟΚΡΙΤΟΥ ΑΧΑΙΩΙ ΕΞ ΑΙΓΙΡΑΣ oder die Inschrift vom hellenistischen Reiterdenkmal des Damon von Patrai, in: T. Schwertfeger, *Der Achaiische Bund von 146 bis 27 v.Chr.* (München 1974) 28.

2 M. Hainzmann, "Pausanias und die Münzprägung von Aigeira", *Meletemata* 13, (Akten des 1. Internationalen Symposiums über "Achaia und Elis in der Antike", Athen 1989) 1991, 195ff.

3 VII 26, 1-11. Das Kultbild der Athene war aus Goldelfenbein, der Name des Künstlers ist nicht bekannt, das marmorne Sitzbild des Zeus soll ein Werk des athenischen Bildhauers Euklid gewesen sein. Zu den auf Münzen überlieferten Götterbildern s. F.W. Imhoof-Blumer und P. Gardner, *Ancient coins illustrating lost masterpieces of Greek Art. A numismatic commentary on Pausanias* (Chicago 1964) weiters N. Papachatzis, ΠΑΥΣΑΝΙΟΥ ΕΛΛΑΔΟΣ ΠΕΡΙΗΓΗΣΙΣ (Athen 1980) IV 159.

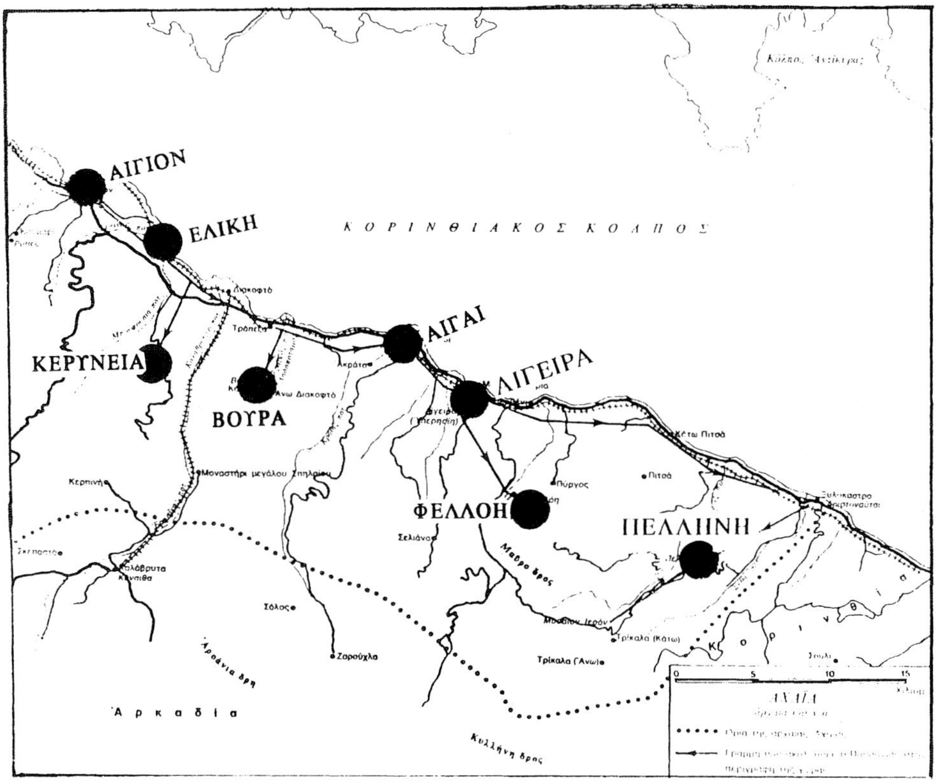

Fig. 1 Achaia, Ostsektor.

von Mionnet[4] als *"caput Aesculapii laureatum"* beschriebenen Münze der Pariser Sammlung eher einen *Zeus*-Kopf erkennen. Natürlich ist ohne entsprechende Attribute zwischen einem bärtigen, lorbeerbekränzten Haupt des Asklepios oder Zeus eine Unterscheidung so gut wie unmöglich; weil wir aber die aigiratischen Münzen nur mit Pausanias und den dortigen archäologischen Funden vergleichen können, scheint mir, angesichts des 1916 von Otto Walter gefundenen kolossalen Zeus-Kopfes[5] und des inzwischen ergrabenen Zeus-Heiligtums,[6] eine Identifizierung mit dem griechischen Göttervater als plausibler.

---

4 II 164 Nr. 118.

5 Foto bei N. Papachatzis (supra no. 3) IV 163; es zeigt die Löcher für die Anbringung des Lorbeerkranzes.

6 Zum Grabungsbefund s. W. Alzinger, Aigeira-Hyperesia II, *Klio* 68 (1986) 50ff. mit der älteren Literatur. Ein letzter Bericht über "Die hellenistischen Tempel von Aigeira" wurde vom selben Autor in den Akten des XIII. intern. Kongresses für klass. Archäologie in Mainz, 1990, 549ff., veröffentlicht.

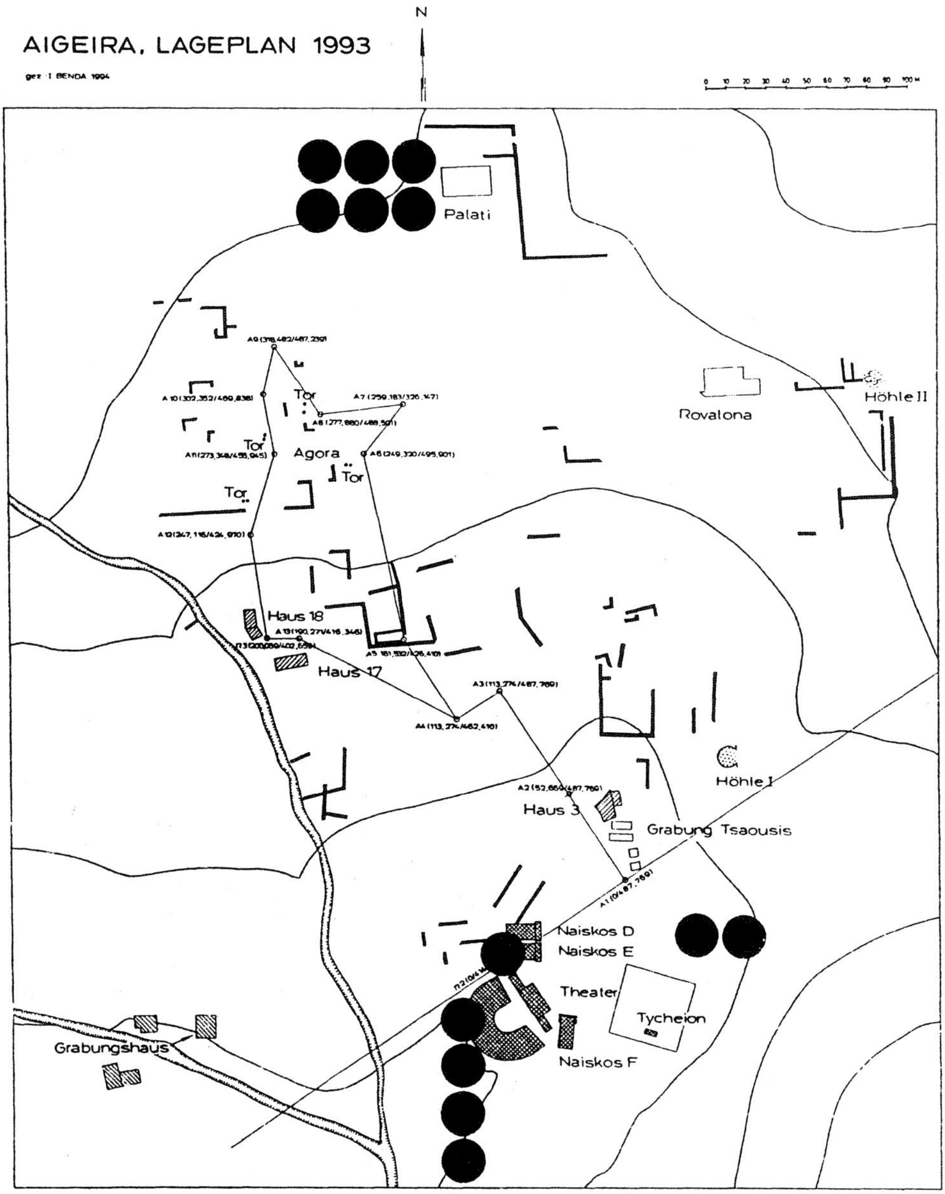

Fig. 2 Aigeira, Fundmünzen biz 1988.

Keine Schwierigkeiten hinsichtlich ihres Bildinhalts bietet die Nr. 2 aus der autonomen Serie, mit dem "Stadtwappen" Aigeiras, dem *Ziegenbock*, welcher hier nur als Protome und nicht wie auf der Rückseite von Typ-3 in voller Gestalt auftaucht. Daß das Beizeichen dieses "type parlant" den

Stadtnamen und die Polis als solche vertritt, wird zudem aus den Bundesprägungen (AR-Serie) Aigeiras deutlich, auf deren Vorderseite nebst Zeus-Kopf und Bundesmonogramm gleichfalls die Vorderhälfte eines Ziegenbocks erscheint. Hier wie dort lesen wir auf der Rückseite Beamtennamen. Ich meine, daß gleichlautende Namen Identität der Person und chronologische Übereinstimmung beider Serien bedeuten. Zu den aus den geläufigen Münzkatalogen bekannten Prägungen konnte zuletzt ich in der Athener Münzsammlung zwei neue (Tabelle 1, Nr. 2b und 2c) entdecken, womit wir bei vorerst sieben Varianten dieses Typs halten.

Die beigeschriebenen Beamtennamen sind es auch, die eine Unterscheidung der autonomen Prägestücke[7] nach älteren (ab ca. 330 v. Chr. Athena) und jüngeren Emissionen (ab 251 v.Chr.?)[8] erlauben, doch wage ich nicht zu behaupten, daß die aigiratischen Behörden über das Jahr 146 hinaus, d.h. in der Folgezeit noch bis 27 v. Chr.,[9] Münzen geschlagen hätten. Mangels entsprechender Materialpublikationen und stratigraphischer Analysen aus den Grabungskampagnen bis 1988, sehe ich auch keine Möglichkeit, auf Basis der hier vorgestellten Neufunde eine chronologische Feindatierung zu geben. Für eine Datierung in die Zeit nach dem ersten Abschnitt des Achäischen Bundes fehlen die notwendigen Anhaltspunkte.

Wenden wir uns nun jenem Prägetyp-3 aus Tabelle 2 zu, von dem wir als einzigem unter den örtlichen Münzfunden mehrere (genau 13 Stück) Belege haben. Er zeigt uns auf der Vorderseite eine nach rechts gewandte, mit Schleier bedeckte Frauenbüste. Die Rückseite schmückt das Wappentier Aigeiras — der Ziegenbock; er wird von einem Ölzweig umrahmt. Zwischen dem nach rechts stehenden Begleittier der Artemis, genauer gesagt den Vorderläufen des Bockes und dem Kranz findet man die Initialen der für die Münzprägung zuständigen Beamten. Der jeweilige Name und das auf der Vs. eingestempelte Ethnikon ergeben, bei sonst gleichbleibendem Münzbild, die Anzahl der Serien. Das geringe Vergleichsmaterial,[10] der schlechte Erhaltungszustand sowie das Fehlen von Abgüssen ließen mich vorerst von einer genaueren Typenanalyse absehen.

---

7 Gruppe I umfaßt in meiner Tabelle alle Münzen der Zeit bis 27 v. Chr., ausgenommen die Bundesprägungen.

8 Daß die jüngere Serie mit dem Beitritt Aigeiras zum Achäischen Bund in Zusammenhang steht, ist anzunehmen. Da Aigion 275 in den Bund eintrat, könnte Aigeira diesen Schritt sehr wohl im Jahr darauf gesetzt haben.

9 *BMC* Peloponnesus (Aigeira no. 17) datiert die "Schleierbüste" in die Epoche 146-31, vorsichtiger hingegen SNG-Cop, mit: "after 251 B.C."

10 Außer den in der Athener Sammlung vorhandenen Belegstücken konnte ich bislang keine weiteren Fundmünzen eruieren.

Table 1 Münzstätte Aigeira: Autonome Prägungen I.

Münzstätte AIGEIRA: Autonome Prägungen I						
"Typ"	Avers	Revers		Zitat	Datierung	Kommentar
		Bild	Legende			
1a	**Athena-Kopf r.**	Ziegenprotome r. in Kranz	AIΓI(ρατων)	SNG-Cop 127; BMC 1-3; Weber 3948	um 330 (?)	Hesperia 41, 1972, 183 Nr.200: AI[Γ(ιρατων)] (!)
1b	"="	"="	AIΓIP(ατων)	Mion. Suppl. IV 20 Nr.120		
2a	**Ziegenprotome r.** AIΓIPATAN	Kranz	AΣK/ΛH	Mion. Suppl. IV 20 Nr.122	ab 274 (?)	SNG: after 251 B.C.
b	"="	"="	AN	Νομ.Συλλ.Αθην.π272		
c	"="	"="	AΠ/OΛ	Νομ. Συλλ. Αθην. 84/3888		
d	"="	"="	KΛE	SNG-Fitzwilliam 3555		
e	"="	"="	ΛA	SNG-Cop 130		
f	"="	"="	ΠPO/ΘY	Cahn 60, 1928,617		
g	AIΓIP[—], ΛA	"="	ΔPA	Mion. Suppl. IV 20 Nr.121		
3a-g	**"Schleierbüste" Iphigenie? r.**	Ziege in Kranz	Beamten-name	**s. Tabelle 2**	251-146 (?)	BMC: 146-31 v.Chr.
4	**Asklepios / Zeus?** - Kopf r. AIΓIPATAN	Ziege in Kranz	AP	Mion. II 164 Nr.118 Eckhel, Doct.num.vet. II 234.	251-146/27(?)	Eckhel: "caput Aesculapii laureatum"

Table 2 "Schleierbüste" / Iphigenie (?) 3a-g; Fundmünzen aus Aigeira (bis 1988).

"Schleierbüste" / Iphigenie (?) 3a-g								
Typ	Kommentar					Avers	Revers	Zitat
3a	SNG: "female head veiled"					AIΓIPATAN	AΛ(–)	SNG-Cop 128
b						"="	AI(–)	(Aigeira Nr. 12)
c						"="	AM(–)	SNG-Cop 129
d	Mion.: "tète voilée de femme"					"="	ΛA(–)	Mion. II 163 Nr.116
e	BMC: "female bust, wearing veil"					AIΓIPAT(αν)	AP(–)	Mion. II 163 Nr.117, BMC 4
f						"="	ΛA(–)	Νομ. Συλλ. Αθην. 271 (unpubl.)
g						[—]	A(–)	(Aigeira Nr. 3)
FUNDMÜNZEN aus AIGEIRA (bis 1988)								
Nr.	Inv.-Nr.	Fundort (Anzahl)	Dm	Gw	Kranz	Avers	Revers	Konkordanz/ Kommentar
1	TH-72-19	**Theater (4)**	17	2,80	x?	[—]	[—]	
2	TH-73-02	"-"	17	4,10	x6	[A]IΓIPATA[N]	AP(–)	3e
3	TH-75-13	"="	16	3,60	x6	[—]	A(–)	3g
4	TH-78-27	"="	18	4,90	x6	[—]	AΛ(–)	3a(?)
5	PA-80-44	**Palati (6)**	17	5,30	x6	[—]	A+(–)	
6	PA-81-02	"="	18	4,40	x6	AIΓIPA[TAN]	[—]	
7	PA-81-10	"="	17	3,60	x?	AIΓ[—]	[—]	
8	PA-82-02	"="	19	4,10	x7	[A]IΓIPAT{αν)	AM(–)	
9	PA-82-05	"="	19	3,80	x6	[A]IΓIP[—]	[—]	
10	PA-82-11	"="	21	3,70	x?	[—]	[—]	
11	PqD5-84-08	**PqD5 (1)**	16	4,70	x6	[A]IΓIPATA[N]	ΛA(–)	3d(?)
12	NA/E-84-06	**Naiskos-E (1)**	17	4,20	x6	[A]IΓIPATA[N]	AI(–)	3b
13	GY-85-19	**"Gymnasium" (1)**	20	3,90	x6	AIΓIPA[TAN]	AΛ(–)	3d(?)
	LEGENDE: Dm= Durchmesser, Gw= Gewicht							

Dank der in Aigeira zum Vorschein gekommenen neuen Fundmünzen (Nr. 3 und 12 aus Tabelle 2) und eines Stückes aus der Numismatischen Sammlung in Athen (Typ 3f) kennen wir nunmehr sieben Varianten dieses Prägetyps. Schon anhand des Ethnikons, das einmal die Kurzform AIΓIPAT und dann wieder die volle Form AIΓIPATAN aufweist, kann man zwei Gruppen, mit zum Teil gleichlautenden Beamtennamen (etwa LA), scheiden. Zwar ist in unserem Fundmaterial bei keiner Münze (vgl. Vs-Umschrift in Tabelle 2) die ganze Beischrift erkennbar; vergleicht man jedoch den Schriftduktus mit den bei SNG-Cop ausgewiesenen Stücken, so gibt es keinen Zweifel darüber, daß die vertikal angeordnete, nach innen gerichtete Vs-Legende ein abschließendes "N" enthalten haben muß.

Typ-3g wiederum unterscheidet sich nicht nur durch das Monogramm "A" von den übrigen; der Beamtenname steht hier — entgegen allen anderen Initialen — horizontal.[11] Könnte man den bei *SNG* Cop 128 zitierten Namen AΛ ebensogut als ΛA lesen, so ist diese Buchstabenkombination auch durch die Fundmünze Nr. 4 bezeugt.[12] Beide Namensformen haben ihre formale und damit wohl auch inhaltliche Entsprechung auf den AR-Bundesprägungen: AΛ jedoch nur in der Kombination AΛ - KI,[13] der andere Name als Λ - A.[14] Ebenfalls auf Bundesmünzen vertreten ist der Beamtenname AP(---), den wir schon von der Asklepios/Zeus-Münze kennen.

Jetzt aber zur *Schleierbüste*, die — ebenso wie die beiden anderen Götterbilder — eine von den Aigeiraten hochgeschätze Kultstatue wiedergeben dürfte. Schon aus den mir bekannten Stücken geht hervor, daß es mehrere Bildtypen gegeben haben muß. Neben der unterschiedlichen Büstenform als Ganzes ist auch eine Differenzierung in der Gestalt des Schleiers sowie des Kopfprofils zu beobachten. Als charakteristisches Merkmal sticht bei allen Darstellungen, selbst bei stark abgeriebener Oberfläche, der Haarknoten ins Auge. Ich habe diese von den Fachkollegen bislang unbestimmte Frauenbüste mit der von Pausanias erwähnten *Iphigeneia* geglichen[15] und fühle mich durch einen Neufund in dieser Interpretation bestätigt, zeigt doch die Fundmünze Nr. 11 ein auf die Nachricht des Periegeten passendes Bildnis einer archaischen Kore mit Schleier.

---

11 Es wäre möglich, daß über diesem Monogramm ein zweiter Buchstabe stand, da in der Regel die Beamtennamen mit jeweils zwei Anfangsbuchstaben signieren. Vielleicht stammt also auch diese Serie vom Münzmeister ΛA(---).

12 Die gleichen Initialen entdecken wir auf zwei Serien des Typs 2, nämlich 2a und 2g, letztere mit dem Beamtennamen auf der Vorderseite.

13 Vgl. M.G. Clerk, *Catalogue of the Coins of the Achaean League* (London 1895) Nr. 16 und 17.

14 Vgl. M.G. Clerk (supra no. 13) Nr. 13.

15 M. Hainzmann (supra no. 2) 202.

Fig. 3 Fundmünze Nr. 11 Table 2. (1:2)

Ohne die von mir seinerzeit vorgebrachten Argumente zu wiederholen, möchte ich nur den für Aigeira legendären Artemiskult in Erinnerung rufen, in dessen Kontext sich Iphigenie so reibungslos einzufügen scheint. Als weitere Stütze für meine Bildinterpretation mag eine jüngst publizierte Münze der Greek Imperials aus Aigeira[16] dienen, deren Vorderseite die vierarmige *Hekate* in phrygischer Mütze und mit Fackeln zeigt. Neben der gleichfalls durch eine Severerprägung bezeugten *Artemis-Agrotera* und der mit Artemis aufs engste verbundenen Iphigenie, ist Hekate bereits die zweite Göttergestalt, die diesem zentralen Kult zuzuordnen ist. Dabei macht es wohl keinen Unterschied, ob wir in ihr eine der synkretistischen Vorstellungswelt entsprechende Artemis[17] erkennen oder sie mit Iphigenie in Zusammenhang bringen, verweist doch Lloyd-Jones[18] auf die Tatsache, daß "in the *Catalogue* [scil. Frauenkatalog des Hesiod] Iphigeneia is not killed, but is turned into Hekate, handmaid of Artemis". So stehen wir vor einem weiteren Zeugnis für den hohen Informationswert antiker Münzbilder, welche uns am Beispiel Aigeiras die Metamorphose eines archaischen Kultes vor Augen führen:

Iphigenie **Artemis**

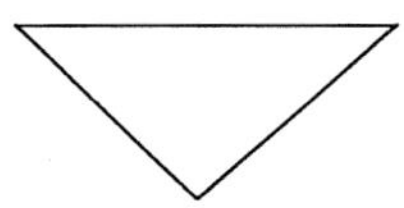

Hekate

16 H. Bloesch, *Griechische Münzen in Winterthur* (Winterthur 1994) Nr. 2140.

17 So lesen wir bei W.H. Roscher [*Ausführliches Lexikon der griechischen und römischen Mythologie* (Leipzig 1886-1890)] I 2, 1896f.: "Daß beide Göttinnen außerordentlich oft mit gleichen Beinamen und in gleichen Funktionen vorkommen, erklärt sich zur Genüge aus der Verwandtschaft ihres Wesens, doch scheint erst in der Zeit des Synkretismus die wirklich allgemeine Identifizierung dieser Göttinnen durchgedrungen zu sein".

18 H. Lloyd-Jones, "Artemis and Iphigeneia", *JHS* 103 (1983) 95.

THE CONTRIBUTION OF THE NUMISMATIC EVIDENCE TO THE DATING OF THE SEAL IMPRESSIONS FROM THE "ARCHIVES" OF THE CITY OF ANCIENT PAPHOS

I. Nicolaou

The excavations at the House of Dionysos in Paphos, conducted by the late Kyriakos Nicolaou, could be compared to a "surprise packet". No doubt, the most sensational discovery remains that of the magnificent late 2nd/ early 3rd century AD mosaics, with figurative and geometric decoration, which cover the floors of fifteen of the forty rooms of this atrium-type residence.[1] Because of the prominence of Dionysiac themes in its mosaics, it was called by the excavator *"The House of Dionysos"*. This house was constructed on an area occupied earlier by a house of the 1st century AD which was destroyed by an earthquake sometime before the mid-2nd century AD. The last house was built on the area of a complex of the Hellenistic period.

The excavations brought to light — apart from the thousands of movable objects (over 5,000) — a hoard of 2,484 silver Ptolemaic tetradrachms[2] (Room XXIII), a workshop for casting bronze Ptolemaic coins[3] (Room LII (LI)), a foundry for casting over lifesize bronze statues[4] (Room XI), a pebble mosaic floor of the late 4th/3rd century BC[5] (near the southwest corner of the atrium) and last but not least more than 11,000 clay seal impressions, which are believed to have belonged to the Archives of the city of Paphos.[6]

---

1 K. Nicolaou, *RDAC* 1963, 56-72; *RDAC* 1967, 100-125; *A Roman Villa at Paphos, Archaeology* 21 (1968) 48-53; C. Kondoleon, *Domestic and Divine, Roman Mosaics in the House of Dionysos* (1995) (here see also for other publications: Introduction n. 7, Chapter 2 n. 6).

2 I. Nicolaou — O. Mørkholm, *Paphos* I (Nicosia 1976).

3 I. Nicolaou, *Paphos* II (Nicosia 1990) 131-133.

4 K. Nicolaou, "Archaeological News from Cyprus, 1970", in *AJA* 76 (1972) 315, *Archaeological Reports 1969-1976*, 59.

5 K. Nicolaou, *ILN* no. 6973 (August 1979) 47; id., "Three New Mosaics at Paphos Cyprus", in *III Colloquio intern. sul Mosaico Antico, Ravenna 6-10 Settembre* 1980 (1984), 219-225, fig. 6-8; D. Salzmann, *Unterschungen zu den antiken Kiesel Mosaiken* (*Arch. Forsch.* 10) (1982) 126 suppl. 3, pl. 64: 1; D. Michaelides, *Cypriot Mosaics* (1992) 13, fig. 1.

6 K. Nicolaou, *ILN* no. 2358 (May 1971) 51-53.

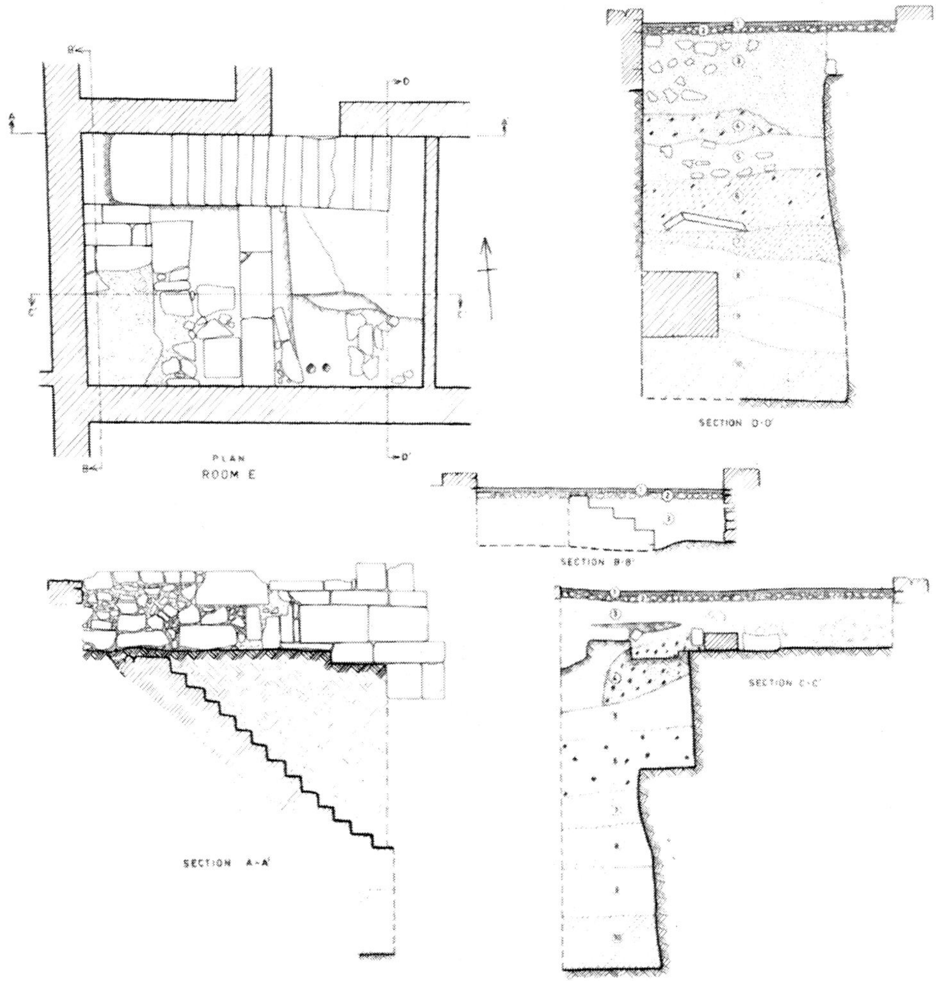

Fig. 1 Plan of Room E, and cross sections.

As some of the mosaics from the House of Dionysos had sunk and cracked in antiquity as a result of earthquakes, it was thought necessary that they be lifted up in order to be reset on sound foundations. Among other mosaics which were lifted up in 1970 was that depicting Hippolytos and Phaedra (Room V(E), 4.85x4.30m). This gave the opportunity of investigating below this mosaic to the full extent of the room. What was found below the mosaic could be considered as a sealed deposit *(Fig. 1)*. There was a clear stromatography but it was a stromatography of a filling. Although it was realised from the very beginning that we had come across a filling, we dug by layer down to the bottom. Counting the mosaic as layer 1, we proceeded digging from layer 2 to 10, (main fill: 4-10); what was considered as layers 11-13 was actually the lower stratum of layer 10, pulverised sandstone soil mixed up with sandstone stones and scrappy material.

The excavations proved that there was an old quarry (?), 5.30 m. deep, which had been filled up with rubble in order to form the foundations of the mosaic. The rubble consisted of earth, either loose or hard, mixed up with fragments of mortar, stones, carbonized wood, painted or unpainted stuccoes, potsherds, coins, lamps, fragments of terracottas, iron nails and clay sealings, all coming from earlier buildings. As soon as we found the first sealings below layer 3, all the excavated earth was sieved, and this continued to be done throughout the excavation of all the layers. The main lots of the sealings were found in layers 4, 5 and 8; sporadic amounts were found in layers 3 (lower), 9 and 10 *(Fig. 1)*. Layers 4-5 and 8 consisted of compact soil full of ashes, dark and greasy, in which the clay seal impressions were found together with coins, terracottas, stamped handles, potsherds and lamps. This same repertory of objects was found in all the layers. Twenty coins[7] were found in the filling of Room V. They are as follows:

Coins found together with the main lots of the sealings (layers 4-5, 8)

Layers 4-5 (depth 0.30-0.60 cm below the mosaic); 11 coins.

1. Ptolemy I Soter, as ruler, (311/10-306/5 BC) (*Paphos* II, acc. no. 21).
2. Ptolemy II Philadelphos (285/4-247/6 BC) (*Paphos* II, acc. no. 42).
3. Ptolemy VIII Euergetes II (146/5-117/6 BC) (*Paphos* II, acc. no. 298).
4. Cleopatra VII, Ptolemy XVI (Caesarion) (47-44 BC) (*Paphos* II, acc. no. 447)
5. Cleopatra VII, Ptolemy XVI (Caesarion) (44-30 BC) (*Paphos* II, acc. no. 467).

6-10. Cleopatra VII, late in her reign (*Paphos* II, acc. nos: 502-504, 508, 509).

11. Jewish coin, under Nero (year 5 = AD 58) (*Paphos* II, acc. no. 614).

Layer 8 (from 1.60 — 1.80 m): 3 coins.

12. 'Ptolemy king of Cyprus' (80-58 BC) (*Paphos* II, acc. no. 416).
13. Cleopatra VII, late in her reign (*Paphos* II, acc. no. 505).
14. Ptolemaic (worn) (*Paphos* II, acc. no. 805).

Layers 9-10, sporadic sealings, (depth ca. 1.80 — 4.50 m): 1 coin.

15. Cleopatra VII, Ptolemy XVI (47-44 BC) *(Paphos* II, acc. no. 450).

---

7 I. Nicolaou, *Paphos* II (Nicosia 1990) 164. Coin acc. no. 626 (OD 20) was the only one found above the mosaic.

Layers 6-7 (depth 0.60-1.60 m), no sealings: 5 coins.
16. Ptolemy X Alexander I (114/3-88 BC) (*Paphos* II, acc. no. 368).
17. 'Ptolemy king of Cyprus' (80-58 BC) (*Paphos* II, acc. no. 423).
18-19. Cleopatra VII, Ptolemy XVI (47-44 BC) (*Paphos* II, acc. nos. 448, 449).
20. Ptolemaic (worn) (*Paphos* II, acc. no. 804).

The presence of coins of the second half of the first century BC is strong: 11 from the reign of Cleopatra with Caesarion, ranging from 47-30 BC. The first half of the first century BC is represented by 2 coins of 'Ptolemy king of Cyprus'. Only the second half of the 2nd century BC is represented: 1 coin of Ptolemy VIII, 1 coin of Ptolemy X Alexander I. The 3rd century BC is present with 1 coin of Ptolemy II Philadelphos, and the late 4th century BC with 1 coin of Ptolemy I, as a ruler.

We turn to the other external evidence: the objects found with the seal impressions (only these are illustrated), and the other objects found in the filling in general.

A. *The Pottery* (total found in the filling: 21)
Layers 4-5[8]
1. Large plate of Eastern Sigillata A ware (*Pl. 7a*).
2. A fragmentary plate of the same ware.
3-4. Two small bowls of local colour-coated ware (*Pl. 7b-c*).
5. Fragment of a casserole of coarse ware.

We get almost this same picture of ceramic finds in all the layers of the filling. Sherds from the pots mentioned above were found in lower layers. A slender jug of Cypriot Sigillata[9] ware was found in layer 7 and a fragment from the rim of a skyphos of Grey Knidian ware[10] was found in layer 10. John Hayes dates the Eastern Sigillata A ware found in Room V "perhaps to the 2nd quarter of the 1st century BC".[11] The local colour-coated ware "is the normal 1st century version, in a yellow buff fabric".[12] Hayes dates the Cypriot Sigillata ware to "about the mid to late 1st century BC".[13] As for the fragment of Knidian ware he notes "pre-Augustan".[14]

---

8 J. Hayes, *Paphos* III (Nicosia 1991) 147-148 nos. 1, 5, 14, 15, 18.
9 Hayes (*supra* n. 8) 148 no. 8
10 Hayes (*supra* n. 8) 148 no. 16.
11 Hayes (*supra* n. 8) 33.
12 Hayes (*supra* n. 8) 27.
13 Hayes (*supra* n. 8) 47.
14 Hayes (*supra* n. 8) 148 no. 16.

B. *Moulded Minor Terracottas* (total found in the filling: 11)

Layers 4-5

Fragment from the statuette of a female seated on a dolphin (?), Aphrodite (?). Pinkish clay. H. 9.2 cm. (ΟΔ 3908) *(Pl. 7d)*. Fragments from limbs of terracotta statuettes (legs, feet, hands). (ΟΔ 3907 a-b, ΟΔ 3913), and from a Maltese (?) doggy. (ΟΔ 3914).

On stylistic grounds these fragments seem to belong to the 1st century BC.

Most of the terracottas were scattered in the lower stratum of layer 10:12. There are five fragmentary pieces (ΟΔ 3950-3954). Another two were found in layer 9 (ΟΔ 3931, 3942). One of these two, ΟΔ 3942, representing Omphale queen of Lydia with the attributes of Heracles, may date, on stylistic grounds, from the mid-2nd/1st century BC. All the rest belong to the 1st century BC.

C. *The Lamps* (total found in the filling: 9)

Only one Red slip lamp (ΟΔ 3956) was found in layer 4 together with the sealings. (Biconical body, shoulders decorated with relief leaf-like pattern arranged in rays, long fragmentary nozzle, flat base. Pr. length 7.4 cm.) *(Pl. 8a)*. It is a type dated to the second half of the 2nd/first quarter of the 1st century BC.[15] Another 8 lamps were scattered in layers: 6 (ΟΔ 3918), 7 (ΟΔ 3919), 9 (ΟΔ 3940, 3941), 10:12 (ΟΔ 3945, 3947, 3955). They are roughly of the same type and of the same date as the one which was found in layer 4 with the seal impressions. Only one, found in the lowest stratum of layer 10 (10:13), (ΟΔ 3948), is of somewhat earlier date: last quarter of the 3rd/first three quarters of the 2nd century BC (biconical body on raised ring-base, pierced lug on shoulder, reddish slip, long fragmentary nozzle. Pr. length 7.5 cm).[16] Two upper moulds of lamps, one in clay (ΟΔ 3922)[17] the other in plaster (ΟΔ 4240),[18] were found in layers 6 and 7 respectively. The lamps produced were of the so-called "Ephesos" type. This type was produced in the last two centuries BC and reproduced throughout the first quarter of the 1st century AD. The two moulds evidence the production of this type in the 1st century BC in Paphos.

D. *The stamped amphora handles* (total found in the filling: 3)

Two Rhodian stamped amphora handles were found in layer 4 (ΟΔ 3934,

---

15 Cf. Th. Oziol, J.Pouilloux, *Salamine de Chypre VII, Les Lampes du Musee de Nicosie* (Paris 1977) 53 no. 14, pl. 7.

16 Cf. Oziol, Pouilloux (*supra* n.15) 41 no. 71.

17 Cf. Oziol, Pouilloux (*supra* n. 15) 63 no. 140.

18 D.M. Bailey, *A Catalogue of the Lamps in the British Museum*, I (London 1975) 100-101, Q 162-Q166, pl. 32.

ΟΔ 3935). The one is fragmentary and the name stamped on it cannot be restored with certainty. The other bears the name ΑΓΑΘΟΒΟΥΛΟΥ, with cluster *(Pl. 8b)*. Agathoboulos is a fabricant attested on handles of Rhodian amphoras in the late 2nd century BC.[19] Another Rhodian stamped handle (ΟΔ 3939) *(Pl. 8c)* found in layer 9, mentions the eponym archon Timotheos. His archonship is dated to the second half of the 2nd century BC.[20]

E. *The Seal Impressions* (identifiable: 11,334)

The internal evidence comes from some seal impressions. About 278 of the total lot bear dates which range from year A (=1) to Λς (=36) *(Pl. 8d-e)*. For the interpretation of these dates we have as guidance the dates which appear mainly on Ptolemaic tetradrachms. Of great help is the hoard of Ptolemaic tetradrachms found in the House of Dionysos.[21] Sealings bearing year 30 to 36 may refer to Ptolemy VI, years 152/1 to 146/5, but also to years 141/0 to 135/4 of Ptolemy VIII or to Ptolemy IX Soter II, years 88/7 to 81/1. Year 30 may refer also to Ptolemy XII Auletes, year 51 BC. Seal impressions with dates K (=20) to ΚΘ (=29) may refer to years of the reign of: Ptolemy I (20=286/5, 21=285/4), Ptolemy II (20-25 = 266/5-257/6), or Ptolemy III (20-26 = 228/7-222/1), Ptolemy V (20-25 = 186/5-181/0), or Ptolemy VI (20-29 = 162/1-153/2), Ptolemy VIII (25-29 = 145-142/1), Ptolemy X Alexander I (20-27 = 95/4-88), 'Ptolemy king of Cyprus' (20-24 = 62/1-58) or Cleopatra VII (20-22 = 33/2-31/0). The dates A(=1) to ΙΘ (=19) appearing on sealings may refer to anyone of the Ptolemies. Thus the problem becomes very complicated. It is again the numismatic evidence which gives us the clue; in the first place the coins found together with the clay sealings, and secondly the other coins found in the filling of Room V. These point to a date between the mid-2nd - 1st century BC and the early 1st century AD. The dates appearing on the seal impressions refer indeed to years of reigns after the mid-2nd century and throughout the 1st century BC. More specifically they relate to the years between the reigns of Ptolemy VIII and Cleopatra VII. This is strongly supported, as we have seen, by the other evidence found in the "deposit" of Room V.[22]

---

19 V. Grace, *BCH* LXXVI (1952), 525: D. Levi, *Annuario* XLIII-XLIV (NS XXVII-XXVIII) (1965-1966), 548 no. 1, fig. 2; cf. D.T. Ariel and G. Finkielsztajn, "Stamped Amphorae Handles" in S.R. Herbert *Tel Anafi* (1994) 190, SAH4; 197, SAH26.

20 S. Sztetyllo, *Nea Paphos I, Les Timbres Amphoriques* (1965-1973), (Varsovie 1976) 70 no. 215, Ariel — Finkielsztejn (supra n. 19), 186, 218 SAH 86, 87.

21 I. Nicolaou, O. Mørkholm, *Paphos* I (Nicosia 1976) 21-25, 106-110.

22 I have discussed here only the evidence provided by the excavations. See, however, H. Kyrieleis, "Θεοὶ ὁρατοί. Zur Sternsymbolik hellenistischer Herrscherbilnisse", K. Braun and A. Furtwängler (eds), *Studien zur Klassischen Archäologie* (Saarbrucken 1986), 56-58.

It seems that the building once housing the "Archives" of the city of ancient Paphos was destroyed by fire and the debris, or part, was dumped in the quarry of Room V, sometime in the late 2nd century AD, in order to produce solid foundations for the mosaic depicting Hippolytos and Phaedra.

Coins: early names, weight studies

COINS AS WEIGHTS IN THE TEMPLE RECORDS OF DIDYMA

John R. Melville Jones

The inscriptions[1] which list some of the objects of value which were stored in the temple of Apollo at Didyma in the third and and second centuries B.C. do not mention individual coins. In this respect they are quite different from the temple records of Delos and Athens, to take the two most notable examples of such documents. But coins are mentioned in these inventories many times for another reason. The weights of valuable objects were expressed in terms of one kind of coinage or another. Some of these entries are straightforward and hardly need comment, others raise interesting problems.

In many of these inscriptions the weights of objects are given in drachmas and obols of Alexander coinage. The practice must have started before Alexander's death, although there is no surviving evidence for it until a few years later. The weight standard of Alexander's coinage was the Attic one, with a drachma of 4.36g, and the coinage struck in his name, during his lifetime and afterwards, was carefully produced, on a weight standard which varied little if at all during the period when it was in use. Some inscriptions from other Greek cities use the phrase 'Attic or Alexander', an expression which shows that, as we should expect, the two words were interchangeable in contexts of this kind.[2]

When the weights of objects are given in Alexander coinage, it can be assumed that they were made of silver. Objects made in bronze or lead or iron were not weighed, and a different system was used for gold. The weights of gold objects were expressed in *chrysoi* or gold coins. No indication of mint is ever given, but no possibility can be considered at this

1 Published by A. Rehm and R. Harder, *Didyma. Zweiter Teil: Die Inschriften* (Berlin 1958) nos. 424 ff. Relevant extracts from these and other inscriptions discussed here are also published in my *Testimonia Numaria* Vol. I (London 1993) nos. 372-3, 484 and 893-5.

2 A good example is *IG* XII, 7, 67, Side B line 55, where it is laid down that a payment is to be made in 'Attic or Alexander coinage which the city uses besides the Attic'.

period other than gold coins of Alexander. These were also of Attic weight, so the use of them to describe the weights of gold, as opposed to silver, objects was a matter of convention. Since the gold *chrysous* weighed two drachmas, expressing the weight of an object in *chrysoi* was not exactly the same thing as expressing its weight in drachmas: for example, if something weighed twenty-one drachmas and two obols, its weight in *chrysoi* was ten *chrysoi*, one *hemichryson* (or drachma), and two obols.

In the inventories from Didyma the Attic/Alexander weight standard is the one most frequently employed. Three others are used, the Milesian, two kinds of Rhodian, and the 'symmachic' standard.

Some of the inscriptions which mention Milesian coins as a weight standard cannot be precisely dated, but one belongs to 205/4 and another must be placed in the second decade of the second century, or later, because it also mentions the 'plinthophoric' coinage of Rhodes.[3] The weight standard of the coins of Miletus was not always the same, but at the end of the third century it seems to be based on a didrachm of about 5g, or a drachma of 2.5g. This weight gives us a satisfactory interpretation of the entries in these inscriptions, which must refer to the regular products of the local mint at the time when each entry was first made. The Milesian standard is used only in recording the weights of silver objects, and gold objects continue to be weighed in *chrysoi*.

Rhodian coinage as a weight standard is first mentioned at Didyma much earlier than Milesian coinage, in an inscription of 272/1.[4] A *phiale* had a weight of one hundred and one Rhodian drachmas. Other silver and gold objects in the same inventory had their weights expressed in Alexander drachmas and, of course, *chrysoi*. It is not surprising that the silver objects should have had their weights recorded in two different ways. We do not know where they came from, and we do not know how old the ticket was which came with each object, or when or where any inscription which it bore might have been engraved upon it.

Like the coinage of Miletus, the coinage of Rhodes was not always struck on the same weight standard year after year. But one inscription[5] gives us very valuable information concerning this matter. Here it is recorded (lines 11-13) that the people of Iasos had offered a *phiale* bearing the inscription '... (so many) ... Rhodian (drachmas), sixty-two Alexander drachmas.' We obviously have an equation here between Rhodian and

---

3 *I. Didyma* 441 (which also mentions *plinthophoroi*), 444, 446, 448-9, 451, 456-7, 463, 477.

4 *I. Didyma* 431, line 6.

5 *I. Didyma* 464, lines 12-13: Ῥοδίας μὲν [.....] Ἀλεξανδρείας δὲ; ἑξήκοντα δύο.

Alexander drachmas. Haussoullier, who first published the inscription,[6] attempted to restore the missing number by reasoning as follows: the full weight of a Rhodian didrachm during the period 304-166 B.C., as established from specimens listed in the British Museum's catalogue, was 6.8g, and the theoretical weight of that drachma was therefore 3.4g. The weight of sixty-two Alexander drachmas of 4.36g is 270.3g, and the number of Rhodian drachmas of 3.4g needed to make up this amount is seventy-nine and a half. Since there is no room on the stone for such a long entry, he suggested that what was actually there was ὀγδοήκοντα, eighty.

This will not do. In the first place, to assume that the weight standard of Rhodian coins was the same over a century and a half is quite wrong. The weights of Rhodian coins varied, and the currency was obviously treated in a quite different manner from Alexander or Attic coinage, where great care was taken to maintain the weight standard from one generation to another. Again, it was not the practice in these or other inventories to round up figures in this way.

Thirdly, the restoration is epigraphically impossible. The photograph of the stone which Rehm and Harder published shows that there is not enough room at the end of the line where the entry appears for a word of ten letters. A much shorter word is needed, with a maximum of six letters. Since the number must be greater than sixty-two, there is only one possibility, a hundred, ἑκατόν. This restoration is also supported by the fact that other *phialai* in these and other inventories have a weight of a hundred drachmas expressed in one currency or another: so a *phiale* of a hundred drachmas was obviously a standard offering.

If a hundred Rhodian drachmas were equal to sixty-two Alexander drachmas, and an Alexander drachma weighed 4.36g, the weight of a Rhodian drachma was 2.7g. This fits the facts.[7] Late in the third century the weight of the Rhodian drachma was reduced from 3.35g or 3.4g to 2.7g or 2.75g, and the new weight standard was employed until the introduction of the 'plinthophoric' series, which may have taken place in the 180s.

The term *plinthophoros* is also used as an indication of a coin weight standard in several of the Didyma inventories. Forty years ago[8] Louis Robert showed that the first part of it, *plinthos*, which has a variety of meanings, must in this case refer to the square depression in which the

---

6 *Études sur l'histoire de Milet et du Didymeion* (Paris 1902) 238-9.

7 This statement is based on correspondence from R.J.H. Ashton, which is gratefully acknowledged.

8 *Études de Numismatique Greque* (Paris 1955) 166-176; see also my article, 'Greek Coin Names in *-phoros*,' *BICS* 21, 1974, 55-74, esp. 56-7.

reverse types of Rhodian coins, both silver and gold, began to be set during the second century. The theoretical weight of the drachma of the silver coins of this series seems to have been 3g or 3.1g.

There has been much argument about the date of the first *plinthophoroi*.[9] Does the inscription which I have been talking about, no. 464, which mentions only 'Rhodian' coins, have any bearing on the question? It is fairly securely dated to 177/6 B.C. because it was created in the fourth year after Metrodorus, a known magistrate. If the *plinthophoroi* were really in existence at that time, would it have been necessary to specify which kind of Rhodian drachma was meant, perhaps by using the word *palaios* to describe the earlier issues? My conclusion is that the inscription does not provide a *terminus post quem* for the *plinthophoroi*. There are two reasons for saying this. Some other inscriptions for which a later date in the second century is more or less certain also use the word 'Rhodian' without specifying whether plinthophoric or pre-plinthophoric coinage is meant. Some of these inscriptions are later than any date which anyone would wish to suggest for the introduction of the *plinthos* on Rhodian coins. The second reason is that it would never be correct to assume that the time at which the weight of an object was inscribed on it was the same as the date of the inventory in which its presence is recorded; objects mentioned in an inscription of 177/6 might have had their weights recorded many years before.

The last piece of numismatic terminology used in the inscriptions of Didyma, and also once at Colophon at the same period, is 'symmachic', συμμαχικόν, a term which implies that the coins which gave their names to this weight standard were connected with a symmachy, or military alliance.[10] In the Didyma inscriptions the word is used to describe the weights of objects. At Colophon, however, a specific sum of 'symmachic' coinage was contributed by a private donor towards the cost of extending the city walls.[11]

---

9 For recent discussions, see R.J.H. Ashton, 'Rhodian Bronze Coinage and the Earthquake of 229-226 B.C.' in *NC* 1986, 1-18, particularly note 10 on p. 10; G.K. Jenkins, 'Rhodian Plinthophoroi. A Sketch' in Georges le Rider *et al.*, Kraay/Mørkholm Essays (Louvain 1989) 101-19.

10 This is a point which should be emphasised. The coinage of a non-military league or *koinon* will not satisfy the requirements.

11 *AJPh* 1935, 358-72, 315-306 B.C.
Column II, lines 149-53
Εὔδημος Πύρρου Μακεδὼν Ἀλεξανδρείου
δραχμὰς μυρίας.
Κρόνιος Μένωνος Μιλήσιος
χρυσοῦς τριηκοσίους,
ἀργυρίου συμμαχικοῦ δραχμὰς τρισχιλίας.

This was not the first time that the word had been used to describe coins. In a Delian inscription of the first decade of the fourth century it appears in a fragmentary entry in a set of accounts, describing a sum of at least eleven hundred drachmas.[12] It is easy to explain here, because we have an approximately contemporary coinage bearing the legend ΣΥΝ, for συνμαχικόν, issued by the mints of Byzantium, Cnidus, Cyzicus, Ephesus, Iasus, Rhodes and Samos in silver, and by Lampsakos in gold. All the coins showed on one side a representation of the infant Herakles strangling the snakes which the jealous Hera had sent to kill him in his cradle, while the other side bore the individual emblem of each city.[13]

The subject of the infant Herakles strangling the snakes also appears on approximately contemporary coins of the Boiotian League, and on some other coins issued about sixty years later at the mint of Croton in Italy, a city which claimed Hercules as its founder. In the latter case it need have no special significance, but in the first two instances it seems reasonable to interpret it as a symbol of resistance to aggression. On the ΣΥΝ coins of Asia Minor it certainly reinforces the message which they bear in writing, that they are the coinage of a military alliance.

It is possible that some of these ΣΥΝ coins were still circulating in the closing years of the fourth century, and a group of them might even then have been described by this name, rather than by the name of a single city, because they came from more than one of the mints which issued them. If there were no better suggestion, we might then be prepared to accept that the money which Cronius gave for wall-building at Colophon consisted of a number of these coins which had somehow come into his hands. But it is impossible to believe that the name would also still have been used to describe an official weight standard on several different occasions at Didyma.

The four inscriptions from Didyma in which the word appears are all inventories of sacred goods which were in the care of the priests of Apollo, gold and silver bowls and garlands, with their weights expressed in drachmas συμμαχικοῦ, with which we must understand the noun ἀργυρίου; the bowls and garlands were weighed against 'symmachic' silver. In only one of these four inscriptions is any other coinage mentioned. This, no. 436, has two entries which each refer to a gold crown with relief decoration, weighing a hemiobol on the Alexander standard.[14]

12 *ID* 95, line 8.

13 For a study of the coinage, with useful bibliography of earlier theories, *see* S. Karwiese, 'Lysander as Herakliskos Drakonopnigon', *NC* 1980, 1-27.

14 This is a very low weight for such an object. If the entry is correct, it is not clear what the explanation may be.

The inscription from Colophon records a decision to extend the fortifications of the city. This is followed by a list of about a hundred donors who contributed various sums. The two entries which are of interest for the present study show that Eudemus son of Pyrrhus, a Macedonian, gave ten thousand Alexander drachmas, while Cronius son of Menon, a Milesian, gave three hundred *chrysoi,* i.e. gold staters or two-drachma coins, and three thousand drachmas of 'symmachic' silver.

The Colophon inscription clearly describes actual coins rather than a weight standard. It is also seems that the 'symmachic' coins are of silver. Furthermore, because that they are mentioned in the same list as Alexander coinage, it is clear that they could not have been coins of Alexander. What then might they have been?

The first thing which needs to be done is to establish the dates of these inscriptions. The Colophon inscription refers to the granting of freedom to the city by King Alexander and Antigonus.[15] Antigonus does not bear the title of king, so it must be before 306 BC. As to a *terminus post quem,* we might choose 315 BC, when Antigonus made his proclamation of liberty for the Greek cities at Tyre, or the general peace of 311 BC.

The Didyma inscriptions are less easy to date. When they were published their editor suggested, principally on the basis of a supposed identification of a certain Lochegus named in one of them, that they belonged to the middle of the 3rd century BC, and that the 'symmachic' weight standard must be that of some coins, not identified, which might have been struck about 260 in connection with the gaining of control over the area by Ptolemy II. The implausibility of this view was at once demonstrated by Louis Robert,[16] who drew attention to the more reliably dated Colophon inscription, with its reference to the same 'symmachic' coinage, and also pointed out that certain features of the Greek dialect used in the Didyma inventories seemed more appropriate to the 4th century than to the 3rd. The prosopographical argument was never strong, since Greeks were so often named after their grandfathers, and another suitable Lochegus held a magistracy in 318/7 B.C. Robert therefore had no hesitation in grouping all the inscriptions together, and in assigning the Didyma inventories to the closing years of the fourth century, like the inscription from Colophon.

It seems therefore that all four inscriptions belong to a period round about 310 BC. What kind of military alliance could have given its name to a coinage used at Miletus at this time? I suggested at one time that this

---

15 Line 7.

16 *Gnomon* 1959, 668-9.

might have been a reference to Alexander the Great, and that 'symmachic' coins were coins struck by cities which he called his allies used for coins struck in his name, or perhaps one particular issue of coins in his name. This proposition has received some support, but the present study should be regarded as a palinode.[17] The combined evidence of the Didyma and Colophon inscriptions speaks against such an interpretation, since what we are searching for is a coinage on a distinctive weight standard. This standard cannot be the Alexander standard, for if it had been the same, there would have been no need to use this alternative name for it.

The first possibility that needs to be considered is that the coinage might have belonged to the Nesiotic League, or League of Islanders, founded by Antigonus in 315/4.[18] The exact composition of the League is uncertain (and one would not necessarily expect that all members joined simultaneously). The question of membership is, however, unimportant, since it is certain that there was such a league at this time.

The Nesiotai cannot, however, provide a solution to the numismatic problem presented by our inscriptions, because there is no coinage which we can point to as being issued by them. The currency of the minor islands was always sparse, and seems to have been non-existent, or nearly so, at this time. Furthermore, the term συμμαχία is never used in any of the official inscriptions which are the principal evidence for the league's existence.

It seems better therefore to start looking for a 'symmachic' coinage among the emissions of Miletus itself, because all the inscriptions which use the word at this period have a Milesian connection. This is in fact what Robert suggested, proposing that it was 'a coinage struck by that city as an ally of Antigonos, who gave it its freedom and a democratic constitution in 313/2 BC.'

Robert's idea is attractive, because the date seems to fit the inscriptions so well, but it is less than totally satisfactory. Greek cities did not strike coins to celebrate receiving democratic constitutions. They struck coins because they needed money to make payments of one kind or another. In addition, there are no coins which can be shown to have been issued to celebrate this event, and there is certainly no sign that a change in the weights of Milesian coins can be linked to it.

---

17 My original suggestion (Louvain 1982) 129, that the term referred to coinage of Alexander the Great, was accepted by M.J. Price, *The Coinage in the Name of Alexander the Great and Philip Arrhidaeus* (Zurich/London 1991) Vol. 1 p. 74.

18 For the Koinon of the Nesiotai, see most recently K. Buraselis, *Das hellenistische Makedonien und die Ägäis* (Munich 1982), 60-87 and 180-88 and J. Seibert, *Das Zeitalter der Diadochen*, (Darmstadt 1983) 117-21.

It is, however, possible to build on Robert's basic idea, that the coins were issued by Miletus, and combine it with a suggestion which I made some years ago in a different context. First of all, however, let us consider what coins Miletus issued in this period. We have nowadays the benefit of a recent and well produced study of the city's coinage from the fourth to the 1st century BC, published ten years ago by B. Deppert-Lippitz, and of an authoritative review of this study by Philip Kinns in *The Numismatic Chronicle* of 1986.[19] Using both of these, it is possible to reduce the number of issues of silver coins from the mint of Miletos at this period to two. The first is a group of tetradrachms, drachmas and hemidrachms, struck to a drachma weight of 3.7g. These could not be the 'symmachic' coins of our inscription. They are placed by Deppert-Lippitz in her Period I (*c*.353-323), and certainly belong to the second half of the 4th century, but the weight standard is one on which many other coins in that area were struck over quite a long period. We call this weight standard 'Rhodian', although there is no evidence that anyone actually used this name for it as early as this. Whatever it was called at the time, it was so widespread and had been in existence for so long that there is no reason why it should now have begun to have been called 'symmachic'.

The second group, however, is more interesting. It consists only of didrachms of 6.4g, indicating a drachma weight of 3.2g. It was dated by Deppert-Lippitz to 290-281 (her Period III), because some of the names of magistrates which appear on the coins can be matched with names in Milesian inscriptions of the 280s and 270s, particularly with those of certain prominent citizens who acted as guarantors for a loan from the Cnidians in 283/2 BC to pay an indemnity to Lysimachus.

The suggestion is not unattractive, but, as Kinns pointed out, an alternative earlier chronology can be proposed. Guarantors for a loan are likely, perhaps even more likely, to be men well on in years, and if the same names really belong to the same men, 'financial weight in the 280s is not incompatible with the filling of public office well before 300 BC.' This argument in itself does not carry much weight, but there is a numismatic one which is much more important. Miletus was not the only city to issue coins on this weight standard at about this time.

The mint of Samos produced didrachms, drachmas, and half and quarter drachmas, struck to a drachma weight of 3.2g. In his study of the silver coinage of Samos, John Barron suggested a date of *c*. 310-300 BC for these, partly on the basis of identifications with known Samian magistrates and

19 H. Deppert-Lippitz, *Die Münzprägung Milets vom vierten bis ersten Jahrhunderts v. Chr.* (Frankfurt 198); review by P. Kinns in *NC* 1986, 233-60.

partly because that was the point at which they seemed to fit into the very well documented silver coinage of that island.[20] He also noted that an unusually large number of die combinations occurred in this issue, a fact which might indicate that the coins were struck over a short period of time in the same workshop. This is also a feature of the Milesian issue which I have just mentioned. The fact that smaller denominations, rather than tetradrachms, were produced also suggests that the money was intended to be spent on minor rather than on major purchases.

Two other mints on the mainland, Teos and Colophon,also issued silver coins on about the same weight standard, or one very slightly lighter, 3.1g or a little less. The coins of Teos are drachmas, with associated half-drachmas. A kantharos on the reverse distinguishes them from earlier heavier issues which have a lyre as their reverse type. The group is tentatively dated in the British Museum's catalogue to a time after 300 BC. This is only an approximation, and there is no reason why they should not have been issued a little earlier.[21]

The coins of Colophon are drachmas, half-drachmas and one-third drachmas or diobols, again on approximately the same weight standard, or slightly lighter. In his study of the coins of this mint, published over half a century ago, J.G. Milne placed them in the period 350-330.[22] Again, there is no very good evidence to support this dating. I would suggest that a date nearer to 310, to group them with other coins of other cities in the area which were issued on the same weight standard, is at least equally appropriate. It is possible, therefore, to say that we have a group of coins from four Ionian mints, Miletus, Samos, Teos and Colophon, which all seem to use the same weight standard, and that the reason for the shared weight standard is that they were issued at approximately the same time.

There is, however, no evidence that these four cities formed a military alliance with each other at this time, so how can this help to elucidate the question of the so-called 'symmachic' coins in the inscriptions from Colophon and Didyma? At this point we should move to another part of the Greek world, and look at another coin which can be brought into the argument. We have a quite exceptional gold issue, a drachma, again weighing 3.2g, from the mint of Carystus. Seven specimens survive of this beautiful coin. It has as its obverse type a bearded head of Heracles, who appears on earlier silver coins of the same mint. The reverse, which shows

---

20 J.P. Barron, *The Silver Coins of Samos* (London 1966) 124-40.

21 For the coins of Teos, *see BMC Ionia* p. 313 nos. 29-31.

22 For the coins of Colophon, *see* J.G. Milne, *Kolophon and its Coinage ANSMN 96* (New York 1941), 59-63.

the reclining ox of Euboea, the 'well-oxed' island, is also found on other coins of Carystus. The gold drachma is therefore a normal product of this city in its appearance, but its metal and weight are abnormal. Gold coinage from city mints was always a rarity in the Greek world. We must always therefore suspect that it was the result of an unusual situation. Sometimes our sources tell us what this was, as in the case of the gold coinage of Athens issued during the second part of the Peloponnesian War. Another example of an emergency issue in gold, a regal one in this case, is the gold coin of Alexander II of Syria, which Justin (XXXIX, ii, 5-6) tells us that Alexander issued at Antioch to pay his troops, using the solid gold statue of Victory in the temple there for this purpose. Only one specimen of it now survives, and the coin of Carystus is also very rare.

The gold drachma of Carystus was at one time dated to *c.* 200 BC, for no very good reason except that it was guessed that it might be celebratory in character, and connected with the 'freeing' of Greece by Flamininus. The event was certainly marked by the striking of a very well known gold coin, bearing a portrait which is probably that of the conqueror, and his name on the reverse, which must have been issued by him, since it does not bear the name of any Greek mint. But there is no reason why Carystus should have celebrated the event in the same way; indeed, Greek cities are not known to have struck gold coins to celebrate any occasion. Gold was a royal metal, but when the cities used it for coining, our first thought must be that they were short of silver.

There is a further reason for refusing to accept such a late date for the Carystian coin. In several inventories from Delos beginning in 225 BC the entry 'a gold drachma of Carystus', which is a precise description of this coin, appears, and it is very likely that the the same entry appeared in passages missing from other inscriptions which go back at least to 260 BC. It may therefore be argued that there is no reason for separating the gold drachma of Carystus from other coins on the 3.2g weight standard. They must be contemporary.[23]

We now have to look for a military expedition which took place in Ionia and on the Greek mainland, and in which Miletus, at least, might have been allied with some other city or with a king. There is only one possibility which can be seriously considered, since Ionian or Samian involvement in the Lamian war is most unlikely. In 313/2 BC Ptolemaeus or Polemaeus, nephew of Antigonus Monophthalmus, after campaigning in Asia, went to Greece and was active there, first on his uncle's behalf and later on his

---

23 For further details, see my article, 'The Gold Drachma of Carystus', *NC* 1980, 28-32.

own.[24] Diodorus tells us that Carystus was 'received into a military alliance' by this Ptolemaeus. Miletus, I would suggest, was the point at which the expedition left Asia, and Samos a place at which it called on its way, and where a further supply of coinage was required.

The issues of Miletus, Samos and Carystus all seem, for different reasons, to have been produced at short notice. No one has yet published an analysis of the coinage of Teos and Colophon in sufficient detail to show whether this is the case with them also. Should the coins of these other mints also be attributed to Ptolemaeus's expedition? This is possible, but it is not necessarily so. Colophon and Teos might have provided troops, and struck coins on an agreed weight standard to pay them, but if we think for a moment about the reasons for the choice and the changing of weight standards at Greek mints, it will be clear that there may well be another reason for its use.

To someone who thinks purely in arithmetical terms, a weight of 3.2g may appear significant, because it is three-quarters of the weight of an Attic drachma. Four of these coins of 3.2 grams could be exchanged for three Attic drachmas, which contained the same weight of silver. But when one tries to guess how this might have advantaged anyone, there is no answer. It is as irrelevant as to say that 3.2g is almost exactly one-hundredth of a Roman pound. The weight standard of all these coins is best considered in the light of what was happening to coinage in the whole of this area at the time. Many mints were beginning to strike issues of posthumous Alexander coins, which were struck consistently on the Attic weight standard, a little over 4.3g for a drachma and 17.2g for a tetradrachm. They formed the international currency of the Greek world, and although over the course of a century or so it is possible to notice a very slight decline in weight, the decline is minimal. Purely civic issues, however, slid downwards in weight. Some explanations which have been offered for this phenomenon are based on the assumption that weights were being adjusted to match what are called the 'Persic', 'Rhodian' or 'Phoenician' weight standards. This assumption is bad in principle, because it assumes that Greek cities tried to strike their coins at weights which would make it easy for them to be interchangeable in trade. This may sometimes have been the case; but coincidences of weight with major external standards are not necessarily significant. The issues of many mints or groups of mints were produced for local circulation rather than for foreign trade, as the relatively small number of them found outside their natural area of circulation shows, and there was therefore little benefit to be gained from matching them to external weight standards.

A better explanation is one which was proposed in a rudimentary form in 1958 by Sture Bolin in a book which was mainly concerned with Roman coins, but made some reference to the early coins of the Greek world as well.[25] Bolin suggested a principle which in some instances is completely credible, that ancient states, when their coins circulated locally and therefore did not have to continue to match any international standard, could strike successive issues at the weight of slightly worn coins in circulation. There would be two advantages in this. The stock of precious metal at the disposal of the state would go a little further, and the existing worn coins in circulation were thus, as it were revalidated, and it would not be necessary to refuse to accept coins which had lost a litle of their original weight.

If this proposition be accepted, we can extend the principle in a way which is useful for the purpose of dating some coins, and say that when the weights of coins are tending to move downwards, issues from neighbouring mints which are on the same weight standard are likely to be contemporary, while a lower weight should indicate a later date. On this assumption the coins of Miletus, Samos, and Carystus which have been mentioned above may be dated to 312 BC. The issues of Teos and Colophon, which are very slightly lighter, may be later. This argument is based on three assumptions: that the coins must be contemporary because they share approximately the same weight standard, that the Colophon inscription must be after 315 BC and before 305 BC, and that the use of the same weight standard at Carystus as at Miletus and Samos for a coin whose abnormal nature suggests a need to strike coinage in a hurry when there was a shortage of silver is best explained by the needs of an army operating in Ionia and Greece. The only expedition of the right date is that of Ptolemaeus.

It is not necessary to insist that the weight standard was created specially for the purpose of striking coins to pay the participants in this military expedition. A more appropriate explanation is that when money was needed, coins were first struck at Miletus. Their weight standard was either the one which was current at the time, because it had already begun to be used on the most recent occasion when coins were needed, or it may have represented a reduction from the weight standard of the last coins to be issued in that area. The reason, in the latter case, would have been that the weight of many of those coins had fallen while they were in circulation,

---

24 For the expedition of Ptolemaeus, *see* Diodorus XIX, 77-8 and 87; XX, 19 and 27; also Richard A. Billows, *Antigonos the One-eyed and the Creation of the Hellenistic State* (Los Angeles and London 1991) 123ff.

25 *State and Currency in the Roman Empire to 300 A.D.* (Stockholm 1958).

and it was time to fix a new standard for the latest issue. The new coins would have been called 'symmachic' at Miletus, because that was the occasion on which they were issued, and the name distinguished them from coins of the last local minting, which presumably went on being referred to as 'Milesian'. We may guess that when the expedition reached Samos there was a need for further coinage, and that more was then produced by the mint of Samos on the same weight standard. At Carystus silver was not available, and a small extra issue was produced in gold, perhaps by melting down precious objects. No other mint in Greece itself is known to have struck coins on this weight standard, so we should assume that when he was there, Ptolemaeus made such payments as he needed to make with coinage which he acquired from the stock of money already in circulation, or that if any was struck for him it is now indistinguishable from the other products of the mainland mints. The term 'symmachic' is therefore, I would suggest, a name which would have been used very briefly for coins issued on this weight standard, and is not likely to have had wide currency in the Greek world away from Didyma and Miletus. It is only by chance that evidence for its use has survived in a few inscriptions from Didyma and Colophon.

EPIGRAPHIE ET NUMISMATIQUE: QUELQUES REMARQUES SUR LES NOMS DE MONNAIES DANS DES INSCRIPTIONS GRECQUES ARCHAIQUES

Hélène Nicolet-Pierre

La familiarité des numismates avec les métaux monnayés, sous les formes inventées vers le début du VIe siècle par les Lydiens et les Grecs d'Asie, adaptées moins d'un siècle plus tard par toutes les cités grecques de quelque importance (de Massalia à Tarse en passant par la Sicile, la Thrace ou les îles égéennes) est-elle de quelque utilité pour la compréhension des inscriptions archaïques souvent si fragmentaires qu'ont à interpréter les épigraphistes et d'une façon plus large, tous les historiens de l'Antiquité?

Nous nous demandions par exemple s'il était possible d'illustrer (au propre et au figuré) l'important recueil de *Nomima*[1] publié l'an dernier: la nature juridique des textes fait que plus d'une fois des sommes y sont mentionnées, pénalités le plus souvent, mais aussi conditions financières, récompenses ou affectations de fonds à divers usages. Leurs dates varient dans des limites à peu près saisissables, entre la fin du VIIe s. et c. 450. C'est à dire que l'on devrait pouvoir mettre en rapport le monnayage archaïque des cités responsables de ces règlementations politiques et juridiques avec la lettre même des textes inscrits. Sous quelle forme, concrètement, étaient payées les amendes? A quelles unités faisait-on appel pour estimer les biens? Des questions de ce type ne sont pas nouvelles. Mais comme la documentation disponible s'élargit peu à peu, tant pour l'épigraphiste que pour le numismate, quelques facettes nouvelles du problème pourront peut-être être éclairées.

Mis à part les *lébètes* crétois, dont les mentions dans les plus anciennes inscriptions en Crète (Pythion de Gortyne) demeurent encore mystérieuses faute de contexte, les unités monétaires les plus anciennement utilisées sont des statères (dont deux attestations remontent au milieu du VIe siècle), des drachmes et des oboles qui apparaissent à la fin du VIe siècle. Nos

1 Henri van Effenterre et Françoise Ruzé, *Nomima, recueil d'inscriptions politiques et juridiques de l'archaïsme grec* I (Collection de l'Ecole française de Rome 188, Rome 1994).

dates sont celles des éditeurs de ces inscriptions[2] et reposent sur leurs critères paléographiques.

Nous nous limiterons à quelques emplois du mot *statère* choisis parmi ses plus anciennes mentions épigraphiques.

1. La plaque d'argent d'Ephèse[3]

On lit deux fois le terme de statère sur la face B de la plaque d'argent trouvée au début du siècle dans les fouilles de l'Artémision d'Ephèse (ligne 3, puis ligne 8, où il est question de huit statères). D'autres unités sont mentionnées dans ce compte: mines, demi-mines, hectés, hémihecta.

D'après la face A, les mines (d'or ou d'argent) représentent du métal *pesé* (verbe: ἐστάθησαν deux fois en entier, deux autres emplois). D'où la question: le mot statère ici désigne-t-il simplement une division pondérale de la mine (l'état du support ne permettant pas de déterminer leur rapport), ou avons-nous au contraire un compte en unités monétaires ?

A la date de l'inscription, vers 550 (la plaque, selon Hogarth, pourrait récapituler des sommes réunies en vue de la construction du temple), statères, et divisions du statère: hectai, hémihecta peuvent être des monnaies telles que celles qui furent révélées par cette même fouille de l'Artémision : depuis plusieurs décennies, les rois de Lydie et les cités ioniennes frappaient monnaie en "or blanc". Les fouilles récentes ont montré qu'il fallait certainement descendre de c. 600 vers 560 le *terminus ante quem* pour l'enfouissement des monnaies de l'Artémision, et donc rajeunir d'autant "l'invention" de ce type de monnaie: la structure sous laquelle bon nombre des pièces furent trouvées étant en fait la plus récente des constructions qui précédèrent le temple de Crésus (560-545) (cf. n. 8). Les poids de ces monnaies s'organisent , comme on sait, en un système parfaitement clair à partir d'un statère d'environ 14g (1/2, 1/3, 1/6, 1/12, etc. jusqu'à 1/96).[4] Le fait remarquable est que la combinaison des types de droit et de revers doit permettre de reconnaître d'emblée la division à laquelle on a affaire, et donc d'éviter normalement le recours à la balance

---

2 Le plus souvent, il s'agit de L.H. Jeffery, *Local Scripts of Archaic Greece* (Oxford 1961) abrégé *LSAG*.

3 D.G. Hogarth, *Excavations at Ephesus* (London 1908) 120-144, pl. XIII; *LSAG* n°53, pl. 66: face A seulement; G. Manganaro *Epigraphica* 36 (1974) 57-77, avec fac.sim. et bibliographie.

4 Etalon dit, sans raison déterminante, "milésien": utilisé à Milet mais aussi dans certaines autres cités d'Ionie et en Lydie. D'autres statères de la même période pèsent un peu plus de 16g (d'où le système "phocaïque"), ou de 17g (système "samien" ancien. Cf. l'article fondamental de H.A. Cahn, "Etalons monétaires en Asie Mineure jusqu'au Ve siècle", dans *Actes CIN Rome* 1961, II, 19-23.

(sauf sans doute pour de très grosses sommes, pour lesquelles le dénombrement était fastidieux et source d'erreurs).

2. Stèle de Chios[5]

Le texte, tronqué par la cassure de la pierre, fait allusion aux fonctions de plusieurs magistrats et prévoit des sanctions (financières?) pour corruption, ainsi qu'une possibilité d'appel devant un conseil. Le montant de l'amende est malheureusement perdu. A la ligne 3 de la face B, était inscrite une somme en statères: montant d'une autre amende, ou dépôt, auprès du démarque, d'une "consignation, si on l'associe à l'appel".[6]

C.M. Kraay ne doutait pas que ces statères ne fussent les premiers statères d'electrum frappés par l'atelier de Chios, caractérisés par le type du sphinx, et de poids milésiaque. Il suivait en cela la chronologie proposée par A. Baldwin[7] en 1914: vers le milieu du VIe siècle. Leur style nous paraissant beaucoup plus évolué que celui de l'electrum d'étalon milésiaque trouvé à l'Artémision d'Ephèse, attribuable aux années 580-560, selon la nouvelle chronologie qui semble s'imposer aujourd'hui,[8] le rapprochement est peut-être discutable. Si la date de l'inscription — gravée dans le deuxième quart du VIe siècle selon L.H. Jeffery, vers 550 pour les éditeurs des *Nomima* — ne pouvait être abaissée jusque vers 530, on devrait songer plutôt aux statères plus anciens frappés en Ionie,[9] ou, à la limite, à un poids de métal précieux, ce qui nous ramènerait au dilemme déjà rencontré ci-dessus à propos de l'inscription d'Ephèse. La parole, pour la date de la loi de Chios, est à la paléographie.

---

5 *Nomima I* n°62; L.H. Jeffery, "The Courts of justice in Archaic Chios", *BSA* 51 (1956) 158, pl. 53 (photo); *LSAG* p. 343, pl. 65, 41 (fac.sim.).

6 Van Effenterre-Ruzé (supra n. 1) 267.

7 *AJN* XLVIII (1914) 12, no. 1-2; C.M. Kraay, *Archaic and Classical Greek Coins* (London 1976) 35 et 316 n. 5.

8 Il est nécessaire, nous semble-t-il, de reconsidérer à la lumière des découvertes récentes à l'Artémision toute la chronologie des monnaies d'electrum antérieures aux créséides: cf A.Bammer, "Les sanctuaires des VIIIe et VIIe siècles à l'Artémision d'Ephèse", *RA* 1991, 63-83. L'évolution du style a pu être beaucoup plus rapide qu'on ne le pensait il y a vingt ans, lorsque la "naissance" de la monnaie lydienne semblait obligatoirement devoir être datée, au plus tôt, du dernier quart du VIIe siècle. Sur la date attribuable à toutes les monnaies frappées au VIe siècle, même le si précieux manuel de C.M. Kraay est sujet à révision.

9 C'est aussi l'hypothèse de N. Hardwick, qui a repris l'étude du monnayage de Chios: "The Coinage of Chios from the VIth to the IVth century B.C.", dans *Actes du XIe Congrès international de numismatique*, Bruxelles 1991 (1993), 1, 211-222. Adoptant pour la loi de Chios une date haute, 575, il constate qu'aucune monnaie connue ne peut en être rapprochée avec un degré suffisant de certitude. La plus ancienne émission qu'il propose de rattacher à l'atelier de Chios est une hecté d'electrum pesant 2,59g, avec un sphinx à droite, et il la situe dans une fourche 550-525.

3. Dédicace de deux Périnthiens à Héra (Samos)[10]

"En tout deux cent douze statères samiens" (lignes 15-19): voilà qui est clair: c'est la valeur de l'offrande de deux citoyens de Périnthe (sur la côte Nord de la Propontide) au grand sanctuaire de Samos, métropole de leur cité. C'est une dîme (on ne sait pas de quoi), et elle est constituée d'objets précieux offerts à la déesse : une gorgone d'or, une sirène d'argent, une coupe d'argent, un lampadaire de bronze, au prix desquels s'est ajouté celui de la stèle et de la gravure de la dédicace.

L'écriture de celle-ci suggérait à L.H. Jeffery, comme fourche chronologique, environ 540-525. Quels statères samiens ont pu, dans cette période, servir de référence pour cette estimation? Ou de monnaie pour l'achat des objets, si les deux Périnthiens ne sont pas eux-mêmes orfèvres?

J.P. Barron a estimé la valeur possible de chaque offrande par rapport à celle de la phiale d'argent, probablement cent drachmes, ici comme ailleurs.[11] Il conclut que 212 statères d'argent, au poids euboïque, équivalant à 848 drachmes, pouvaient couvrir le prix des objets et de la stèle. Autre conclusion: Samos ne frapperait plus d'electrum à l'époque de cette dédicace, pour laquelle il retient la date de c. 525. Ce serait au contraire le début des émissions d'argent, dont le tout premier groupe est constitué d'hectés de poids euboïque (deux paires de coins, Barron 1-2, "c. 530-526").

Aucune monnaie samienne d'argent ne représente matériellement, à l'époque archaïque, un "statère" pesant quatre drachmes de poids euboïco-attique. On sait en revanche que des statères d'électrum (et leurs divisions) ont été frappés à ce poids au VIe siècle: en témoignent le trésor de Samos de 1894[12] et des trouvailles isolées dans l'île.[13] Une date d'enfouissement autour de 550, pour le trésor de Samos, est vraisemblable, à cause des parentés de style et de fabrique entre ses pièces et celles de l'Artémision d'Ephèse. Mais ces statères d'electrum n'auraient-ils pas continué à circuler au-delà du milieu du siècle, à être frappés aussi peut-être? Cela permettrait de mieux justifier le stratagème prêté au tyran Polycrate (533-522), qui aurait frappé des monnaies d'électrum fourrées de plomb, et acheté à ce vil prix la levée du siège de sa ville par une troupe spartiate (Hérodote

---

10 G. Klaffenbach *MDAI* 6 (1953) 15-20; *LSAG* 365 et pl. 71, n°35; J.P. Barron, *The Silver Coins of Samos* (London 1966) 18; D.F. McCabe, J.V. Brownson, B.D. Ehrman (eds), *Samos Inscriptions.* Texts and List (Princeton 1986) no. 218 (avec bibliographie à compléter).

11 Ainsi la phiale d'argent trouvée à Beroia, dédiée vers 500 à l'Athéna mégarienne, pèse 432g: D.W.J. Gill, *AJA* 94 (1990) 624-625.

12 *IGCH* 1158.

13 Deux statères sont signalés par Barron (supra n. 10) 15 n. 3.

III,56,2, en 525/4). Des pièces de plomb retrouvées dans l'île portent effectivement au revers les deux rectangles creux caractéristiques des statères samiens archaïques. Ceux-ci devaient être encore bien connus comme "monnaies samiennes" dans les années 540-525 où fut gravée la dédicace des Périnthiens. Il nous paraît tout à fait possible qu'il s'agisse de 212 statères d'electrum: des offrandes plus riches que celles qu'imaginait Barron purent justifier davantage la gravure d'une stèle commémorative. Samos était la métropole de Périnthe: cette parenté mythique est peut-être rappelée par le terme d'*oikeioi* dans l'inscription, à moins encore, comme l'a suggéré L.H. Jeffery,[14] que les deux dédicants n'aient été des personnages officiels en charge d'un *oikos* de Périnthe au sanctuaire d'Héra, d'un "trésor" sur le modèle de ceux que l'on connaît bien à Delphes ou Olympie.

4-5. Les lois d'Erétrie[15]

Dix statères d'amende dans le texte de loi n°3 d'Erétrie, avec le contexte relativement clair d'une procédure qui condamne à payer dans les délais, sinon prévoit des sanctions.

La lecture d'une bonne partie de la première ligne, très endommagée, du texte 3 (*IG* XII,9, 1274, pl. VI) est due à E.Vanderpool et W.P. Wallace (*l.c.* n. 15, p. 387): "the last three words in the line are practically certain — δέκα στατε̃ρας ὀφέλεν. Quant à la date de ces lois, d'abord placées par L.H. Jeffery dans une fourche large, "c. 550-525", elle se situerait plutôt vers 525 ou même un peu après.[16]

W.P. Wallace dans *Num.Chron.* 1962 remarquait déjà: "The character of the staters, whether electrum or silver, Aiginetic or Euboic, is not specified, and this must surely mean that the staters in question are local, Eretrian, staters." Aussi propose-t-il d'y reconnaître, comme premières émissions d'Erétrie, les monnaies du type de Jenkins, Acq. BM, dans *Num.Chron.* 1955, 136 (n°7), pour l'attribution desquelles l'auteur hésitait entre Erétrie et sa colonie chalcidienne de Dikaia.

Il nous paraît en tout cas hors de doute qu'il s'agit de payer ces amendes en métal monnayé.[17] Déjà des monnaies non érétriennes circulaient en Eubée dans la deuxième moitié du VIe siècle: on pense bien sûr aux

---

14 *LSAG* 365, n. 4.

15 *Nomima* I, n°9; E. Vanderpool et W.P. Wallace, "The sixth cent. laws from Eretria", *Hesperia* 33 (1964) 381-391 et pl. 67-69.

16 Cf. F.Cairns *ZPE* 54 (1984) 145-155, qui l'abaisse: "525 or after", avec l'accord exprès, dit-il, de L.H. Jeffery.

17 F. Cairns est revenu récemment sur une position indéfendable et admet (*Phoenix* 45 (1991) 298-299) que ces statères puissent être, non un poids de métal, mais des monnaies (d'Erétrie).

didrachmes athéniens dits "*Wappenmünzen*", frappés par les Pisistratides: leur présence est attestée par plusieurs trésors: *IGCH* 3 (Eubée 1935?), 9 (Erétrie c. 1870), 10 (Pascha 1883). Mais plusieurs émissions attribuables à Chalcis, Erétrie et Karystos prouvent aussi l'activité des ateliers eubéens dès les années 530-520.[18]

Le premier texte de la même série d'inscriptions (qui selon F.Cairns attesterait une "pre-coinage situation at Eretria") ne prend tout son sens que si les *chrèmata* en question sont aussi des monnaies. Les deux adjectifs qui accompagnent ce terme de χρήματα, si courant pour désigner toute espèce de richesses, sont éloquents: les monnaies (peut-être diverses) doivent être "vérifiées" (δόκιμα, donc ayant cours à Erétrie[19]), et "saines" (ὑγιᾶ), c'est à dire, à notre avis, "non fourrées" — la méfiance envers les pièces fourrées a dû naître en même temps que les monnaies elles-mêmes. On rappelait ci-dessus les pièces de plomb recouvertes d'or frappées par Polycrate de Samos. Coïncidence peut-être, on connaît aussi un statère archaïque d'Erétrie en argent fourré, trouvé dans les fouilles d'Eleusis avec des *Wappenmünzen* (*IGCH* 5, conservé à Athènes).[20]

6. Plaque de bronze de Monte San Mauro[21]

De Sicile, un seul document archaïque dans les *Nomima* I mentionnerait le terme de statère, restitué dans une inscription du dernier quart du VIe siècle (525-500). En fait, si des "talents" -probablement siciliens[22] — au nombre de deux et de trois, sont clairement attestés (fragments 5 et 6) sur ces tablettes de bronze très ruinées, les lettres -ερα du fragment 5 peuvent être la fin d'un mot autre que le nom du statère. On doit suggérer ἱερά εἶναι, qui indiquerait la consécration de l'amende infligée (Cf. la lecture de Jeffery *LSAG*, 242, n°2).

18 Cf. les types illustrés par Kraay (supra n. 7) pl. 15, n°262-263, 267, 271 (cette dernière pièce = Asyut Hoard 1969, Price-Waggoner n°250).

19 Sur ce terme (à l'époque hellénistique), on peut lire en particulier les réflexions de O. Picard dans *Hommages à Lucien Lerat* II (Paris 1984) 679-690.

20 M. Oeconomides et H. Nicolet, "Note sur la trouvaille d'Eleusis 1883", *AAA* XIV (1982) 92-94, ill.

21 *Nomima* I, n°01; *LSAG* 242 et 247 n°2; F.Cordano, "Le leggi calcidese di Monte San Mauro di Caltagirone", *Miscellanea greca e romana* X (Roma 1986) 33-53 et pl. I-X.

22 Le talent sicilien ancien pèserait un peu plus de 200g d'argent. Une pénalité de deux talents équivaudrait donc presque à une mine euboïque.

7. Stèle d'Axos (Crète)[23]

L'inscription aujourd'hui mutilée comportait vraisemblablement un contrat de travail, avec pénalité prévue en cas de rupture de l'accord ou de non exécution dans les délais de travaux pour lesquels le contrat était conclu. On lit encore assez clairement le montant de l'amende, exprimé en statères (30 ou 40: on peut restituer [τρι]άκοντα ου [τετταρ]άκοντα).

L'éditrice datait l'écriture de son texte de la fin du VIe ou du début du Ve s. Ni Axos ni les autres cités crétoises ne frappaient monnaie alors. Cependant les monnaies d'Egine étaient connues dans l'île: le vase trouvé près de Matala (port de Phaistos) en 1943 contenait 70 statères d'argent d'Egine et 1 statère de Théra.[24] Kydonia, colonie d'Egine sur la côte nord, a aussi frappé à la fin du VIe siècle des statères très proches des "tortues" éginètes. C'est l'étalon éginétique qui sera adopté par toutes les cité crétoises dès le début de leur monnayage propre (par Gortyne et Phaistos au milieu du Ve s., par exemple). Nous pouvons donc être raisonnablement sûrs que les amendes en statères de notre contrat d'Axos, comme celles des autres "codes" crétois étaient exprimées (et payées?) en statères éginétiques.

Sur les six textes épigraphiques que nous avons retenus, trois des plus anciens emplois du terme "statère" proviennent d'Asie Mineure. Ceci n'a rien d'étonnant: les textes littéraires et les découvertes archéologiques suggèrent d'y situer le berceau du monnayage qui se développe ensuite dans toute l'Egée et au-delà.

L'interprétation de toutes ces mentions de statères n'est pas évidente, dans la mesure où la datation des écritures d'une part, celle des émissions monétaires archaïques anépigraphes, de l'autre, demeurent affectées d'un certain coefficient d'incertitude.

A ce problème s'ajoute la richesse sémantique du mot lui-même, qui dans ses emplois "monétaires" représente aussi bien un poids de métal, une unité de compte définissant une valeur, que le support concret chargé de matérialiser cette valeur (la monnaie frappée). On sait que poids et métal pouvaient également varier d'un Etat à l'autre: aussi devons-nous tenter de comprendre chaque cas particulier. Dans ces conditions, comment archéologues et numismates pourraient-ils ne pas continuer à mettre en commun leur ingéniosité, pour essayer de saisir des miettes d'une histoire difficile?

---

23 *Nomima* I, n°29. Trouvés en 1947, les deux fragments jointifs qui proviendraient de l'acropole d'Axos ont été publiés par L.H. Jeffery dans *JHS* 69 (1949) 25-38, fig. 10-12; *LSAG* 310 et 316 n°23.

24 *IGCH* 1. La date d'enfouissement doit être abaissée jusque vers 500.

Mint studies: iconography, attribution and activity

Η ΑΡΧΑΙΚΗ ΝΟΜΙΣΜΑΤΟΚΟΠΙΑ ΤΗΣ ΚΕΑΣ ΠΡΟΒΛΗΜΑΤΑ ΑΠΟΔΟΣΗΣ

Ch. Papageorgiadou-Banis

Στην αρχαιότητα η επιλογή των εικονογραφικών τύπων που χαράζονταν στα νομίσματα κάθε πόλης ήταν μιά πολύ σημαντική υπόθεση. Το ίδιο το νόμισμα ήταν φορτισμένο με πολλές έννοιες και είχε ιδιαίτερη σημασία για την πόλη και τους πολίτες της, ενώ συγχρόνως μετέφερε κάποια πολύ συγκεκριμένα μηνύματα στις γειτονικές ή πιο απομακρυσμένες περιοχές. Επρεπε συνεπώς, τα εμβλήματα και τα σύμβολά του να αποτελούν σημείο αναφοράς τόσο για τους γηγενείς όσο και για τους ξένους.

Η νομισματική εικονογραφία ωστόσο φάνηκε ότι ήταν εξίσου καθοριστική και για τις επερχόμενες γενεές των μελετητών των αρχαίων νομισμάτων. Ιδιαίτερα για τα ανεπίγραφα νομίσματα της αρχαϊκής περιόδου εκείνο που συνέβαλε κατά κύριο λόγο στην απόδοσή τους ήταν η αποκρυπτογράφηση των εικονιστικών συμβόλων.

Ωστόσο, πολύ συχνά, η παραπάνω διαδικασία δεν έχει τα αναμενόμενα αποτελέσματα. Χαρακτηριστικότερο παράδειγμα της αδυναμίας μας αυτής αποτελούν τα κυκλαδίτικα νομισματοκοπεία, για τα οποία οι περισσότερες από τις αποδόσεις και τις ταυτίσεις που έχουν κατά καιρούς προταθεί, είτε δεν έχουν τύχει κοινής αποδοχής, είτε έχουν αναιρεθεί από τα αρχαιολογικά ευρήματα.[1]

Η κοινή θρησκευτική παράδοση, προσανατολισμένη κυρίως στον Διόνυσο και τον Απόλλωνα, οι περιορισμένες τεχνικές δυνατότητες, οι οποίες επέβαλαν ορισμένες θεματικές επιλογές, τα μετακινούμενα εργαστήρια και τεχνίτες, φορείς συγκεκριμένων τεχνικών γνώσεων, είχαν ως αποτέλεσμα τη δημιουργία νομισματικών κοπών, οι οποίες μοιράζονταν

---

1 Θα πρέπει ίσως να αρχίσει μια εκ νέου, συνολική μελέτη για τα κυκλαδικά εργαστήρια, με όσα νεώτερα στοιχεία έχουν τυχόν προκύψει, ώστε να υπάρξει μια πιο ολοκληρωμένη εικόνα. Δυστυχώς, μετά από τις θεμελιώδεις μελέτες των πρώτων νομισματολόγων, που συνδέθηκαν και με τις πρώτες περιηγήσεις και μεγάλες ανασκαφές στις Κυκλάδες, η περιοχή εγκαταλείφθηκε και μόνο σπαραδικά εμφανίζονται πλέον νέες σχετικές έρευνες.

κοινά εικονογραφικά και τεχνικά χαρακτηριστικά, τα οποία δεν διευκόλυναν καθόλου την απόδοση τους σε συγκεκριμένα νομισματοκοπεία. Εαν δε σε αυτά προσθέσουμε και την άποψη που διετύπωσε ο C.M. Kraay και άλλοι, ότι δηλαδή γινόταν συνειδητή προπάθεια ώστε στα νομίσματα των μικρότερων κυκλαδικών εργαστηρίων να απεικονιζονται τύποι παρεμφερείς με αυτούς της Αίγινας, ώστε να κυκλοφορούν παράλληλα με αυτά και να γίνονται δεκτά στις αγορές ως συμπληρωματικά τους,[2] τότε αντιλαμβάνεται κανείς τα προβλήματα που αντιμετωπίζει η όποια προσπάθεια απόδοσης.

Μία από τις περιπτώσεις που έχει ταλαιπωρήσει κατά καιρούς τους ερευνητές είναι και η τετράπολις Κέα, στην οποία, κατά την αρχαϊκή περίοδο αναπτύχθηκαν τρία διαφορετικα νομισματοκοπεία (*Pl. 9*).[3]

Θα πρέπει να επισημάνουμε καταρχήν ότι η μία από τις πόλεις, η Ποιήεσσα, δεν φαίνεται με τα υπάρχοντα δεδομένα να είχε αυτόνομη νομισματική δραστηριότητα, αν και στην περιοχή της έχουν βρεθεί αρκετά σημαντικά ίχνη της αρχαϊκής περιόδου.[4]

Αντίθετα, για τις άλλες πόλεις η νομισματική έρευνα αποδείχθηκε καρποφόρα, αν και εξαιρετικά προβληματική. Σε γενικές γραμμές, εκτιμάται ότι οι κοπές και των τριών ξεκινούν σχεδόν συγχρόνως, στα τελευταία χρόνια του 6ου π.Χ.αι., ενώ ελάχιστα αργότερα, αν όχι σχεδόν παράλληλα, κοντά στον κυρίως τύπο προστίθεται ένα μικρό δελφίνι, το οποίο προς το τέλος των σειρών, μετά από μια εικοσαετία σχεδόν, μετατρέπεται σε κυρίως έμβλημα.[5]

Οι κοπές της Κορησίας φαίνεται να είναι οι λιγότερο προβληματικές, και αν και παραμένουν σχεδόν άγνωστες και εξαιρετικά περιορισμένες μπορούν να αποτελέσουν τη βάση για τη διερεύνηση της δραστηριότητας και των άλλων πόλεων.

Στην Κορησία αποδόθηκαν εξ αρχής, με βεβαιότητα τα αρχαϊκά νομίσματα που απεικονίζουν μια σουπιά, έχοντας ως σημείο αναφοράς την αναγραφή του εθνικού Ο ανελλιπώς από τις πρωιμότερες κιόλας κοπές της πόλης, όπως άλλωστε και την απεικόνιση του ίδιου περίεργου και σπάνιου αυτού τύπου στα υστερότερα νομίσματα της (*Pl. 10a*).

Η επιλογή του συγκεκριμένου εμβλήματος, το οποίο δεν φαίνεται να

2 C.M. Kraay, *Archaic and Classical Greek Coins* (California 1976) 45. Ο C.H.V. Sutherland, "Overstrikes and Hoards. The Movement of Greek Coinage down to 400 B.C." *NC* (1942) 12, σημ. 11, θεωρούσε ότι ακόμα και το ίδιο το σφαιρικό σχήμα των πρώτων νομισμάτων της Καρθαίας, καθώς και άλλων εργαστηρίων εκτός Κυκλάδων, είχε επιλεγεί όχι μόνο για την ομοιότητα με το αιγινητικό, αλλά και επειδή διευκόλυνε το ξανακτύπημα των σφαιρικών "χελωνών".

3 Ch. Papageorgiadou – Banis, *The Coinage of Kea* (Athens 1997).

4 G. Galani, L. Mendoni, Ch. Papageorgiadou, "Επιφανειακή έρευνα της Κέας" *Αρχαιογνωσία* 3, 1982 (1987) 237-250.

5 Ch. Papageorgiadou – Banis (όπ. π., σημ. 3).

συνδέεται με κάποια τοπική παράδοση, είναι αρκετά παράδοξη. Η άποψη του Babelon[6] ότι συνδέεται με τη λατρεία του Απόλλωνα Σμινθίου δεν φαίνεται να ευσταθεί. Ο Babelon στηρίχθηκε σε μια αγγειογραφία, στην οποία απεικονίζεται ο Απόλλωνας να πετά με το άρμα του πάνω από τη θάλασσα. Ωστόσο, η παρουσία της σουπιάς, μαζί με άλλα μαλάκια και ψάρια, μπορεί και ίσως πρέπει, να ερμηνευθεί ως η καλλιτεχνική έκφραση του θαλασσινού στοιχείου και όχι ως σύμβολο του θεού.

Αλλωστε, η παρουσία της σουπιάς στα νομίσματα θα μπορούσε να εξηγηθεί και από την έντονη φυσική παρουσία των μαλακίων αυτών στην παραλιακή Κορησία, ή ακόμα να υπoννοεί κάποιο οικονομικό κέρδος από την αλιεία και το εμπόριό τους, ή ίσως, ακόμα περισσότερο, να αναφέρεται και σε κάποια μορφή πολιτικής σχέσης με τη γειτονική Ερέτρια, στα νομίσματα της οποίας απεικονιζόταν το χταπόδι.[7]

Σε αντίθεση με την Κορησία, η Καρθαία, με του σωζόμενους επιβλητικούς ναούς της, η πλέον επιφανής από τις πόλεις της Κέας, υπήρξε το μόνιμο πρόβλημα των νομισματολόγων. Αιτία για αυτό ήταν ο εξαιρετικά κοινός τύπος που έφερε στα νομίσματά της, ο αμφορέας (*Pl. 10b*).

Η μία σειρά των νομισμάτων της, αυτή όπου απεικονίζεται αμφορέας και δελφίνι, δεν δημιουργεί προβλήματα απόδοσης καθόσον σε ένα από αυτά τα νομίσματα, που σήμερα βρίσκεται στο Παρίσι, αναγράφεται και το εθνικό ΚΑΡΘ. Ο Bröndstedt, ο οποίος είχε βρει νομίσματα αυτού του τύπου και κατά τη διάρκεια των ερευνών του στο νησί, στηριζόμενος σε αυτό το νόμισμα, απέδωσε στην Κέα και όλες τις κοπές που έφεραν ως τύπο μόνο τον αμφορέα, χωρίς το δελφίνι. Αρκετά παραδόξως όμως τα κατέτασσε στα "nummi incertae sedis civitatum Cei insulae".[8] Τις απόψεις του Bröndstedt ακολούθησαν και υποστήριξαν ο E. de Cadalvène,[9] ο W. Wroth στον κατάλογο του Βρετανικού Μουσείου[10] και ο F. Imhoof-Blumer.[11]

Ωστόσο, εξισου επιφανείς νομισματολόγοι προτίμησαν να αποδώσουν τα νομίσματα με τον αμφορέα στην Ανδρο. Ο B. V. Head[12] και ο E.

6 E. Babelon. *Traité des monnaies grecques et romaines II*, 1 (Paris) 1291, 1292, σημ. 1.

7 Στην περίπτωση αυτή θα είχαμε και κάποιο χρονολογικό πλαίσιο ένταξης αυτών των νομισμάτων. Δυστυχώς όμως οι ιστορικές μαρτυρίες για την περίοδο της μεγάλης δύναμης του ερετριακού κράτους είναι ασαφείς. Σύμφωνα με τον κατάλογο των Θαλασσοκρατοριών του Ευσέβιου, η θρυλούμενη ερετριακή επικυριαρχία στα νησιά μπορεί να συνδεθεί με τη μεγάλη ναυτική επέκταση της πόλης που τοποθετείται στα 505 με 490 π. Χ.

8 P. O. Bröndstedt, *Reisen und Untersuhungen in Griechenland* (Paris 1826).

9 E. de Cadalvène, *Recueil de médailles grecques inédites: Europe* (Paris 1828).

10 W. Wroth, *Catalogue of the Greek Coins in the British Museum. Crete and the Islands* (London 1886).

11 F. Imhoof-Blumer, *Griechische* Münzen (*München* 1890)

12 B.V. Head, *Historia Numorum. A Manual of Greek Numismatics* (Oxford 1911).

Babelon[13] αρχικά, ενώ λίγο αργότερα ο Δ. Πασχάλης, με τη σύμφωνη γνώμη του Ν. Σβορώνου, στο άρθρο του για τη νομισματοκοπία της Ανδρου στο πρώτο τεύχος της ΔΕΝΑ, το 1898, έκλινε οριστικά υπέρ αυτής της απόδοσης.

Αρκετά αργότερα, ο C. T. Seltman,[14] με μια αρκετά ριζοσπαστική στροφή, απέδωσε τα νομίσματα με τον αμφορέα στην Αθήνα, κατατάσσοντάς τα στα πρώτα εραλδικά. Ωστόσο η υπόθεση αυτή συνάντησε αμέσως πολλές αντιδράσεις και σύντομα εγκαταλείφθηκε.[15]

Ωστόσο, η διαμάχη μεταξύ των υποστηρικτών της μιας ή της άλλης απόδοσης, στην Καρθαία ή την Ανδρο, δεν έληξε. Στα νεώτερα χρόνια οι Kroll, Waggoner[16] και Bloesch επανήλθαν υποστηρίζοντας την απόδοση στην Καρθαία,[17] ενώ ο R. Holloway προτίμησε την Ανδρο.[18]

Τελευταία, στις μελέτες των K. Sheedy[19] και Χ. Παπαγεωργιάδου[20] προτείνεται και πάλι η απόδοση στην Καρθαία.

Θα πρέπει να σημειωθεί ότι η όποια απόφαση σχετικά με την απόδοση αυτών των νομισμάτων στηρίζεται σε εξαιρετικά λεπτές διαφοροποιήσεις, ενώ τα στοιχεία εκείνα που συνηγορούν υπέρ της μιάς ή της άλλης απόφασης ουσιαστικά αυτοαναιρούνται ή έρχονται σε αντίθεση με άλλα ήδη δεδομένα.

Από τεχνικής πλευράς η διαφοροποίησή των δύο τύπων είναι μηδαμινή. Τεχνικές διαφορές, όπως το σχήμα των πετάλων, ή ο τύπος των εγκοίλων δεν υφίστανται, καθόσον και τα δύο νομισματοκοπεία βρίσκονται στον ίδιο χώρο και ακολουθούσαν τις ίδιες βασικές αρχές των κυκλαδικών εργαστηρίων. Για τον ίδιο λόγο, εξίσου ατελέσφορη αποδεικνύεται και η μελέτη της μετρολογίας. Συνεπώς για την επίλυση του προβλήματος οφείλουμε να παραμείνουμε στην εικονογραφία.

---

13 E. Babelon (όπ. π., σημ. 6).

14 C.T. Seltman, *Athens. Its History and Coinage before the Persian Invasion* (Cambridge 1924).

15 Ενδεικτικά αναφέρω τις ενστάσεις του E.S.G.R. Robinson στην Βιβλιοκριτική του, *NC* (1924) 239-241 και του J.H. Jongkees, "Notes on the Coinage of Athens" *Mnemosyne* 3, 12 (1945) 81-83, ο οποίος μάλιστα επανέρχεται στην Καρθαία.

16 Πρέπει να επισημανθεί ότι οι απόψεις τους δεν εκφράστηκαν σε συγκεκριμένες μελέτες για τη νομισματοκοπία αυτών των νησιών, αλλά ανάμεσα σε προβληματισμούς γενικότερου ενδιαφέροντος.

17 S. Hurter, E. Pászthory, H. Bloesch, "Archaischer Silberfund aus dem Antilibanon", Festschrift für Leo Mildenberg (Wetteren 1984) 111-125

18 R.R. Holloway, *Archaic Coinage in the Cyclades*, ANS Summer Seminar 1957 (αδημοσίευτες σημειώσεις).

19 K. Sheedy, forthcoming.

20 Ch. Papageorgiadou — Banis (όπ. π., σημ. 3).

Πρέπει να παραδεχθούμε ότι υπάρχουν κάποιες σημαντικές διαφοροποιήσεις ανάμεσα στις δύο νομισματικές σειρές. Σε αυτήν με τον αμφορέα μόνο, χωρίς δελφίνι, το αγγείο αποδίδεται με το σώμα πιο σφαιρικό, χαμηλό λαιμό και δυνατές λαβές, ενώ στηρίζεται σε μια πλατειά βάση. Στη σειρά όπου απεικονίζεται και το δελφίνι έχουμε την εντύπωση ενός ραδινότερου αγγείου. Ο αμφορέας χαρακτηρίζεται από λεπτότερο και ψηλότερο σώμα και λαιμό, λεπτές λαβές και κωνική βάση. Ωστόσο, οι διαφορές αυτές εξομαλύνονται εάν υπάρχει διαφορά χρονολόγησης, όπως άλλωστε δείχνουν και τα τεχνικά χαρακτηριστικά.

Στα νομίσματα με τον αμφορέα μόνο τα πέταλα είναι σφαιρικά, ενώ τα έγκοιλα, του τύπου Union Jack, έχουν αρκετό βάθος. Αντίθετα, στα νομίσματα, όπου απεικονίζεται και το δελφίνι, τα πέταλα είναι πιο λεπτά και πεπλατυσμένα, ενώ τα έγκοιλα είναι πιο αβαθή και με πιο εξελιγμένους τύπους.[21]

Συνεπώς, οι όποιες τεχνοτροπικές διαφοροποιήσεις που εμφανίζονται, μπορούν να ερμηνευθούν όχι από την ταυτότητα του νομισματοκοπείου, αλλά από τη χρονολογική διαφορά των σειρών. Τα νομίσματα χωρίς δελφίνι προηγούνται χρονικά όχι μόνο αυτών όπου απεικονίζεται και το δελφίνι, αλλά και όλων των άλλων γνωστών κοπών της Κέας.

Η εξαιρετικά σημαντική και πρώιμη, σχετικά με τις άλλες πόλεις του νησιού, νομισματική δραστηριότητα της Καρθαίας θα μπορούσε να ερμηνευθεί και με το μεγαλεπήβολο αρχιτεκτονικό πρόγραμμα που είχε αρχίσει στα τέλη του 6ου π. Χ. αι., στην τελευταία δεκαετία του ίσως, με τους ναούς του Απόλλωνα και της Αθηνάς, και συνεχίστηκε με γοργούς ρυθμούς και τα επόμενα χρόνια.

Από την άλλη πλευρά, εάν αποσυνδέσουμε τη σειρά με τον αμφορέα από την Καρθαία, διαταράσσεται σημαντικά το σχήμα που παρακολουθείται στις άλλες πόλεις, δηλαδή μία νομισματική σειρά, ελάχιστα πρωιμότερη πιθανόν, που φέρει μόνο το κυρίως έμβλημα της πόλης, η οποία ακολουθείται ή είναι σχεδόν σύγχρονη με μία άλλη στην οποία έχει προστεθεί και το δελφίνι. Στην περίπτωση αυτή θα πρέπει να δεχθούμε ότι η Καρθαία δεν ακολούθησε τις άλλες πόλεις στην έναρξη της νομισματοκοπίας τους, αλλά ξεκίνησε στη δεύτερη φάση τους, όταν προστίθεται και το δελφίνι, γεγονός που δεν φαίνεται αρκετά λογικό εάν λάβουμε υπόψη μας την ευμάρεια της πόλης.

Εξάλλου, θα ήταν πραγματικά απορίας άξιο, γιατί σε δύο τόσο

21 Πρέπει να σημειώσουμε ότι, αντίθετα με όσα παρατηρούνται στις άλλες πόλεις της Κέας, όπου συνήθως χρησιμοποιούνται οι ίδιοι τύποι εγκοίλων και για τις δύο σειρές, πράγμα που προϋποθέτει την σχεδόν σύγχρονη κοπή τους, στην Καρθαία οι τύποι των εγκοίλων των νομισμάτων με αμφορέα δεν εμφανίζονται ποτέ στα νομίσματα με αμφορέα και δελφίνι.

γειτονικές περιοχές, όπως η Ανδρος και η Κέα, να χρησιμοποιηθεί ως έμβλημα ο ίδιος τύπος, πράγμα που δεν εμφανίζεται ξανά όχι μόνο στις Κυκλάδες, αλλά και σε ευρύτερες περιοχές, και τη στιγμή που γνωρίζουμε τη σημασία της νομισματικής εικονογραφίας για τις αρχαίες πόλεις.

Θα πρέπει λοιπόν, ακολουθώντας τα νομισματικά σύμβολα, να επανέλθουμε στις αρχικές απόψεις και να ακολουθήσουμε τις προτάσεις του Bröndstedt αποδίδοντας τα νομίσματα με αμφορέα στην Καρθαία.

Η περίπτωση της Καρθαίας είναι ίσως η περισσότερο γνωστή και πιο εντυπωσιακή, εξίσου όμως αμφισβητούμενη και ίσως πιο περίπλοκη και με ευρύτερο προβληματισμό είναι η νομισματοκοπίας της Ιουλίδας. Δεν πρόκειται πλέον για μια "διαμάχη" ανάμεσα σε δύο γειτονικά νησιά για την κυριότητα ενός τύπου. Πρόκειται ουσιαστικά για την εκ βάθρων επαναδιαπραγμάτευση μιάς πληθώρας βοτρυοφόρων νομισμάτων (*Pl. 10c*).

Το σταφύλι αποτελεί ένα εξαιρετικά διαδεδομένο νομισματικό τύπο στον ελληνικό χώρο. Η λατρεία του Διονύσου, η καλής πιότητας παραγωγή κρασιού και το εμπόριο του, αλλά και το άκρως διακοσμητικό και εύκολο σχήμα του έκαναν, σε πολλές περιοχές, την επιλογή του ως νομισματικό σύμβολο, την πλέον ενδεδειγμένη.

Ο προβληματισμός για την απόδοση στην Ιουλίδα περιορίζεται στις σειρές όπου δεν απεικονίζεται το δελφίνι. Ανάλογα με τον τρόπο απόδοσης του σταφυλιού, ενιαίου τριγωνικού ή τριμερούς, έχουν υποστηριχθεί κατά καιρούς διαφορετικές απόψεις. Οι W. Wroth και ο E. Babelon απέδιδαν χωρίς διάκριση κια τους δύο τύπους όχι μόνο στην Ιουλίδα, αλλά και στην Καρθαία.[22] Αντίθετα, ο Imhoof-Blumer ήταν ο πρώτος που διευκρίνισε ότι το τριμερές σταφύλι ανήκει στην Τήνο, τύπο τον οποίο ο Σβορώνος απέδιδε στη Μύκονο, αφήνοντας το τριγωνικό τσαμπί στην Ιουλίδα. Στην ίδια άποψη επανήλθε πολύ αργότερα, το 1976, η Artemis-Gyselen,[23] την οποία ακολούθησε και ο R. Etienne.[24]

Θα πρέπει ωστόσο να αναφερθεί και η άποψη του R. Holloway,[25] η οποία φαίνεται να περιπλέκει ακόμα περισσότερο τα πράγματα. Ο Holloway κατέληξε στο συμπέρασμα ότι όλα ανεξαιρέτως τα βοτρυοφόρα θα έπρεπε να απομακρυνθούν από τα νομισματοκοπεία στα οποία είχαν αποδοθεί μέχρι τότε. Εκτός από τις καθαρά τεχνοτροπικές διαφορές και κάποιες αντιρρήσεις στην κατάταξη του Imhoof-Blumer, επεκαλείτο ένα

---

22 E. Babelon, *Traité des monnaies grecques et romaines II 1* (Paris) και W. Wroth, *Catalogue of the Greek Coins in the British Museum. Crete and the Islands* (London 1886).

23 L. Gyselen, "Les monnaies archaïques de Ténos" *RBN* (1977) 5-15.

24 R. Etienne, *Ténos et les Cyclades du milieu du IVe s. av. J. C. au milieu du IIIe siècle ap. J. C*, MEFRA 263 bis (Paris 1990).

25 R. Holloway, (όπ. π., σημ. 18).

βασικό λόγο για αυτήν την πρόταση. Την ύπαρξη ενός δυσανάλογα μεγάλου αριθμού υποδιαιρέσεων σε σχέση με τους υπάρχοντες στατήρες, πολλές από τις οποίες είχαν βάρος γύρω στα 2.50 γρ., βάρος το οποίο δεν εντάσσεται σε κανένα από τους γνωστούς σταθμητικούς κανόνες, και ιδιαίτερα στον αιγινητικό. Η αλήθεια είναι ότι οι υποθέσεις του Holloway πράγματι ευσταθούν και θα πρέπει όντως να γίνει κάποτε μια συνολική διαπραγμάτευση των βοτρυοφόρων νομισμάτων ώστε να καταλήξουμε σε νέες αποδόσεις.

Οσον αφορά στην Κέα όμως υπάρχουν δύο σημεία τα οποία μας επιβάλλουν να δεχθούμε την απόδοση στην Ιουλίδα ορισμένων τουλάχιστον από αυτά τα νομίσματα.

Το πρώτο είναι βέβαια η εξισορρόπηση με τις κοπές των άλλων πόλεων και η παράλληλη σειρά με το δελφίνι, βάσει της οποίας καθορίζεται και ο τύπος του σταφυλιού, δηλαδή ο τριγωνικός, που θα πρέπει να αποδώσουμε στην Ιουλίδα. Θα πρέπει να επισημάνουμε ωστόσο ότι, παρά την ορθότητα των απόψεων του Blumer ως προς το σχήμα του σταφυλιού, τελικά δεν ευσταθούν όλες οι προτάσεις του. Το δεύτερο σημείο είναι τα τεχνοτροπικά παράλληλα, και ιδιαίτερα τα έγκοιλα, ορισμένα από τα οποία επανεμφανίζονται και στην Καρθαία και στην Κορησία.

Θα πρέπει λοιπόν όσον αφορά στις αποδόσεις στην Ιουλίδα να εξετάζεται κάθε νόμισμα χωριστά λαμβάνοντας υπόψη τόσο τις διαφοροποιήσεις του σταφυλιού, όσο και των εγκοίλων. Στην περίπτωση που γίνει μιά προσεκτική διάκριση σε αυτή τη βάση, τότε παρατηρούμε ότι αναιρούνται ακόμα και τα μετρικά προβλήματα που έθεσε ο Holloway, καθώς στην Ιουλίδα παραμένουν μόνο νομίσματα των οποίων τα βάρη εντάσσονται στο αιγινητικό σύστημα.[26]

Τα τελευταία χρόνια, η αποκρυπτογράφηση της νομισματικής εικονογραφίας επισκιάστηκε από άλλες, περισσότερο "τεχνοκρατικές" προσεγγίσεις στα νομισματικά ερωτήματα. Ωστόσο, με βάση τον ποβληματισμό που προκύπτει από τη μελέτη των εργαστηρίων της Κέας, όπου, ιδιαίτερα για την αρχαϊκή νομισματοκοπία, η εικονογραφία παραμένει εξαιρετικά σημαντική, θα πρέπει ίσως να επανεξετάσουμε τις αποστάσεις μας από αυτήν.

26 Ch. Papageorgiadou — Banis (όπ. π., σημ. 3)

ΤΡΙΚΚΑΙΩΝ ΑΘΛΑ*

A. Moustaka

The dekadrachms of Syracuse, which were minted during the final decades of the 5th century BC by two of the foremost engravers of the era, Kimon and Euainetos, have often been the object of scholarly attention,[1] both because of their artistic perfection but equally because of the problems of interpretation they present, i.e. their proper dating, the use for which they were intended, and their significance in the historical events of the period.

Although this is certainly one of the most thoroughly debated subjects in the field of Greek numismatics, we shall once more take the opportunity to briefly describe the basic characteristics of this coinage. As is well known, the dekadrachms follow the iconographic tradition of the tetradrachms which had begun to be minted in Syracuse as early as the late Archaic period.[2] In keeping with artistic developments of this period, these tetradrachms bore on their obverse a representation of a charioteer in a quadriga being crowned by Nike, while on the reverse there appeared the celebrated head of Arethusa encircled by four dolphins.

The only iconographic difference between these coins lies in the symbols located in the exergue beneath the relief line which divides the field of the main representation on the obverse. In the case of the dekadrachmon, along with a series of themes which are also found on the tetradrachms —

---

* For discussion and other help I would like to express my warmest thanks to C. Arnold-Biucchi, V. Dimitriadi, A. Gulaki-Voutira, M. Tiverios.

1 P.R. Franke-M. Hirmer, *Die griechische Münze* (München 1964) pl. 34, 104 (Euainetos) and pl. 40-41, 116; 42, 118 (Kimon). The bibliography on this subject is very extensive; I refer readers to the recent article of W. Fischer-Bossert, *AA* 1992, 39-60 which gathers together the most important titles. In the present article I shall refer to specific works only when this is absolutely necessary.

2 See E. Boehringer, *Die Münzen von Syrakus* (Berlin 1925); *SNG* ANS Part 5, Sicily III (1988), pl. 1 ff.

lions, sea monsters, dolphins or ears of wheat[3] (whose symbolism cannot be discussed here), there is represented for the first time an entire panoply of armour consisting of a shield, crested helmet, a pair of greaves and a breast-plate. What is notable, however, is that some of these coins bear in the immediate vicinity of the panoply, although not always in precisely the same spot, the inscription ΑΘΛΑ (*Pl. 11a-b*).[4]

As early as the 18th century, J. Eckhel[5] tried to connect the dekadrachms with the performance of the "ἀγῶνες ἀργυρικοί". In 1891 Sir Arthur Evans[6] chose to view them as commemorative medals in honour of the great victory of the Syracusans over the Athenians in 413 BC, and associated them with the Asinaria, the games which were held on the banks of the Asinaros river at Syracuse. Evans saw the armour depicted on the coins as representations of the spoils won by the Syracusans in their battles with the Athenians and suggested that they were probably the prizes awarded in these athletic contests. Since, however, we have no actual testimonia regarding these games, Evans had to hypothesize their existence, basing his assumption on the word ΑΘΛΑ, which he took to mean "prizes" or "trophies", thus establishing an immediate connection between the word ΑΘΛΑ and the arms depicted on the coins.

Evans' interpretation gained wide scholarly acceptance and was only criticised by J. Liegle[7] in 1941 who saw the entire representation on the obverse (the quadriga) as an iconographic unity to be taken in conjunction with the depiction on the exergue. Thus he maintained that the arms were prizes given to victors in chariot races. He also supported a dating 10 years earlier. Liegle's theory, however, did not win acceptance.

A fuller treatment of the subject within the more general context of the significance of the dekadrachms was given by M.R. Alföldi.[8] In contrast to all previous interpretations which viewed the dekadrachms[9] as commemorative medals Alföldi, after a methodical analysis of the conditions under which the most important series of dekadrachms were minted in

---

3 E.g. Franke-Hirmer (supra n.1) pl. 26, 8 (Damareteion — lion); pl. 28, 82 (tetradrachm — sea monster); pl. 33, 101 (tetradrachm of Euainetos — dolphin); pl. 38. 109R (tetradrachm of Phrygillos — ear of wheat).

4 In some coins the inscription is located beneath the panoply in the center, in others it is found to the left over the shield; see E.S.G. Robinson, *A Catalogue of the Calouste Gulbekian Collection of Greek Coins*. Part 1 (Lisboa 1971), pl. 34, nr. 312 and 36, nr. 318.

5 J. Eckhel, *Doctrina numorum veterum* (Vienna 1792-1826) 243.

6 A. Evans, *NC* 1891, 205-376, esp. 339 ff.

7 J. Liegle, Euainetos 101. *BWPr.* (Berlin 1941) note 5, p. 25.

8 M.R. Alföldi, *Dekadrachmon. Ein forschungsgeschichtliches Phänomen* (Wiesbaden 1976).

9 For the dekadrachms of the hellenistic period see recently C. Arnold-Biucchi, *RivItNum* 1993, 243-249.

antiquity, concluded that they also possessed real monetary value. As for the coinage which concerns us here Alföldi, diverging from the proposals of Evans, did not accept the interpretation of the arms as war booty but saw them rather as the actual armour of the Athenian general Nikias. Therefore she attributes a symbolic significance to the panoply as representing a favourable omen for the outcome of the new war Syracuse was then waging with Carthage and which had broken out in 409 BC.

Since the appearance of Alföldi's article the evidence from recently found coin hoards[10] now makes it quite clear that the dekadrachms must have been minted only in the last five years of the 5th century BC. This fact has led some investigators, such as C.M. Kraay,[11] to disassociate them from the wars with the Athenians and to interpret them rather as coins which were exclusively due to the economic policies of Dionysios of Syracuse (405-367 BC),[12] who required enormous monetary resources in order to pay the mercenaries he had hired to wage war against Carthage.

That we have dared to treat it yet again, after such a host of publications and opinions regarding this hotly debated topic, is due partly to the fact that very recently, in an extensive article, W. Fischer-Bossert[13] added a new opinion to the debate. He attempted to show that the panoply is actually a depiction of Homeric weaponry so that, as a consequence, the portions of the panoply which were represented should be seen as "Homeric trophies". Thus Dionysios' mercenary troops were being called upon to emulate the prowess of Homer's warriors, their ultimate reward being elevation to the sphere occupied by the heroes of the Homeric epic. Shortly after the publication of Fischer-Bossert's views, his opinions were criticised by S. Garraffo.[14]

Undoubtedly, the basic significance of the word ΑΘΛΑ, with which the interpretation of the scene depicted is so closely linked, derives from the Homeric era where it had the meaning of prizes in the agones.[15] However, at least from the 6th century onward the word is used synonymously with

---

10 See M. Thompson, O. Mørkholm, C.M. Kraay, *An Inventory of Greek Coin Hoards* (New York 1973) Nr. 2120 (Ognina Hoard), Nr. 2090 (Pacchino Hoard).

11 C.M. Kraay, *Archaic and Classical Greek Coins* (London 1976) 224.

12 On Dionysios of Syracuse see G.K. Jenkins, *BICS* 8 (1961) 86; Chr.Boehringer, "Zur Finanzpolitik und Münzprägung des Dionysios von Syrakus", in: *Greek Numismatics and Archaeology. Essays in Honour for M. Thompson* (Wetteren 1979) 9-32.

13 Supra n.1.

14 S. Garraffo, *RivItNum* 95 (1993) 167-186, 180:"...non crediamo necessario pensare alla organizzazione di homerische Wettkämpfe da parte di Dionisio". However, Fischer-Bossert seemed as well, in private conversation with me, to rescind, at least in part, his proposed interpretation of a reference to Homeric martial contests.

15 See Liddell-Scott, 32 ff s.v. ἆθλον.

the games themselves. One has only to think of the "Ἆθλα ἐπί Πελία" of Stesichoros,[16] the "Πατρόκλους ἆθλα" on the dinos of Sophilos[17] or, even later, the "ΤΩΝ ΑΘΗΝΗΘΕΝ ΑΘΛΩΝ" represented on the Panathenaic amphorae.[18] However, the word 'ΑΘΛΑ' in general refers symbolically to the "νικητήριον",[19] a term which does not apply exclusively to the "victory prize" awarded to the contestant who came first in the contest, but was also used for the prizes awarded to the second and third place winners.

Apart from the dekadrachms, only on one other coin (a stater from Metapontum[20] dating from 480-470 BC which bears on its reverse the figure of Acheloos with the body of a man and the head of a bull standing in a markedly hesitant pose) do we read the inscription "ΑΕΘΛΟΝ-ΑΨΕΛΟΙΟ". On the obverse it bears an ear of wheat and a grass-hopper. This coin has been interpreted as being a prize for an athletic contest, otherwise unknown, held in Metapontum in honour of Acheloos. It is perhaps superfluous to state that the basic difference between the inscription on this coin and that on the Syracuse dekadrachm lies in the fact that the word which concerns us here (ΑΘΛΑ) is rendered in the singular on the Metapontum coin and is so placed that it covers the entire coin and not just a portion of it. Therefore the question arises if the coin from Metapontum was exclusively designed to be a prize awarded to the victor in an athletic contest.[21]

The presence of this inscription on coins from the mainland of Greece was unknown until recently when it was found on an obol in a private[22] collection (*Pl. 12a; cover*). Although not of excellent quality, the coin does allow us to view the subject from yet another angle. It bears on its obverse a horse moving toward the right within a dotted circle. In the field, above its back, a small object is visible which is not easy to interpret because of wear. On the reverse, which is also somewhat worn, there is a standing, laurel crowned male figure wearing a long chiton and himation who, turning slightly leftward (though not fully in profile), moves to the left carrying a musical instrument in his left hand. To the right and left of the figure we read the letters of the ethnic: **T]RI[K]KA**. Next to the figure and

---

16 D.L. Page, *Poetae Melici Graeci* (Oxford 1962) 179 b.

17 Athens, National Museum 15499: *ABV* 39 ff.

18 For the Panathenaic amphorae, see recently: P. Valavanis, Παναθηναϊκοί ἀμφορεῖς ἀπό την Ἐρέτρεια (Athens 1991) with further bibliography.

19 *RE* 11,2 (1896) 2058-2063 (Reisch).

20 P. Noe, *The Coinage of Metapontum* II, *NNM* 47 (New York 1931), 7ff, pl. 23, 311. Franke-Hirmer (supra n. 1) fig. 230, pl. 82.

21 On this subject see Fischer-Bossert (supra n. 1) 45, note 54. Also see below.

22 Weight: 0.5 gm, Diameter: 1.2 cm.

parallel to the fall of the himation on the left, we can also make out the clumsily written inscription: ΑΘΛΑ.[23]

Even without the assistance provided by the inscription (albeit partially preserved) of the ethnic on the reverse, the coin unquestionably comes from the region of "horse bearing" Thessaly because of the characteristic depiction on the obverse of an especially popular theme found in the coinage of many Thessalian cities. Thus, around the beginning of the 4th century BC Trikka[24] in Hestiaiotis minted silver obols which depict such themes, i.e. a horseman or a horse.[25] By way of analogy, in the coinage of Larissa various symbols were placed at precisely the spot in the field where the extremely worn (and therefore difficult to interpret) object is found on our coin.[26] Moreover, in regard to the representations on the reverse of the obols of Trikka, the engraver generally followed prototypes from the neighbouring city[27] of Larissa. Thus, at Trikka, the eponymous nymph is portrayed in a series of different attitudes similar to her counterpart at Larissa: holding a mirror or hydria, or playing ball, to mention just a few of the depictions which have reference to local myths.[28]

However the scene on the reverse of the newly found coin does not seem to be "borrowed" from the iconography of Larissa. Here the laurel-wreathed figure represents Apollo, a divinity whose cult is closely associated with Thessaly. But even though Apollo is not found on coins from Larissa itself, we frequently encounter the laurel-wreathed head of the god on scenes represented on various other Thessalian coin-types.[29] Of greater significance, however, is the fact that the god is here represented in a specific guise: that of a musician. We encounter depictions of Apollo Kitharodos frequently in Thessaly, both in the late Classical period (there

---

23 Although the last letter is difficult to discern in the photograph, the reading A should be considered secure.

24 For the silver coinage of Trikka see: *BMC Thessaly to Aetolia* (London 1883). For the copper coins the basic source remains E. Rogers, *The Copper Coinage of Thessaly* (London 1932) 16-18. There was recently a summary presentation of the basic coin types of the city by S. Lavva in the Πρακτικά του 1ου Συμποσίου Τρικαλινών Σπουδών (Τρίκαλα-Καλαμπάκα-Μετέωρα), Τρικαλινά 8 (1988) 289-300. (I owe this reference to my colleague A. Kontoyiannis).

25 In spite of every effort it has not been possible to identify coins from the same die with the stepping horse on the obverse among the coins from Trikka, nor has it been possible to identify die-links between coin-types of Trikka and those of Larissa.

26 E.g., for a lion-headed spout on a coin-type from Larissa, see *BMC* 25, 15 pl. IV 11.

27 For the coinage of Larissa in the 5th century BC see F. Herrmann, *ZfN* 33 (1921) 33-69.

28 For the importance of Thessalian coins as a source of information about the cults and the mythology of the region see P. Philippson, *Thessalische Mythologie* (Zürich 1944) and A. Moustaka, *Kulte und Mythen auf thessalischen Münzen* (Würzburg 1983).

29 See Moustaka (supra n. 28) 36-38, Cat. pp. 111-114.

are well-known examples from Thessalian reliefs with representations of the Apolline triad,[30] the best known example of which is the one from Pharsala[31]) as well as in a rare silver coin of the 4th century BC said to be from Trikka's neighbouring city, Metropolis.[32] Lastly, as P.R. Franke has recently reported, Apollo again appears as Kitharodos in five Thessalian coin series representing different statuary types from the Neronian period.[33] Although these coin types are easily related to the Roman iconography of the divinity they are not, however, unconnected with the local Thessalian tradition which concerns Apollo in his role as a musician. Consequently, we do not think it is unreasonable to suggest, on the basis of the evidence here presented, that these representations point to the existence of a specific musical tradition in Thessaly.

Recently, a discovery from Larissa itself has served to throw further light on this relatively obscure aspect of the Thessalian region. This involves a large krater (*Pl. 13a-b*) by the Painter of Munich 2335 which dates to the third quarter of the 5th century BC. M. Tiverios[34] has succeeded in connecting this krater with the Periklean Panathenaea. Because of the nature of the scenes depicted on it — on the one hand a hoplite race, on the other a musical contest (flute-playing or singing accompanied by the flute) — this krater must have been made specially to order by the Athenian vase painter at the request of a citizen of Larissa, who in either an indirect or direct way (i.e. by having personally competed in some contest) took part in the Panathenaic games. The suspicion that this krater was specially commissioned is also supported by the fact that the far more significant contest of the kitharodoi is absent from the musical scenes depicted on the krater. In the context of this study Tiverios[35] stressed that especially in regard to the flute-playing contests there are definite indications that in the Panathenaic games non-Athenians could also be proclaimed victors,[36] a fact which lends support to the view that the probable winner in the aulodia was the Thessalian who commissioned the vase. In addition,

30 On this subject see the recent work by M. Flashar, *Apollon Kitharodos* (Köln-Weimar-Wien 1992) 30-32.

31 H. Biesantz, *Die thessalischen Grabreliefs* (Mainz 1965) 31, Nr. 52, pl. 48.

32 *BMC* 36,2 pl. VII 8; MuM Liste 164 Jan 1957, Nr. 17. Moustaka (supra n. 28) Nr. 4.

33 P.R. Franke, Νέρων, Απόλλων και Θεσσαλία in Διεθνές Συνέδριο για την Αρχαία Θεσσαλία. Μνήμη Δ. Θεοχάρη (Athens 1992) 370-375, pl. 81.

34 M. Tiverios, Περίκλεια Παναθήναια. Ένας κρατήρας του Ζωγράφου του Μονάχου 2335 (Athens 1989).

35 See Tiverios (supra n. 34) 130-132.

36 For musical contests in Athens see recently H. Kotsidou, *Die musischen Agone der Panathenäen in der archaischen und klassischen Zeit* (Munich 1991).

according to Huchzermeyer[37] the Thessalians were at a very early period familiar (along with the Boeotians, Lacedemonians, Ionians and Argives) with the use of the aulos.

Another piece of information which points to the close relationship of Thessaly with the musical arts is of particular interest since it derives from a very early period, the last quarter of the 6th century BC, and refers to the life and work of the lyric poet Anakreon.[38] Coming from his native city, Teos in Ionia, to Peisistratid Athens, Anakreon brought about a genuine revolution in the field of lyric poetry by introducing the barbiton, which became the preeminent musical instrument in the Dionysian festivals, the komos revels and symposiums, to judge from its many depictions on vases of the late Archaic period which feature symposiasts. Among these is a kylix by Oltos in the British Museum,[39] on which Anakreon himself, bearded, garlanded and in a drunken state, is identified by an inscription; he is accompanied by a group of singing youths.

The significance of this poet for the Thessalian region is due to the fact that — as we know from the epigrams — after the death of Hipparchos, Anakreon left Athens and dwelt for a time in the court of the Aleuadai whose seat was at Larissa.[40] It is obvious that Anakreon's residence there would have had an influence beyond the confines of the city itself, and that he would leave his mark on the development of musical culture throughout Thessaly.

On the basis of these hypotheses, the laurel-wreathed, himation-wearing male figure on our new coin from Trikka now acquires further significance. As I have already mentioned, the instrument Apollo is holding is not a kithara.[41] It is admittedly difficult to decide whether it is a barbiton or a lyre, since the quality of the rendering does not help us at this point. However, in regard to another detail as well the depiction does not immediately fit into the known representations of Apollo Kitharodos: while in all other examples to which we have referred the god is depicted

---

37 H. Huchzermeyer, *Aulos und Kithara in der griechischen Kunst bis zum Ausgang der klassischen Zeit* (Münster 1931), pp. 28 and 72.

38 On Anakreon see *RE* 1,2 s.v. Anakreon (1894) 2038 (Crusius). Also S. Papaspyridi-Karouzou, *BCH* 66-67 (1942-43) 248 and K. Schefold, *Die Bildnisse der antiken Dichter, Redner und Denker* (Basel 1952). For the portraits of Anakreon also see G.M.A. Richter, *The Portraits of the Greeks* (London 1965) 75-78.

39 London, BM E 18. *ARV*[2] 62, 68. Also see Schefold (supra 38) pl. 51, 1.

40 For these epigrams from the Palatine Anthology VI 136=fr. 109, see *RE* (supra n. 38) note 31.

41 For musical instruments in antiquity, see M. Wegner, *Das Musikleben der Griechen* (Berlin 1949); for stringed instruments in particular see M. Maas and J. McIntosh Snyder, *Stringed Instruments of Ancient Greece* (New Haven-London 1989).

with his chiton belted high here his garment falls free in a manner reminiscent of the symposiasts mentioned earlier.

The epigraphical evidence we possess for Trikka (as well as for other cities in Thessaly) is quite meagre. Thus, the presence of an inscription on the coin we are presenting here acquires particular significance since it furnishes us with evidence about the performance in this city of otherwise unknown musical competitions.[42] Furthermore, on another little known coin from the beginning of the 4th century BC, now in the Berlin Museum[43] (*Pl. 12 b*), which probably was minted in Trikka, a seated musician is represented holding what appears to be a lyre, thus adding support to our identification of the instrument on our coin. The male figure on the Berlin coin is also somewhat unusual, in that he wears his himation draped around his naked torso. Because of this he can be seen as a precursor of the seated type of kitharodos who appears, as we stated earlier, on the coins of Nero.

It is not perhaps by chance that a Thessalian city chose to include the inscription ΑΘΛΑ on one of its coins. The iconographic and stylistic connections of many of the Thessalian coins with Sicilian coin-types, particularly during the second half of the 5th century BC (to which we are unable to devote further attention here[44]), reveal the tremendous influence the former coins had on local coin production. Here the question arises concerning the precise dating of our obol: if the dekadrachm is older, which we think is quite likely, then we have a terminus post quem for the Trikka coin of 405 BC. Obviously, the answer to the question of dating must for the time being remain open as new numismatic data from coin hoards is constantly adding to our knowledge.

---

42 Very little is known about the performance of musical competitions in Thessaly, as can be seen from the meagre references in I.C. Ringwood, *Agonistic Features of Local Greek Festivals Chiefly from Inscriptional Evidence* (Poughkeepsie 1927) 15-21.

43 To date it has only been depicted in the book by H. Biesantz, (supra n. 31) pl. 72, 13. According to information I have received from H.-D. Schultz, whom I warmly thank, the coin is not bronze, as claimed by Biesantz in his list of plates, but silver and 1.00 gm in weight. Of the letters of the ethnic, the beginning T and final A can be read with considerable certainty, while between them there is space for 5 or 6 letters. Its identification as a coin-type from Trikka is quite probable for another reason as well: the representation on the obverse of a female head turned toward the right is very reminiscent of similar female heads from other coins of this city; see Rogers (supra n. 24) 553, fig. 310.

44 M. Oikonomidou has exhaustively described the great influence the coins of the Greek colonies in the West, and especially Syracuse, had on the iconography of the coinage of Greece and the East: *The Griffon* N.S. 1985-86, 8-127, especially pp. 121-122. She associates this phenomenon with the fact that Thessalian cavalrymen participated in great numbers in foreign campaigns and brought back with them coins from Sicily which then had an influence on local issues. For a photocopy of this article I thank Ms. E. Tsourti.

Our original speculation about the significance of the word ΑΘΛΑ on the dekadrachms from Syracuse should now be re-examined on the base of these new findings. Aside from the fact that in the case of Syracuse we are dealing with a special coinage of an apparently celebratory character (while the Thessalian piece is an ordinary obol), the presence of the same inscription in entirely different contexts suggests that the interpretation of the arms depicted in the panoply as athletic trophies does not comprise the sole interpretive possibility. This view is strengthened by the fact that on the dekadrachms inscriptions are found only sporadically. For this reason we consider it more likely that the inscriptions refer to the coin itself. This conclusion is supported by analogy with the numerous bronze vessels, primarily hydriai but also lebetes, bearing dedicatory inscriptions, on which the word ΑΘΛΟΝ or ΑΘΛΑ is frequently found[45] and which date from the 7th to the 4th century BC. As we have seen in the case of the coin from Metapontum,[46] its interpretation as a prize in an athletic contest is very probable. Furthermore, we know that as early as the time of Solon monetary prizes for athletic contests were not unheard of.[47] Also, in regard to musical competitions, we know from inscriptions that gold and silver wreaths of specific value[48] were given as prizes. Furthermore, it also appears that in later musical competitions established from the 5th century BC onward (though perhaps ones of secondary importance) cash prizes were awarded.[49]

According to Evans, it is very likely that the Syracusan coins themselves were meant as prizes,[50] a view which is further supported by the new coin from Trikka. This certainly accords with the proposal of M.R. Alföldi that the dekadrachms actually served as currency. Regarding the representation of the arms itself, Alföldi connects them with the arms of the general Nikias, bestowing on them an additional symbolic value as tokens of victory. Another question which now presents itself is if the representations of these arms can be distinguished from the other representations found

---

45 For the main publication of this material see P. Amandry, *BCH* 95, 171, 602-625, E. Vanderpool, ΑΔ 24, 1969 Μελ. 1-5, pl. 1-4 and L.E. Roller, *Stadion*, 1981, 1-18. There is also exhaustive reference to these finds in the doctoral dissertation of E. Kephalidou, Ο νικητής αθλητής. Εικονογραφική μελέτη με έμφαση στην αττική αγγειογραφία (Thessaloniki 1996) 97-119.

46 See above note 21

47 See *RE* I,1 (1894) 848 (P.J. Meier)

48 *IG* II^2 22311, also see A.W. Johnston, *BSA* 82 (1987) 125 ff.

49 Aristotle, *Athenian Constitution* 60, 3; also see *RE* II, 2 (1896) 2060 (Reisch).

50 Also see the reference of S. Garraffo, *RivItNum* 95 (1993) 181: "Ma ΑΘΛΑ cosi come aveva intuito l' Evans poteva essere anche i decadrammi stessi..."

on the exergues of the dekadrachms and tetradrachms mentioned above. The question as to what at least were the games for which these coins were issued, must still remain unanswered.[51]

At any rate, since the inscription has now been freed from the burden of uniqueness, the word ΑΘΛΑ, along with the pictorial representations on the coins, can now be seen to reflect the intense efforts by the city of Syracuse to promote itself as a νικητήρια ανταμοιβή της αρετής. The dekadrachms of Syracuse consequently should be viewed as awards for military or athletic prowess, while in the case of Thessalian Trikka this new coin can be seen as an award in the art of music.

51 Perhaps, instead of searching for a specific contest, we should view the representation on the coins as possessing more general symbolic significance.

THISOA BY MOUNT LYKAION: FURTHER LIGHT ON AN ARKADIAN PROBLEM

Jennifer Warren

There has been much focus of interest in recent years on Arkadian problems, such those arising from the synoikism of Megalopolis, in the work of scholars such as Roy, Jost, and archaeologists of the Dutch School, te Riele and his colleagues.[1] I am delighted to have the privilege of honouring Mando Oeconomides with a contribution about the bearing that Arkadian coinage can have on such a problem.

There were two Arkadian cities named Thisoa, (or Theisoa, the alternative form), Θισόα ἡ πρός Ορχομένῳ, Thisoa near Orchomenos, in the north, and Θισόα ἡ πρὸς Λυκαίῳ, Thisoa on the slopes of Mt. Lykaion, in the southwest *(Fig. 1)*; they have duely been accorded two entries in Pauly-Wissowa by Ernst Meyer.[2] Apart from six inscriptional references[3] and a

---

1 See J. Roy, "Tribalism in Southwestern Arcadia in the Classical Period," *ActaAntHung* XX (1972) 43-51 (= Roy); M.Jost, *Sanctuaires et Cultes d'Arcadie* (*Études péloponnésiennes* 9, Paris 1985) (= Jost), and see her bibliography, 9-21; G.-J.-M.-J. te Riele, J.J. Feije, Y.C. Goester, "Archaeological investigations at Lavda in Arcadia, 1," *Pharos* I (1993) 175-208 (= *Pharos* I), and see bibliographies, 180-81, 198-99; Y.C. Goester, J.J. Feije, "Archaeological investigations at Lavda in Arcadia, 2," *Pharos* II (1994) 37-89 (= *Pharos* II). I am indebted to Mrs Goester for kindly keeping me informed about the investigations in this area; to Professor Jost for generous permission to use an adaptation of her map of Arkadia in *Sanctuaires et Cultes d'Arcadie* ; and to Mr Stuart Laidlaw for invaluable photography.

2 *RE* VI A1 (1936) 292-93; also *RE* Suppl. IX (1962) 1393.

3 (1) Delphi, first half of 4th cent. B.C. Dedication by a Thisoan from Arkadia, son of Hetairichos. *SEG* XIV. 455; Jost, 211, n. 4: "il désigne vraisemblablement un citoyen de Thisoa d'Orchomène plutôt qu'un habitant de Thisoa de Cynourie (une bourgade dont on ne sait rien...)." (2) Delphi, fourth century account. Βαθυκλῆς Θισοαῖος | ἐκ Μεγάλας πόλιος | δραχμὰς δύο. *FdD* III. 5. 4; J. Bousquet, *BCH* 66-7 (1942-3) 96-7, II lines 23-5. (3) Delphic *theorodokoi* inscription, third century. *BCH* 45 (1921) 15, III line 5; 52; *SEG* XXIII (1968) 322; W.E.Thompson, *REA* 84 (1982) 87. (4) and (5) Karkalou (Thisoa by Orchomenos). Two inscribed bronze tablets forming an honorary inscription, dated by letter forms to the beginning of the second century. *IG* V. 2. 511, 510; Dittenberger, *SIG*³ 623, published the two together as forming an honorary decree. (6) Lavda. Fragment of a stamped terracotta tile found in 1987 in the excavations of the Dutch School. ΘΙΣ[ ]. G. Touchais, *BCH* 112 (1988) 631-32, fig. 34; H.W. Catling, *AR* 34 (1987/8) 23; *SEG* XXXVIII (1988) 357; M. Jost, *Ktema* 11 (1986) 154, n. 92.

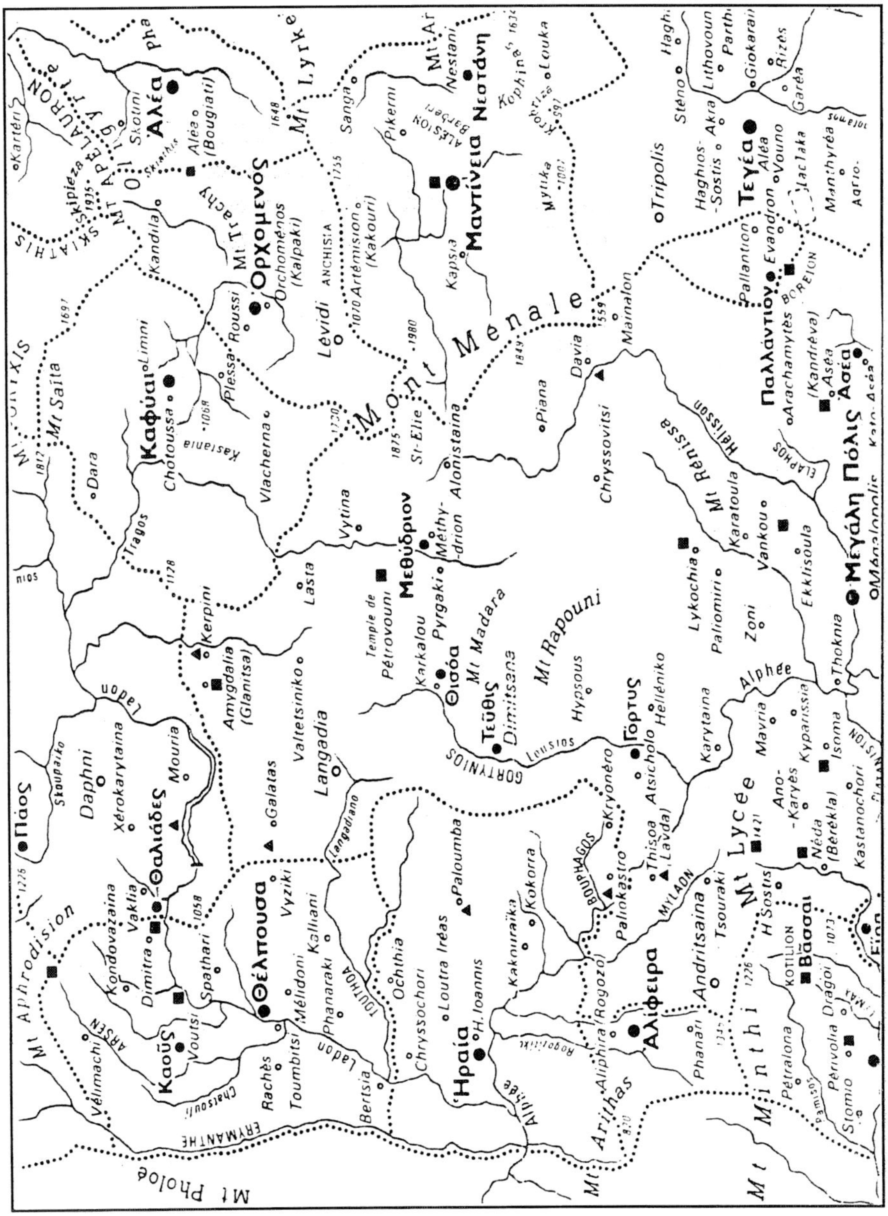

Fig. 1 Map of Arkadia (part).

citation by Stephanos of Byzantium,[4] our only non-archaeological evidence for these two towns are five mentions in Pausanias.[5] In Book 8 in the passage in which he lists the *poleis* which took part in the synoikism of Megalopolis in the fourth century, Pausanias mentions both Thisoas; he writes: ἐκ δὲ Κυνουραίων τῶν ἐν Ἀρκαδία Γόρτυς καὶ Θεισόα ἡ πρὸς Λυκαίῳ καὶ Λυκαιᾶται καὶ Ἀλίφηρα. ἐκ δὲ τῶν συντελούντων ἐς Ὀρχομενὸν Θεισόα Μεθύδριον Τεῦθις.[6]

Obscure though both towns are, it was the northern Thisoa that has had the greater claims on our attention, that is, until the recent Dutch excavations at Lavda.[7] Situated between Methydrion and Teuthis (as Pausanias tells us[8]), its location at Karkalou was confirmed by the discovery by Oikonomos, excavating the site in 1911,[9] of an honorary decree of the Thisoans datable to the first half of the second century.[10] Earlier, in 1851, Curtius[11] had expressed uncertainty as to which of the two Arkadian towns called Thisoa had struck the Achaian League bronze coins in the name of the Thisoans, which Sestini had described at the beginning of the nineteenth century;[12] Curtius thought that the northern Thisoa was more probably the location, since this was further away from Megalopolis, and therefore more likely to have been independent. Hiller von Gaertringen in 1913, in *IG* v. 2, 127, attributed the coins to the northern Thisoa as a certainty, and this was repeated by Dittenberger in 1917 in *SIG* [3] 623. He in turn was followed by Meyer in 1936 in Pauly-Wissowa.[13] Later J.Roy in 1972, was to write of a Thisoan Arkadian in a dedication at Delphi[14] that he "probably belonged not to Cynurian Thisoa, of which very little is known, ...but to Thisoa near Orchomenos, which was an independent state in the Hellenistic period (*IG* V.2. 510, 511)."[15] More recently still S. Dušanić in 1978 went so far as to state that "la Thisoa du Lycée avait cessé d'exister

4 Θείσοα, πόλις Ἀρκαδίας. Παυσανίας ὀγδόῳ. ὁ πολίτης Θεισοάτης, ὡς Λυκοάτης.

5 Paus. 8.27.4; 27.7; 28.3; 38.3; 38.9.

6 Paus. 8.27.4. See fig. 1.

7 See below n. 18.

8 Paus. 8. 28.3, 4.

9 G.P. Oikonomos, *Prakt* 1911 243-44.

10 *IG* V. 2. 510, 511. See supra n. 3.

11 E. Curtius, *Peloponnesos: eine historisch-geographische Beschreibung der Halbinsel, I* (Gotha 1851) 393, n. 10.

12 *Sopra le Medaglie antiche relative alla Confederazione degli Achaei dissertazione di Domenico Sestini* (Milan 1817) 42, no. 49; 43, no. 50.

13 See supra n. 2.

14 *SEG* XIV 455.

15 *ActaAntHung* XX, 48, n. 36.

avant 362 (cf. J. Roy, *Acta ant. Hung.* 20 (1972) 48, note 36)."[16] And in 1985 unsurprisingly, M. Jost had then referred to the Thisoa of Kynouria as "une bourgade dont on ne sait rien."[17]

In the southwest of Arkadia between Andritsaina and Karytaina on the northern slopes of Mount Lykaion is a fortified acropolis site visited and described by several eminent travellers to Greece such as Leake, Cockerell and Haller von Hallerstein, and Gell.[18] Between 1985 and 1988 the Netherlands School of Archaeology in Athens conducted excavations on the hill of Lavda.[19] It has long been debated whether this was the site of the ancient Lykoa or Thisoa.[20] In the 1986 season was found pottery from the second century BC, and in 1987 fragments of Megarian bowls,[21] and of special interest, a fragment of a tile bearing the inscription Θισ[ ].[22] It is highly tempting therefore to identify the site as Thisoa rather than Lykoa, though the site of Lykoa has yet to be identified.[23]

If it is accepted that the site is Thisoa, then to the evidence of second century BC occupation, the pottery and the Megarian bowl fragments, that was found can be added the Achaian League bronze coinage of Thisoa, and this in turn indicates that Thisoa was at that time an autonomous city state. For it is possible to demonstrate with little doubt that the Achaian League bronze issues belong to the southwestern Thisoa, and therefore probably the acropolis site Lavda on the slopes of Mount Lykaion, and surely not to the Thisoa near Orchomenos.

From my study of the bronze coinage of the Achaian League, now in advanced state of preparation, an unexpected picture of that coinage has emerged. (I was privileged to give a paper on the coinage, with special reference to the mints of Achaia and Elis, to the First International

---

16 *BCH* 102 (1978) 351, n. 22.

17 Jost, 211 n. 4. But since the Dutch discovery of the ΘΙΣ[ ] tile at Lavda (see supra n. 3), see eadem, "Thisoa du Lycée, réputée abandonnée lors du synoecisme, vient d'être identifié avec certitude", *Ktema* 11 (1986) 154.

18 J.J. Feije, *Pharos* I (1993) 183-85.

19 Topographical reconnaisance: *BCH* 104 (1980) 610-11; *BCH* 105 (1981) 651-65. Excavations: *BCH* 110 (1986) 693; *BCH* 111 (1987) 532; *BCH* 112 (1988) 632; *BCH* 113 (1989) 614; *AR* 1986-7, 21; *AR* 1987-8, 23. See also *Pharos* I.

20 Y.C. Goester, G.-J.-M.-J. te Riele, C.T.F. Vermeulen Windsant, *BCH* 105 (1981) 651 n. 4; G.-J.-M.-J.-te Riele, *Pharos* I (1993) 177-81.

21 S. Rotroff dated the start of their production in Athens some time between 240 and 220 B.C. (*The Athenian Agora* XXII. *Hellenistic Pottery. Athenian and Imported moldmade bowls* (Princeton 1982) 10). G. Siebert placed the invention of mouldmade bowls ca. 230 B.C. (*Recherches sur les ateliers de bols à reliefs du Péloponnèse à l'époque héllénistique* (Athens/Paris 1978) 156).

22 See supra n. 3.

23 G.-J.-M.-J. te Riele, *Pharos* I (1993) 180; J.J. Feije (supra n. 18) 188-196.

Symposium on Achaia and Elis in Antiquity, in 1989 here in Athens.[24]) As I explained there, it appears that as the result of a federal decree the coinage was started at four major mints and then spread over the Peloponnese, so that, in effect, the striking of the coinage by the forty-five mints was a single episode, although probably lasting over at least some months. As I collected specimens of this rare and obscure coinage, it became evident that the same hand could be seen to have cut dies for two or more mints, and that this phenomenon was repeated many times over. Almost invariably evidence of the work of a hand at two or more mints, or of copying, has occurred at adjacent mints, or at least at mints that are not far distant. For example there is one distinctive hand that cut obverse dies with a triangular Nike for Tegea, Pallantion, Asea, Kaphyai, Dipaia, and one die for Helisson, and another hand that cut most reverse dies of Corinth, several for Sikyon and some for Pellene and Alea.[25] In both cases the cities, with the exception of Kaphyai, were adjacent or close. There is no evidence for centralised minting; rather in both cases a die cutter has moved round an area working in first one city, then another. Similarly, of course, in *theorodokoi* inscriptions it is generally possible to follow the path of the *theoroi* as they moved from city to city.[26]

The designs of the Achaian League bronze coins are simple: on the obverse a nude Zeus Nikephoros standing to the left, on the reverse a female seated to the left wearing a chiton and peplos and holding out a wreath; both figures rest their left hand on a long sceptre behind. The design of the human face is far simpler and yet we are confident in recognising family likenesses. In asserting that the same engraver can be seen to have worked at two or more mints, of which I believe there to have been some 20 cases, I am aware of being open to the charge of subjectivity; yet would counter that this charge if at all justifiable can be only minimally so.

I have traced 12 Achaian League bronze coins of Thisoa, struck from probably 8 obverse dies and 11 reverse dies;[27] modest though these statistics are they are not untypical of the smallest Achaian *poleis* that struck the coinage. Significantly, we find that there are certain definite

---

24 A.D. Rizakis (ed.), *Achaia und Elis in der Antike. Akten des 1. internationalen Symposiums Athen 19-21. Mai 1989. ΜΕΛΕΤΗΜΑΤΑ* 13 (Athens / Paris 1991) 151-54.

25 For illustrations see my forthcoming study.

26 See W.E. Thompson, *REA* 84 (1982) 87-94.

27 Also there were two examples mentioned by Sestini (supra n. 12) 43, no. 51; idem, *Descrizione delle medaglie antiche greche del Museo Hedervariano. Parte Europea* (Florence 1830) 85, no. 20) and one by Warren (*NC* 1864, 92) which I have not been able to identify with any of the coins known today.

affinities between the engraving of some of the Thisoan dies and others of Heraia, Gortys, and Hypana; that there has been reuse of one - and possibly more - obverse die of Gortys at Thisoa; and that there is an obverse horizontal disposition of the personal name characteristic of the mints of a defined area including Thisoa. Heraia is on the western periphery of Arkadia; Hypana is in Triphylia, to the southwest of Heraia, and Gortys stands on the river Lousios which runs southwards into the Alpheios, while the acropolis of Thisoa itself — at least if the identification with Lavda is correct, — rises above the south bank of the Alpheios just to the west of its junction with the river Lousios. As mentioned above, Pausanias in his listing of the 40 *poleis* that were synoikised to form Megalopolis in the fourth century, wrote: of the Kynourians in Arkadia: Gortys, Theisoa by Lykaion, the Lykaiatai, Aliphèira; of those belonging to Orchomenos, Theisoa, Methydrion, Teuthis.[28]

Note the striking similarities between these reverses of Thisoa,[29] Gortys[30] and Heraia[31] *(Pl. 14)*: the wreath is held low so as not to interrupt the legend, there is the same treatment of the drapery, and a seat with a back but no third leg shown (these are common variants in the coinage). It seems likely that the three coins of Thisoa, Heraia and Gortys illustrated were by the same hand. Again the Zeus on an obverse of Thisoa, with thin legs and the left leg pointing to the base of the sceptre could be by the same hand as that on a coin of Hypana in Triphylia[32] *(Pl. 14)*.

All the coins of Thisoa bear the personal name ΠΟ/ΛΥ//ΗΡ/ΗΣ on the obverse. Two coins from the same obverse die, from Paris *(Pl. 14)* and the BM respectively, are struck from an obverse of Gortys with the name ΝΙΚ/Ο̣/Σ/ΤΡΑ̣/Τ̣Ο//Σ reengraved; omicron, alpha and tau of the underlying name are discernible, and rho is common to both names. However no coin of Gortys yet recorded is from the die in the original state. It seems possible that the obverse die shared by two more coins of Thisoa, in Leiden and the ANS respectively,[33] was also recut over another die of Gortys, although no letters from the first state of the die were discernible, because eta rho of the Thisoan personal name are engraved to the left, suggesting that this was to reuse the rho of the orginal die; also the second eta gives the appearance of having been engraved over another letter and its right vertical stroke falls

---

28 Supra p. 98 and n. 6.

29 Paris K3327.

30 Olympia SW 305; P.R. Franke, *Antike Welt* 15 (1984) 19, Abb. 22 ("Elis").

31 Paris G93.

32 Thisoa: Berlin 8751; Hypana: *BMC* 151.

33 For these and other details see my forthcoming study of the Achaian League bronze coinage.

awkwardly on the line of the sceptre. This is, to my knowledge, the only instance of the reuse of dies of one city by another in the entire Achaian League bronze coinage. Gortys is neighbour to the southwestern Thisoa and both were Kynourian cities; the northern Thisoa on the other hand lies between Teuthis and Methydrion. Obviously the engraver could have carried a die or dies from Gortys to the northern Thisoa, bypassing Teuthis, but is it not more likely that he took them straight to the southwestern Thisoa?[34]

Further, the practice of engraving the personal name on the obverse not vertically, as is the norm in the coinage, but horizontally, whether in one line or more, is found on the Achaian League bronze coins of all of a group of contiguous western Peloponnesian mints: Heraia (ΘΕΟΞΕΝΟΣ), Alipheira (ΤΕΙΣΙΜΑΧΟΣ), Gortys (ΝΙΚΟΣΤΡΑΤΟΣ), Thisoa (ΠΟΛΥΗΡΗΣ) (all in Arkadia), and Hypana (ΘΡΑΣΥΜΑΧΟΣ) in Triphylia. The practice is first found on some issues of Argos and Asea, whence it must have spread westwards, but except on one issue of Elis, is not found elsewhere in the coinage. This again indicates that it was the Thisoa in southwestern Arcadia, in other words the Kynourian Thisoa, that struck the Achaian League bronze coins.

Consider, on the other hand, the engraving of the Achaian League coins of Orchomenos and the cities that had belonged to it. Orchomenos lay at a considerable distance to the northeast of its three satellites, and its Achaian bronze coins show no association with any of theirs; in fact the disposition of the legend shows an eccentric deviation from the norm, with ΑΧΑΙΩΝ on the obverse instead of the reverse left, the personal name on the reverse left instead of right, and the ethnic, abbreviated, on the reverse right. (This divergence from the standard disposition is, surely, copied from Epidauros.)

Of the three cities that had belonged to Orchomenos (τῶν συντελούντων ἐς Ὀρχόμενον) the northernmost, Methydrion, certainly and uniquely, had the dies of the two recorded specimens engraved by an engraver who cut dies for Megalopolis itself. For Teuthis, the southernmost of the three, the legend disposition on the sole coin that I have seen is circular, and unique in the entire coinage; there are slight similarities with coins of Heraia, suggestive of the use of a coin of Heraia as model, rather than that an engraver from Heraia moved to Teuthis. It was between Methydrion and

34 Mrs Goester has drawn my attention to the natural barrier that the river Alpheios makes between Gortys and Lavda, and the limited possibilities for crossing it by bridge today (*Pharos* I 201). However since Gortys and Thisoa were Kynourian cities, it is difficult to believe that there were not regular communications between those two *poleis* in antiquity.

Teuthis that the northern Thisoa lay. Thus as well as there being cogent positive reasons for attributing the Achaian bronze coins to the south-western Thisoa, there are equally cogent negative reasons, especially in the legend dispositions, for not attributing them to the northern Thisoa. And since all the coins bear the same personal name ΠΟΛΥΗΡΗΣ, there is no question of apportioning them between the two *poleis*.

Mrs Yvonne Goester, who is publishing the coins found in the Dutch excavations at Lavda 1985-8, has generously communicated to me descriptions of them. Most are late Hellenistic, which fact supports the other archaeological evidence for use of the site at that period.[35] No Achaian League bronze coin was among them. In view of the extreme rarity of that coinage, and the comparatively modest number of coins found at Lavda, this is not surprising. However, among the lamentably small number of recorded find spots of Achaian League bronze coins there are seven instances of coins being found at the issuing mint, so the find of a Thisoan coin at Lavda would be welcome.

While it is clear that both Thisoas flourished during the Hellenistic period, there is no problem in the fact that that the northern Thisoa did not coin. (Nor in fact did Lykoa.) All the major Peloponnesian *poleis,* which had struck the silver Achaian League coinage also struck the bronze coinage, with the exception, surely politically motivated, of Sparta. But of the minor *poleis,* it is demonstrable that a certain number did not. Why was this? I believe that a simple answer can be provided. It appears that the striking of the coinage was discretionary, not obligatory, but those minor *poleis* that decided to do so had realised that there was a profit to be made from a bronze coinage[36] that would be acceptable not only locally but throughout the Achaian League area. In this respect striking the Achaian League bronze coinage offered an exceptional fiscal opportunity.

When Megalopolis was synoikized in the fourth century, some of the villages had all of their inhabitants removed to form the new city, but in other cases a proportion of the citizens moved, leaving others to carry on as a *kome*.[37] Plutarch, as is well known, tells us that Philopoimen on his

35 See most recently J.J. Feije, "Lavda. The site, the walls," *Pharos* II, 87. It may be suggested that since Paus. 8.27.4 in his list of those *poleis* synoikised to form Megalopolis (see above p. 98) used the ethnic, not the city name, exceptionally in this instance: Λυκαιᾶται (despite the reference of Polybios 16.17.5. to Lykoa), they were a people living on the slopes of Mt. Lykaios rather than a *polis.* See B. Helly, "Une cité d'Arcadie. Thisoa du Lykaios," *Cahiers d'histoire publiées par les universités de Clermont-Lyon-Grenoble* (1969) 377-8 (though Pausanias does list Thisoa as a *polis,* and its identifcation as Lavda is probable). Y.C. Goester, "Lavda: the coins", *Pharos* III (1995) 131-139.

36 Profit to be made from bronze coinage: *OGIS* 339; see C.J. Howgego, *NC* 1990,18.

37 Paus. 8.27.7; see M. Jost, *RA* 1974, 185-86.

return from Crete, probably in 194 BC, caused the secession of many of the small outlying villages from Megalopolis, his native city, with which he was at the time at odds.[38] But Plutarch did not name the *komai*. It has been widely assumed that they were the small Arkadian *komai* that struck the Achaian League bronze coins, such as Thisoa. But Errington was right to observe that the coins cannot be associated too closely with Philopoimen. We cannot be certain that these towns from which the coins are extant were the Megalopolitan towns that supported Philopoimen, or even that they were the only ones to do so, or that they struck the coins shortly after seceding. In fact other evidence suggests that they were not struck until the 170s or 160s. Furthermore there were other small towns or *komai* that were outside Arkadia that struck the coinage: Tenea in Corinthia, Korone and Kolonides in Messenia, Hypana in Triphylia. Pausanias in the second century AD mentioned the *komai* of his day.[39] The essential point, however, is that all the small Peloponnesian towns, Arkadian and others, that struck the Achaian League bronze coinage in the first half of the second century were at that time acting autonomously as *poleis*. Such was the Kynourian Thisoa in the southwest of Arkadia.

38 Plutarch, *Philopoemen* 13. 5; see R. M. Errington, *Philopoemen* (Oxford 1969) 90-1.
39 See supra n. 37.

Hoards, circulation and dies

LATE ARCHAIC HOARDS IN THE CYCLADES AND SOME THOUGHTS ON A REGIONAL PATTERN OF TRADE*

K. A. Sheedy

The scale and importance of mercantile activity in the Greek world are themes which have continued to preoccupy archaeologists. A good deal has been recently said, for example, concerning the trade of archaic and classical fine wares.[1] Developments in the archaic period are recognised as significant, but the interpretation of their impact has drawn widely different opinions. Snodgrass has argued that trade had very limited consequences for archaic Greek society.[2] A perceptibly more dynamic role is sought by Murray who notes that "by the mid sixth-century there had developed in the Mediterranean a complex international market economy involving the exchange of a wide variety of goods and services; in contrast to an earlier age, large scale activity was now at least as important as the exchange of luxury items".[3] In this brief study I would like to focus on aspects of two phenomena commonly associated with this international market. The first is the appearance of well organized trade routes. There had always been recognized routes for communication throughout the Aegean and the wider Mediterranean but in the sixth century we have archaeological evidence for the existence of a network of well established paths for the regular transport of sometimes specialised goods and services. The second phenomenon is the introduction of local silver coinages by a variety of Greek and non-Greek states. Murray has suggested

---

* This paper represents an early 'airing' of ideas from a chapter within a forthcoming book. I trust it will be of some interest to Mrs Oeconomides who has done so much to further my studies here in Athens.

1 Cf. the debate which is represented by the following: J. Boardman,"The Trade in Greek decorated pottery", *OJA* 7 (1988) 27-33; D.W.J. Gill, "Silver Anchors and Cargoes of Oil: Some Observations on Phoenician Trade in the Western Mediterranean", *BSR* 56 (1988) 1-12; A.W. Johnston, "The Vase Trade: A Point of Order", *Acta Hyperborea* 3 (1991) 403-409.

2 A.M. Snodgrass, *Archaic Greece. The Age of Experiment* (London 1980) 123-159.

3 O. Murray, *Early Greece* (London 1980) 226.

that "the invention of this new medium of exchange, coinage, is closely connected with the international movement of materials and men".[4] Precious metals had always been a significant item for trade and exchange (though it is not until the advent of coinage that we have the means to document the movement of at least a portion of this commodity). Most states needed to import silver to strike coins, but the functions of archaic coinage were largely perceived in terms of the needs of the state in which they were produced — even though state expenditure was not the only reason for minting.[5]

In this paper I wish to re-examine the archaic coin hoards found in the Cyclades and to consider their value as evidence for the existence of a route between the southern Cyclades and south west Asia Minor. I will also attempt to demonstrate that these hoards provide valuable information about the nature of trade and exchange along this route. There has been relatively little interest shown in attempting to integrate numismatic studies into the analysis of pre-Roman Mediterranean trade and exchange, and indeed into the investigation of the ancient economy. In the well-known volume of essays, *Trade in the Ancient Economy*, for example, which was in effect a staunch defence of the Finley model of the ancient economy, not one of the contributors dealt with coinage.[6] Coinage cannot be used as a general index of trade between those states responsible for its minting, but it can, with the help of information from context, be used to indicate the flow of silver as a commodity from region to region, and it can in general terms indicate the route along which it was carried.

The hoard is a basic tool in the study of numismatic evidence, and much has been written about how we should interpret the contents of a hoard and then hoards collectively.[7] Numismatists have traditionally attempted to classify hoards according to the perceived intent of the hoarder.[8] It is, however, notoriously difficult to say with any conviction, when confronted with the actual coins, that one is looking at an emergency hoard, or a savings one, or a mercantile hoard. I should like then to advocate a different approach, and some new terms. I wish to propose a broad division of archaic and early classical hoards on the basis of the origin of the coins they contain. It is a division between what we may call 'diversified' and

4 Murray (supra n. 3) 223.

5 C.J. Howgego, "Why did ancient states strike coins", *NC* 1990, 1-25.

6 P. Garnsey, K. Hopkins and C.R. Whittaker, *Trade in the Ancient Economy* (London 1983).

7 Cf. P.J. Casey, *Understanding Ancient Coins: An Introduction for Archaeologists and Historians* (London 1986) 51-67.

8 Cf. J.G. Milne, *Greek and Roman Coins and the Study of History* (London 1939) 91-110.

'accordant' hoards. A diversified hoard contains coins from a range of mints in a number of different regions. Accordant hoards, on the other hand, mostly hold coins from only one state and a few of its near neighbours, or from several cities within the same region. *IGCH* 2, 3, 5, 9, and 10, all found in Attica or Euboea, for example, contain only the coins of Athens and (in all cases) a few from the neighbouring cities of Euboea, and can be termed 'accordant'. *IGCH* 1636 (Mit Rahineh) and 1640 (Benha el Asl), both found in Egypt, contain coins from a good number of mints in various regions, and can be easily described as diversified. It is a distinction which unlike that between mercantile and savings hoards is not based on the recognition of any pattern of hoarding behaviour.

This division quickly brings to the fore certain geographical distinctions. There clearly are areas in which the majority of hoards are accordant, and others where they are diversified. It is even possible to identify an eastern belt of diversified hoards which extends from south western Asia Minor through the Levant to Egypt. It also has a sub-branch, the southern Cyclades, which must be considered separately and which I leave to one side for the moment. South Italy might appear to be another candidate. The great Taranto hoard of 1911 (*IGCH* 1874)contained over 600 coins; most came from local mints but over 20 non-Italian cities are represented. Colin Kraay suggested that this part had come via Egypt.[9] There is certainly nothing else like it from the immediate region. From Sicily the recently published Selinus hoard has a cluster of 80 coins from Aegina and 39 from Corinth which were probably brought west together; the rest of the hoard is made up of Sicilian coins.[10] These are diversified hoards, but they are at present unique examples in each of their areas.

Not all archaic and late classical hoards found in this eastern belt of diversified hoards are diversified, though it is significant that accordant hoards are usually only encountered together with diversified hoards of any significant number in one area, and that is south west Asia Minor. These diversified hoards do follow a general pattern in terms of their composition but various tendencies associated with geographical areas can be identified. These components and tendencies are fairly well known and I need only give a thumbnail sketch in this context.[11] An important general component is always the coins from North Greece, especially the

9 C.M. Kraay, *Archaic and Classical Greek Coins* (London 1976) 326.

10 C. Arnold-Biucchi, L. Beer Tobey and N.M. Waggoner, "A Greek Archaic Silver Hoard from Selinus", *ANSMN* 33 (1988) 1-35.

11 Here I draw on the survey given by M.J. Price and N. Waggoner, *Archaic Greek Silver Coinage. The Asyut Hoard* (London 1975) 13-22, 117-120.

mints of the Thraco-Macedonian tribes, and this remains true until ca. 450 when the flood of Attic coins becomes the rule. In the hoards of Egypt, coins of northern origins are almost inevitably the most important component numerically; they make up 38% of the Demanhur hoard, for example, and over 47 % of the Benha el Asl find.[12] But they are not quite so dominant in Asia Minor (cf. *IGCH* 1165, discussed below). The representation of Ionian mints is evenly scattered and only small numbers of coins are involved. The main mints are Miletos and Ephesos and the islands of Samos and Chios. Slightly more of these coins, as one might expect, are found in nearby south west Asia Minor. The representation of mints from Mainland Greece is predictable. The coins of Athens are regularly found, even if the numbers are small. The coins of Corinth and Euboea are rarely found in Asia Minor, but turn up in the hoards of the Levant and Egypt. Aeginetan coins are almost always found in these hoards but their numbers are surprisingly modest. The mints of the Cyclades are well represented in name though not in numbers in the Egyptian hoards, but fewer are found in the hoards of the Levant and Asia Minor. Cypriot coins start making their appearance around the beginning of the 5th century, and are generally a consistent element. The coinage of Persia is rarely found in western Asia Minor finds, and only a few coins turn up in Egyptian and Levantine hoards. The final element is the coinage of the mints of south west Asia Minor, the beginning of the diversified hoard territory (and the only region in this belt that possessed its own mints). This area is poorly represented even in finds from the region itself; Phaselis in Lycia and the mints of Rhodes are often contributors of single coins.

The existence of a corridor of trade which passed from North Greece down to Egypt has been often pointed out.[13] I am not proposing in the following discussion that we are simply to imagine merchants setting off from North Greek ports and finally arriving in Egypt bringing the coins they had obtained on departure. I am arguing that these regions were linked through the movement of a variety of commodities as well as services, and that the evidence of coins suggests that silver (and gold) was a significant element in this network of exchange. North Greece was, of course, an important source of silver and gold, but it is noticeable that North Greek coins do not appear in any hoard which we know to have been found in Ionia or even in the Troad. The reported finds known to me are all in south west Asia Minor; the earliest is the Cos hoard (*IGCH* 1173)

---

12 Price and Waggoner (supra n. 11) 118.

13 Cf. R.E. Jones, *Greek and Cypriot Pottery* (Athens 1986) 662-673, 690-703 reviewing provenance studies on East Greek pottery.

of ca 480 BC. As noted above, it is not until we reach this south west region that diversified hoards occur at all; there are few if any reported finds of coins in Ionia that are not from Ionian cities, or from the Troad, Persia and Lydia (in other words what I have called concordant hoards). On the other hand when we reach the belt of diversified hoards the basic ingredients found in eastern hoards of this type are all present.

The cities of Ionia were among the most wealthy and advanced of all Greek cities; they were leading traders, and noted producers of a variety of manufactured luxury goods. We know from the establishment of colonies in the Black Sea, together with their dominant presence in the commercial centre at Naukratis, that these cities (especially Miletos and Ephesos) were the home or base for a significant body of merchants.[14] The Greeks, however, had failed to make much impact on the mainland south of Ionia, and with a few exceptions such as Knidos, most of the important Greek settlements were on the islands of the Dodecanese, notably Rhodes. Caria and mountainous Lycia remained in the hands of powerful local dynasts. These areas exchanged foodstuffs and raw materials for East Greek manufactured products and luxury items. They were an important consumer of silver, and it is likely that silver prices were higher here, and certainly from here on to Egypt, than in Ionia or elsewhere further north. Silver collected as bullion, principally in the north but with the addition of pieces that could be picked up through a continuous process of trading from port to port, was amassed until it could be profitably exchanged for something in greater demand. This occurred when south west Asia Minor was reached, and hence the beginning of a pattern of diversified hoards.

One or two numismatic comments on south west Asia Minor are clearly needed at this point. A number of the hoards under discussion are known only by the general designation, western or southern Asia Minor.[15] The hoard 'profile' for the south west Asia Minor region, by which I mean Caria, the Carian islands or the Dodecanese, Lycia, and along to Cilicia, is derived from finds of archaic and classical date whose provenance is attested. The earliest diversified hoard is *IGCH* 1165 of ca. 500 BC found in western Asia Minor sometime before 1893. Initially noted by the Athenian merchant J.P. Lambros, it was not fully published until 1971.[16] It contained an Ionian electrum fraction possibly from Lampsacus, together with silver fractions from cities such as Ephesos, Miletos, Phocaea, Abydos in Asia

14 An overview is provided by J.M. Cook, "The eastern Greeks" in *CAH* III.3 (Cambridge 1982) 196-221.

15 Cf. O. Mørkholm, *IGCH* p. 151-153.

16 O. Mørkholm, *SNR* 1971, 79-91.

Table 1 Santorin Hoard c. 1821 IGCH 7. Burial: c. 500 BC; Contents: 760 AR.

IGCH listing				Sheedy 1997
Aegina 541		st	541	Aegina
Cycladic				
Andros or Ceos	1	st	1	Unc. Aegean? (amph. without handles)
Naxos	15	st	14	Naxos
–		st	1	Unc. Aegean? (ob. head of satyr)
Paros	2	st	2	Paros
Siphnos	3	st	3	Siphnos
Thera?	23	st	23	Thera or Unc. Caria or Lycia
Asia Minor or Cyclades				
Cyzicus	2	st	2	Uncertain (ob. fish)
Dardanus?	1	st	1	Unc. Caria (ob. cock)
Miletus?	48	st	48	Mylasa or Kaunos
Unc. Caria?	41	st	41	Unc. Caria
Unc. mint	1	st	1	Uncertain
	82	fr	82	Unc. Lycia? (boar's head)

Minor, Athens (didrachm stater and 2 obols), and a fraction from Karthaia in the Cyclades, as well as 39 fractions, many quite small, which are unattributed and which are mostly if not all from Asia Minor mints.

There is really only one other area in which diversified hoards occur, the southern Cyclades. Four archaic hoards and one of early classical date are reported from the Cyclades. The early classical hoard (*CH* 2, 24) was found on Paros and consists only of Aeginetan staters. An archaic hoard of the early fifth century, *IGCH* 13, found on the same island, consists of local drachms. This leaves one found on Thera in 1821 (the Santorin hoard; *Table. 1*), another from Melos reportedly found a few years later (1825?), and one thought to have been found in the region, the Cyclades hoard of around 1889 (*Table. 2*). The Santorin hoard (*IGCH* 7) is best attested; its contents were listed by H.P. Borrell but illustrations and the location of the specimens were not given. Borrell is the only witness to the Melos hoard (*IGCH* 8); he described its contents as "bearing the same types as those in the Santorin hoard but which were evidently of more modern date" without providing a list.[17] It is then only of real use in providing general statistical support to

17 H.P. Borrell, "Unedited Autonomous and Imperial Greek Coins", *NC* 1843-4, 134.

Table 2 The Cyclades Hoard c. 1889 IGCH 6. Burial: c. 500 BC; Contents: 145+AR.

Greenwall's listing (1890)	
Aegina	114
Ceos (Carthaea)	4
Delos? (Dolphins opp.)	9
Delos? (Dolphins same)	2
Paros	2
Siphnos	4
Miletos? (lion)	2
Chios?	4
Cos?	4

IGCH listing				Sheedy 1997
Aegina 114		st	114	Aegina
Cyclades				
Andros or Ceos	4	st	4	Karthaia
Paros	2	st	2	Paros
Siphnos	4	st	4	Siphnos
Thera?	11	st	9	Thera
Asia Minor				
Dardanus?	1	st	–	(not in hoard?)
Miletos?	2	st	2	Unc. Caria
Chios	3	st	3	Unc. Caria or Lycia*
Cos	4	st	4	Unc. Caria or Lycia*
–		st	2	Unc. Caria or Lycia* (dolphin)
				* same mint

plus unidentified small denominations

conclusions drawn from the other two finds. The third hoard, the Cyclades (*IGCH* 6), was partly seen in London by Greenwell.

These three hoards evidently had the same three basic components. The first and by far the most dominant consists of Aeginetan staters. Of the 145 + coins in the Cyclades hoard 114 were Aeginetan staters and of the 760 coins in the Santorin hoard 541 were from Aegina. The second component is the coinage of local Cycladic mints. The Santorin and Cyclades hoards contained coins of Karthaia, Paros, Siphnos, Naxos and Thera. These are the same mints whose coins are found in Egyptian hoards. What is perhaps surprising is how few of these coins were in the island finds. The mint of Thera is represent by only a possible 23 staters from a total of 760 found in the hoard from the island itself. The other Cycladic mints give only one or two coins. The final component consists of a significant number of coins from Asia Minor. This is certainly the most interesting element, but it is also that which has been largely forgotten; these hoards are inevitably noted solely in regard to the preponderance of Aeginetan coins. Before looking at these coins in detail I should like to make some general comments on the three hoards as a whole.

Firstly, there are no North Greek coins. This is also true of finds from the Greek mainland. Metal analysis of Aeginetan, Corinthian and Attic coins indicates that the regional demand for silver was largely met by the Cycladic island of Siphnos, and later by the Attic mines at Laurion, as well as by other unknown sources that may possibly be northern Greek.[18] Secondly, the Cycladic hoards are not known to have contained coinage from mints on the Greek mainland.

Let us now turn to the Asia Minor coins. We can divide these into two groups, those from Ionia or the Troad, and secondly those from south west Asia Minor. The first group is small and, as I hope to demonstrate, illusory. I begin with the Santorin hoard in which two silver staters of Cyzicus, another of Dardanus in the Troad, and fractions of Miletos have been tentatively identified. The so called Cyzicus coins, which were struck on the Aeginetan standard, cannot be certainly placed with any mint, but are almost certainly not from Cyzicus; they show the head and then tail of a fish *(Pl. 15a)*. The coin attributed to Dardanus displays a cock on the obverse; this unique silver coin seems to be that once in the Montagu Collection and now in London. The electrum type of Dardanus is a cock but the style of bird is not the same, and no other silver coins of this mint are known. It was struck on the Aeginetan standard, and it has a Union Jack reverse incuse device. I would like to suggest that an origin in south west Asia Minor is more likely. The 48 staters attributed to Miletos showing the forepart of a lion have been assigned to Mylasa, the early Carian capital, following a suggestion once made by Robinson, and more recently to Kaunos.[19]

Despite the listing in *IGCH* it seems that the Cyclades hoard did not have another of these 'Dardanus' cock staters; none at least are reported in Greenwell's original account. The two staters with the head of a lion *(Pl. 15b)* tentatively given to Miletos, are unlikely to be from this mint; they

18 N.H. Gale, W. Gentner and G.A. Wagner, "Mineralogical and Geological Silver Sources of Archaic Greek Coinage", in D.M. Metcalf and W.A. Oddy (eds), *Metallurgy in Numismatics* I (London 1980) 3-49.

19 E.S.G. Robinson, "A Hoard of archaic Greek coins from Anatolia", *NC* 1961, 114, No. 37; Price and Waggoner (supra n. 11) 91, No. 667-668; to Kaunos: U. Westermark and R. Ashton, *SNG* Finland I, 64-65, noting that the stater, no. 64, was reportedly found in a grave at Kaunos, and the fraction, no. 65, was found nearby.

have the weight of Aeginetan didrachm staters. Their fabric recalls the unique cock stater and I suspect that they might also be Carian. It has also been claimed that coins of Chios and Cos *(Pl. 15c)* are present, but in each case the coins possess a reverse type consisting of two separate punch incuses, one smaller than the other, which distinguishes then from the usual coins of these mint, and these Ionian attributions are commonly rejected. I will have more to say on the subject in a moment. For now we need only conclude that there is in fact no firm evidence for the presence of Ionian or Troad coins in these hoards, and none from these regions are known to me in finds from the Greek mainland.

The second group consists of those coins from south west Asia Minor. The Santorin hoard contained an impressive 41 staters attributed to Caria showing the fore-part of a horse *(Pl. 15d)*. A stater *(Pl. 15e)* and 82 *(Pl. 15f)* fractions with the head of a boar on the obverse and an incuse reverse in this find remain problematic but the fractions might be attributed to Lycia.[20] To this total we should add the 48 staters once given to Miletos that are now attributed to Mylasa or Kaunos. Over 20% of this great hoard can thus be seen to have been issued by mints in south west Asia Minor. Unfortunately, the smaller coins from the Cyclades hoard were not seen by Greenwell though their existence was acknowledged. I believe that these were fractions of the same type as those found in the Santorin hoard (i.e. mostly boar's head type). Sixth century fractions from Aegina do not appear to be common and almost none have been found in hoards. The minting of fractions in the Cyclades is mostly a practise of the fifth century.

I turn now to a small group of coins known from a number of hoards, but especially those from the Cyclades. I have already noted sphinx coins and those showing a crab, which are regularly attributed to Chios and Cos respectively, and which were found in the Santorin hoard.[21] From the same find we can also add those staters showing two dolphins jumping in the same direction. These coins are not Theran, though they are grouped in accounts of this hoard with the usual staters of this Cycladic island which show two dolphins jumping in alternate directions. All of these coins are united in having a reverse produced with two punches of unequal size. They have been separately attributed to a variety of mints. As nearly all were struck on the Aeginetan standard and bear types which look characteristically Aegean, Aegean islands have been favourite places in which to place them. On the evidence of a die link it can be demonstrated that they were all struck at the one mint. I believe that they were probably

20 SNG France, 2799.

21 Cf. Kraay (supra n. 9) 34, pl. 4: 86-90.

issued in either Caria or Lycia. A fuller discussion of these coins, their mint and its location must be kept for another occasion.[22] The main point to be stressed is that the recognition of this mint significantly reduces the range of states which were once believed to be represented in the Cycladic hoards. It moves the focus away from Ionia.

We find in these Cyclades hoards evidence of an unusual phenomenon. On the one hand they attest to the drawing away of silver from a region, south west Asia Minor, which the diversified hoards indicate was itself a significant market for the import of precious metals. On the other we find that the range of mints represented in the diversified hoards of south west Asia Minor are largely absent from the Cycladic hoards. These island finds show a proportion of Carian (and perhaps Lycian) coins which is unmatched in the hoards of any other region, including at the moment most finds from south west Asia Minor itself. Evidently there was some special pattern of exchange by which silver from this region of Asia Minor in the form of local issues was being bought into the Cyclades, an area whose coin circulation was dominated by the coinage of Aegina. It also seems likely, given the very unique composition of the Cycladic hoards, that this exchange had a very particular aspect which distinguished it from the usual practice of trade in the Aegean.

Three marble peplophoroi now in the British Museum were found in the Lycian city of Xanthos.[23] H. Metzger has attributed them to a parapet around the most elaborate Heroon of the city's akropolis, Building G.[24] They closely resemble a marble Nike found on Paros, which has been dated to the decade 470-460 BC.[25] Ridgway has called attention to the similarity in the modelling of the dress, which she describes as being distinguished by the "unarticulated, chiton-like treatment of the peplos".[26] The resemblance suggests the hypothesis that the established sculptural centres of the Cyclades, especially Paros, supplied marble, masons and probably sculptors to the capitals of the Lycian dynasts. The local dynasts proved to be important patrons for monumental architectural and sculptural projects, and here one thinks in particular of Lycian grave monuments.[26] In this context we may note that the well-known Harpy

---

22 Sheedy forthcoming (Studies in honour of M.J. Price).

23 R. Tölle-Kastenbein, *Frühklassische Peplosfiguren Originale* (Mainz am Rhein 1980) 98-101, cat. 133 a-c, pl. 59-63.

24 H. Metzger, *FdX* 2 (1963) 51, pl. 35-36.

25 B.S. Ridgway, *The Severe Style in Greek Sculpture* (Princeton 1970) 37, fig. 57.

26 Ridgway (supra n. 24) 37 n. 5.

27 A.G. Keen, "The Dynastic Tombs of Xanthos — Who was Buried Where?", *AS* 42 (1992) 53-63.

Tomb from Xanthos, a dynastic monument of the early classical period, was made from Parian marble.[28] The iconography was appropriate to the culture and aspirations of the rulers but the sculptural styles and the use of the medium, marble, were Greek.

The Cyclades were a famous source for the best fine white marble. The quarries of Naxos and especially Paros were already well established in the second half of the sixth century. Marble could have been shipped to Caria and Lycia by a number of routes; one of the most direct was perhaps via the southern Cyclades. I would suggest then that the three great Cycladic hoards reflect the existence of this quite specialized trade. Lycian and Carian patrons may have been paying in part with local coin for the import of stone and stone carving expertise. The simple existence of this trade between the islands and south west Asia Minor may have also led to the infiltration of local coins which had been acquired by means other than direct payment for stone.

I am aware that I have covered a great deal of territory. At the risk of dealing too briefly with complex issues I have tried to use this paper to suggest ways in which numismatic evidence might be integrated into models of trade and exchange. Indeed, only with the incorporation of the numismatic evidence will it be possible to approach some form of appreciation of one of the key features of late archaic trade and of trade in the ancient world in general, that in precious metals.

---

28 Ridgway (supra n. 24) 95-96, fig. 127.

RECONSTRUCTING THE CIRCULATION OF ROMAN COINAGE IN FIRST CENTURY B.C. MACEDONIA

R. A. Bauslaugh

The following paper is based on a comprehensive die study of the silver coinage with the types of Aesillas the Quaestor begun in 1984 and now in press in the American Numismatic Society's monograph series *Numismatic Studies*.[1] The Aesillas coinage has been the center of intense scholarly debate; and only an exhaustive collection of close to 1,000 tetradrachms and drachms has provided the necessary evidence to explain many of the enigmatic features of the Aesillas issues and reconstruct correctly their surprising pattern of production.

There are, however, some things about the Aesillas coinage that are straightforward and undisputed. To begin with, it is agreed that early in the first century B.C. the Romans issued an Attic weight coinage in the name of the Macedonians. On the obverse, the coinage features a portrait of Alexander the Great. To the left and below the portrait is the legend, in Greek, MAKEΔONΩN, meaning [coinage] "of the Macedonians" *(Pl. 16a)*. This is the basic Aesillas type. At some point, however, the obverse legend was temporarily changed to a bilingual Latin and Greek combination, CAE PR MAKEΔONΩN or "Cae... Pr[aetor] of the Macedonians" *(Pl. 16b)*.

The Aesillas reverse features the famous club of the Macedonians' putative ancestor, Herakles, flanked by two symbols of the authority of a Roman financial officer or *quaestor*: to the right, a chair or *sella* and to the left, a money chest or *cista*. Above the club and symbols of quaestorial office is the name, in Latin, AESILLAS, accompanied by the letter Q for *Q[uaestor]* placed in the right field between the name and the *sella* (*Pl.*

1 A preliminary paper on the evidence emerging from the die study was given at the Tenth International Numismatic Congress in London (1986) and an important new overstrike was published in *ANSMN* 32 (1987), pp. 11-21. The finished manuscript, *Silver Coinage with the Types of Aesillas the Quaestor, American Numismatic Society Numismatic Studies*, vol. 22 is due out in 1997. Among the many scholars and museum officials who have generously assisted my research on Aesillas, and many other topics, is Dr. Oeconomides, to whom this paper is gratefully dedicated.

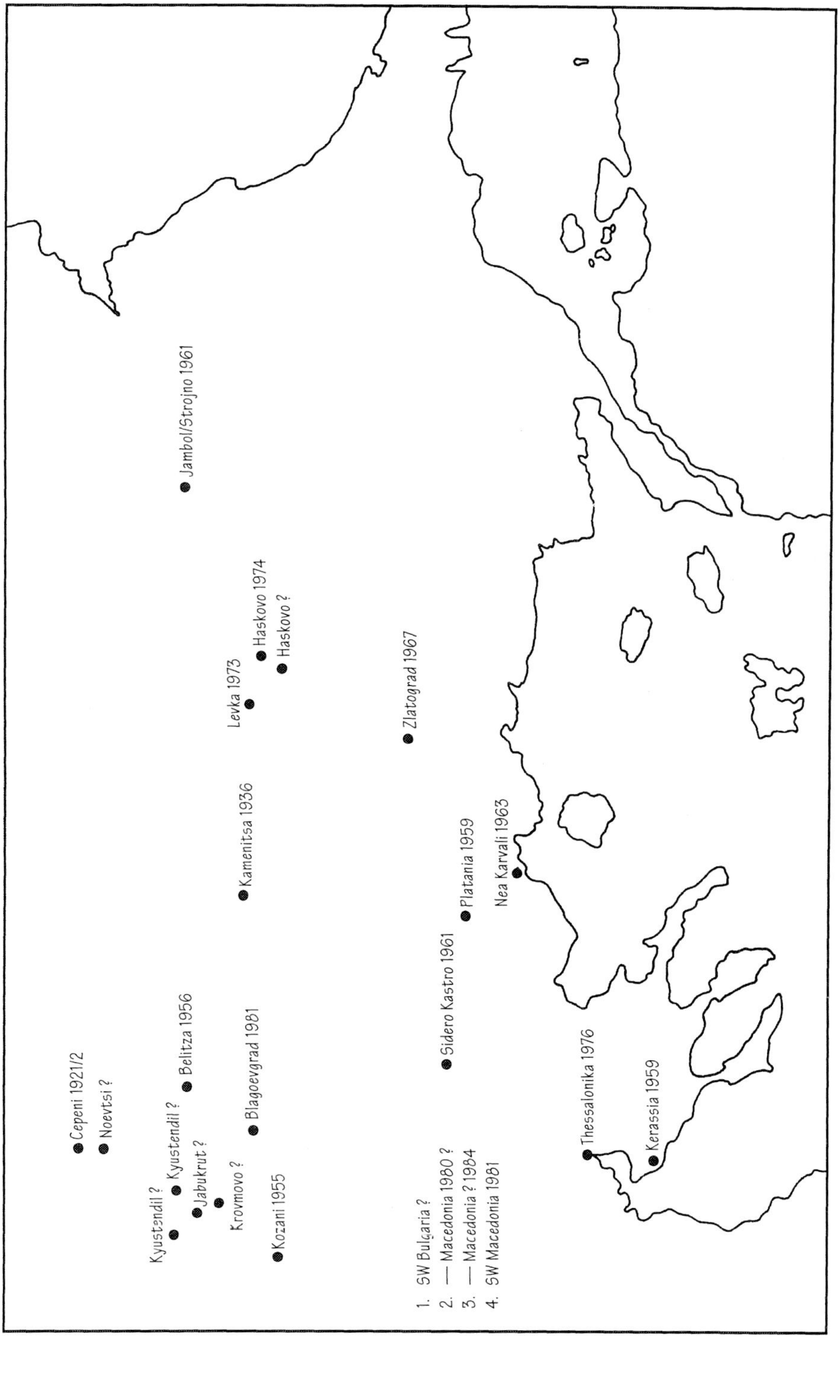

Fig. 1 Map of hoard locations in Northern Greece and Bulgaria.

16a). There is, however, an exception. On just two reverse dies the legend AESILLAS is replaced with SVVRA LEG PRO Q for *Sura Leg[atus] Pro Q[uaestore]* or "Sura Legate [acting] in the capacity of Quaestor" *(Pl. 16c)*.

All of the reverse elements are surrounded by a laurel wreath and both the obverse and reverse dies regularly have controls in the form of letters, monograms, and pellets either alone or in various combinations. The coinage was struck on a slightly reduced version of the Attic standard, with tetradrachms averaging 16.44g (from 708 weighed examples) and the rare drachms averaging 3.93g (6 weighed examples).[2] The Aesillas coinage was not as large a coinage as some scholars have suggested.[3] After eleven years of collecting information, I have identified just under 1,000 different tetradrachms struck from 102 obverse and 372 reverse dies, together with 6 ancient imitations or forgeries, all from different dies, and 8 genuine drachms from 7 different obverse and reverse dies, together with one imitation drachm known from 6 examples.

When the technical numismatic information now available about the Aesillas coinage is combined with the surviving archaeological and historical evidence, a clearer picture emerges of the circulation of Aesillas issues themselves and of the role they played in the expansion of Roman power across the Balkan Peninsula. Two main questions concern us here. First, how does the numismatic evidence correspond to and agree with the archaeological record represented in hoards containing Aesillas and other Roman issues, particularly denarii? And secondly, how can the archaeological and numismatic evidence help to clarify Roman policy and aims in early first century B.C. Macedonia and Thrace?

Aesillas tetradrachms have been reported in 23 hoards found in Northeastern Greece and southcentral Bulgaria.

2 Examples that are pierced or broken or suspected of being imitations — ancient or otherwise — have been excluded from these tabulations.

3 E.g. Crawford, *Coinage and Money under the Roman Republic, Italy and the Mediterranean Economy* (1985), p. 197, calls the Aesillas coinage "very large" and assigns it to the decade "from the mid-80s to the mid-70s." Burnett, *Coin Hoards* VII, p. 56, makes the same characterization on the basis of his belief that the Aesillas issues were all minted within "two or three years at most" (p. 57); and admittedly, production of ca. 102 obv. dies in 3 years could well be described as "huge." The exaggeration is, however, nothing new; in 1906, Hill claimed that "coins with the name of Aesillas alone are among the commonest that have come down to us" (*Historical Greek Coins*, p. 159).

TETRADRACHMS OF THE AESILLAS TYPE IN HOARDS[4]

Hoard	*IGCH*	*No.*	*GROUP*	*Burial Date*[5]
1. [Kozani (Gr) 1955[6]	457	1	III	240-230]
2. Strojno (Bulg) 1961[7]	924	1	III	ca. 90[8]
3. Zlatograd (Bulg) 1967	969	1	I	ca. 90[9]
4. SW Macedonia (Gr) 1981[10]		8	I-III	ca. 90[11]
5. Siderokastro (Gr) 1961	642	hundreds	I-III, VI, VIII	ca. 90T[12]
6. Haskovo (Bulg) 1974[13]		2	x[14]	Early 1st cent.
7. Kerassia (Gr) 1959?	653	1	VI	post 76T
8. Haskovo (Bulg) ?[15]		1	x	ca. 75
9. Thessalonika Environs (Gr) 1976[16]		40	x	ca. 75
10. Macedonia? (Gr) 1986[17]		16	IV, V, VI, VIII	ca. 70
11. Blagoevgrad Vicinity (Bulg) 1981[18]		ca. 200	VI, VII,[19] VIII	ca. 65

4 Hoards are listed chronologically; *IGCH* = *An Inventory of Greek Coin Hoards*, ed. by M. Thompson, O. Mørkholm, C. Kraay (New York, 1973); *No.* = the number of Aesillas issues reported to have been originally in the hoard; *GROUP* = the internal placement of the specific Aesillas issue within the reconstructed order of production arranged by the author (see above, n. 1).

5 Burial dates are taken from the *IGCH* or other publication unless specified; T indicates the dates assigned by Margaret Thompson in *IGCH*.

6 See O.H. Dodson and W.D. Wallace, "The Kozani Hoard of 1955," *ANSMN* 11 (1964), pp. 21-8, who cannot explain the presence of the Aesillas tetradrachm in this hoard and consider it intrusive (pp. 21, 23); H. Mattingly, "L. Julius Caesar, Governor of Macedonia," *Chiron* 9 (1979), p. 155, n. 35, also suspects modern intrusion.

7 See in addition to *IGCH* 924, E. Schönert-Geiss, *Griechisches Münzwerk Die Münzprägung von Maroneia, Schriften zur Geschichte und Kultur der Antike* 26 (Berlin, 1987), pp. 105-6 and I. Prokopov, "Sur la circulation des tétradrachmes d'argent du questeur Aesillas dans les régions du Sud-Est de la Bulgarie et leur datation" [in Bulgarian] *Numizmatika* 19 (1985), p. 9, no. 13.

8 For the date given here, see discussion below, p. 124; without knowing of the Aesillas issue in the hoard,. Thompson, dated it "c. 125-100?" in *IGCH* 924.

9 Dated ca. 90 by Prokopov; see details below, p. 124.

10 See A. Burnett, *Coin Hoards* VII, 133, pp. 54-67.

11 Dated ca. 75 by Burnett (*loc. cit.*); but see discussion below, p. 124.

12 For problems with the reported contents and the dating of this hoard, see discussion below, pp. 125-126.

13 *Coin Hoards* I, 92.

14 x = the actual coins were not available for study or the source provided no reliable information about the Aesillas examples.

15 *Coin Hoards* VI, 44; Prokopov (above, n. 7), p. 9, no. 11.

16 *Coin Hoards* V, 55.

17 A partial photographic record and information about this hoard, which appeared and was dispersed in international commerce in 1986, was provided to me by Simon Bendall and Charles Hersh.

18 See I. Prokopov, "A Scattered Hoard of Tetradrachms belonging to Aesillas the Quaestor" [in Bulgarian], *Numizmatika* 20 (1986), pp. 11-15.

19 Prokopov has recently reported the presence of at least one CAE PR issue (GROUP VII) in this hoard.

Hoard	*IGCH*	*No.*	*GROUP*	*Burial Date*[5]
12. Nea Karvali (Gr) 1963[20]	660	14+	V, VI, VIII	55-50
13. Macedonia? (Gr) 1980[21]		10	V, VI, VII, VIII	ca. 50
14. Belitsa[22] (Bulg) 1956	976	7	x	Before 50?
15. Platania (Gr) 1959	663	2	VI, VIII	ca. 49
16. Kjustendil (Bulg) ?[23]		2	x	?
17. Cepeni (Bulg) 1921/2	64	ca. 100	x	?
18. Kamenitsa[24] (Bulg) 1936	970	15	x	?
19. Zhabokrat (Bulg) ?[25]		"dozens"	x	?
20. Kroumovo (Bulg) ?[26]		x	x	?
21. Levka (Bulg) 1973[27]		3	x	?
22. Noevtsi (Bulg) ?[28]		2	x	?
23. Kjustendil District (Bulg) ?[29]		2	x	?

Unlike the New Style Athenian tetradrachms or the autonomous tetradrachms of Thracian Maroneia and Thasos, with which they were commonly hoarded, Aesillas issues circulated and were hoarded within a comparatively small region bounded in the south by the city of Thessalonika, in the east by the valley of the Hebrus River, in the north by the Balkan Mountains of central Bulgaria, and in the West by the Strymon River valley. No hoards containing Aesillas tetradrachms have been reported from modern Romania or the former Yugoslavia or anywhere in Asia Minor, the Aegean islands, or central Greece. As should be immediately clear, all 23 hoards, regardless of their assigned burial dates, were reportedly found in the territory of ancient Macedonia and Thrace.

If we disregard the obviously intrusive Aesillas piece in the Kozani 1955 hoard that must have been buried between 240 and 230 B.C.,[30] the earliest

20 Formerly referred to as the "Cavalla (or "Kavalla") 1963 Hoard;" for the change, see Y. Touratsoglou, "The Adam Zagliveriou/1983 Hoard in the Museum of Thessalonika (Athenian 'New Style' Tetradrachms in Macedonia)" [in Greek and English], *Nomismatikon Chronikon* 8 (1989), p. 19; and *The Coin Circulation in Ancient Macedonia* (ca. 200 B.C. -268-286 A.D.), *The Hoard Evidence* (Athens, 1993), chart. IIa.

21 Burnett *Coin Hoards* VII, 139, pp. 54-67.

22 *IGCH* 976 and Mattingly (above, n. 6), p. 155, spell the name of this hoard "Belica; " but Thompson, *The New Style Coinage of Athens* (New York, 1961), p. 522, and "Athens Again," *NC* (1962), p. 314, spells "Beliza," as does D.M. Lewis, "The Chronology of the Athenian New Style Coinage," p. 285; but cf. Prokopov, (above, n. 7), p. 9, no. 8.

23 Prokopov, (above, n. 7), p. 9, no. 4.

24 *IGCH* 970 spells the name of this hoard "Kaminica;" cf. Prokopov, (above, n. 7), p. 9, no. 9.

25 Prokopov, (above, n. 7), p. 9, no. 5; Zhabokrat is located in the district of Kjustendil.

26 Prokopov, (above, n. 7), p. 9, no. 6; Kroumovo is located in the district of Kyustendil.

27 *Coin Hoards* VI, 49.

28 Prokopov, (above, n. 7), p. 9, no. 2; Noevtsi is located in the district of Pernik.

29 Prokopov, (above, n. 7), p. 9, no. 3.

30 See above, n. 6.

hoards containing Aesillas tetradrachms were all buried about 90 B.C. Fortunately, thanks to the generous sharing of unpublished illustrations and information by Bulgarian numismatists Dimitrov Draganov of the Museum of History in Jambol, and Ylia Prokopov of the Museum of History in Kjustendil, we can now study the contents of four hoards dated to the early years of the first century B.C. and compare the exact Aesillas issues included with the overall sequence of issues reconstructed from the comprehensive die study of the coinage.

The traditional organization of the Aesillas type coinage assumed that the CAE PR MAKEΔONΩN type came at the beginning, the bulk of undistinguished MAKEΔONΩN issues followed, and the extraordinary SVVRA LEG PRO Q issue came at the end when either death or supercedure relieved Aesillas from the quaestorship. However, a completely different structure has emerged from a comprehensive die study that breaks the traditional connection between the CAE PR and SVVRA issues and reverses the order of their production. What actually happened is that the coinage began with issues that had no obverse marks at all, followed with the addition of theta, then *beta* and reverse *beta*, and then very briefly replaced AESILLAS with SVVRA LEG PRO Q. Next, the *theta* issues with AESILLAS returned and were produced for some time before being temporarily replaced by the CAE PR issues that were minted both with *theta* and without it. Finally, the coinage ended with a last series of plain AESILLAS issues that have a distinctively sloppy style and consistently lighter weight. In all, there appear to be eight distinct groups of issues.

RECONSTRUCTED ORDER OF AESILLAS ISSUES

GROUP I: *O*1-*O*6 (OBV: no *theta* [except 5B, 6C-D]; REV: with/without A)
GROUP II: *O*7-*O*13 (OBV: *theta*; REV: with/without A, and pellets
GROUP III: *O*14-*O*15 (OBV: β, and [reverse β]; REV: *beta* below wreath)
GROUP IV: *O*16-*O*19 (OBV: *theta* with S I; REV: AESILLAS and SVVRA LEG PRO Q
GROUP V: *O*20-*O*31 (OBV: *theta*; REV: with/without pellets)
GROUP VI: *O*32-*O*83 (OBV: *theta*; REV: without pellets)
GROUP VII: *O*84-*O*87 CAE PR MAKEΔONΩN (OBV: *theta*/no *theta*; REV: without pellets)
GROUP VIII: *O*88-*O*102 (OBV: *theta*; REV: with pellets)

Now, returning to the hoard record, we can begin by comparing the exact Aesillas issues reported to be in hoards dated to about 90 B.C. What appears immediately is the repetition of examples from the first three groups in the reconstructed coinage (GROUPS I-III).

The Zlatograd 1967 hoard (*IGCH* 969) is today in the Plovdiv Museum. Prokopov reports that it contains 7 late Hellenistic Thasian tetradrachms, 1 Thracian imitation of Thasos, and 1 Aesillas tetradrachm. According to Prokopov, who generously provided an illustration to me and who now has a comprehensive die study of the Hellenistic coinage of Thasos in press, the burial date of the hoard, to judge from the Thasos issues, should be ca. 90 B.C. Not surprisingly, the Aesillas example belongs to the earliest group of issues that do not have *theta* added to the obverse (GROUP I: *O3-R9*; *Pl. 16d*).

The 195 tetradrachms of the Strojno 1961 hoard (*IGCH* 924) are today in Jambol and have been studied and published by Elizabeth Schönert-Geiss in her recent study, *Die Münzprägung von Maroneia*, where she concludes that the Strojno hoard was also buried ca. 90 B.C.[31] Included were 2 ΜΑΚΕΔΟΝΩΝ ΠΡΩΤΗΣ tetradrachms, 62 Maroneian, 126 Thasian (including 9 Thracian imitations), 4 New Style Athens down to ΤΙΜΟΣΤΡΑΤΟΣ-ΠΟΣΗΣ (or 102/1 B.C. on Otto Mørkholm's 32 year downdating of Margaret Thompson's "high" chronology[32]), and 1 Aesillas *(Pl. 16f)*. Dimitrov Draganov has generously provided a cast of the Aesillas tetradrachm; and again, as we saw in the Zlatograd hoard, the Aesillas issue in Strojno comes from an early group in the coinage (GROUP IV) and has a very close connection with both GROUP II of the Aesillas type coinage and the SVVRA LEG PRO Q issue, which also belongs to GROUP IV. You can see this by noticing the reuse of the same reverse die that was first used during GROUP II (Cf. *Pl. 16e, f)* and the S I added to the obverse in the field to the right of Alexander's neck. The latter is a very unusual feature also found on the extraordinary SVVRA LEG PRO Q issue *(Pl. 16c)* that agrees perfectly with the placement of both the Jambol and the SVVRA issues early in the Aesillas coinage.

---

31 On Schönert-Geiss see above, n. 7. It should be explained that the total of 195 tetradrachms given here differs from *IGCH* 924 (193) and Prokopov (above, n. 7), p. 9 (also 193), because Schönert-Geiss, pp. 105-6, restudied the hoard with the assistance of Dimitrov Draganov in the Jambol Museum. Together they add two examples of Maroneia and one of Aesillas and reject one of ΜΑΚΕΔΟΝΩΝ ΠΡΩΤΗΣ; and that accordingly changes the totals given in *IGCH*. Schönert-Geiss also reduces the number of Thasian "imitations" from 18 (*IGCH* 924) to 9.

32 See O. Mørkholm, "The Chronology of the New Style Coinage of Athens," *ANSMN* 29 (1984), pp. 29-42; cf. Touratsoglou (above, n. 20), pp. 17-18 and F. de Callataÿ, "Athenian New Style Tetradrachms in Macedonian Hoards," *AJN* 3-4 (1991-2), p. 12, with n. 7.

Thirdly, the Southwest Macedonia 1981 hoard published by Andrew Burnett (*Coin Hoards* VII, 133) reportedly contained 32 tetradrachms: 5 LEG MAKEΔONΩN issues, one rare MAKEΔONΩN, 15 New Style Athens, and 8 AESILLAS. Burnett dated the burial to ca. 75 on estimation of comparative wear of the coins; but this is too late. More reliable indications come from the facts (1) that the Athenian issues end with HPAKΛEIΔHΣ-EYKΛHΣ or 105/4 on Mørkholm's 32 year downdating of Thompson's New Style chronology and (2) that all eight of the Aesillas tetradrachms come from GROUPS I-III of the coinage. This, I believe, suggests strongly that the SW Macedonia hoard also belongs close to ca. 90 B.C.

Finally, there is the very large Siderokastro 1961 hoard (*IGCH* 642). After its discovery some twenty kilometers south of the Bulgarian border the hoard was immediately broken up and dispersed, with the result that neither the original size nor its exact contents are known for certain. Margaret Thompson estimated the total at between 420 and 650 tetradrachms, including a small quantity of LEG MAKEΔONΩN issues, 120-150 New Style Athens, and 300-500 Aesillas. After working very diligently to reconstruct the original contents of the hoard, Thompson concluded that "the Siderokastoro hoard is a combined deposit: Athenian and Leg Makedonon pieces put aside in the late 130's or early 120's and Aesillas tetradrachms merged with them at a considerably later date."[33]

Obviously, Thompson's conclusion about the Siderokastro hoard was influenced by her belief that the Athenian New Style issues dated some thirty-two years earlier than is almost certainly the case. But to make matters worse, Thompson was also misled by the incorrect dating of the LEG MAKEΔONΩN and MAKEΔONΩN issues.[34] However, in 1986, Andrew Burnett showed that the LEG MAKEΔONΩN issues must be much later than earlier numismatists had thought. From the evidence of the SW Macedonia 1981 hoard just discussed, he argued, surely correctly, that the LEG MAKEΔONΩN and MAKEΔONΩN issues preceded the Aesillas coinage by only a short time.[35] All of this helps to set the record straight. But what neither Thompson nor Burnett realized in their scrutiny of the evidence is that the Aesillas issues originally in the Siderokastro 1961 hoard have almost certainly been mixed with Aesillas issues from other sources.

The problem is this. Thompson collected a total of 58 casts and photographs of Aesillas tetradrachms said to come from Siderokastro.

33 Above, n. 22: "Athens Again," p. 320; cf. *IGCH* 642.

34 See P. A. MacKay, "Macedonian Tetradrachms of 148-147 B.C.," *ANSMN* 14 (1968), pp. 15-40.

35 *Coin Hoards* VII, p. 55-56.

Even though this may amount to as little as 10% of the original number, it is nevertheless a substantial number of Aesillas tetradrachms. The problem is that the assembled issues divide very clearly into two parts. The first involves early issues from the GROUPS I-III of the die study, and the second late issues from GROUPS VI and VIII. The two parts are separated by at least 24 dies (or about 1/4 of the total production). To further confuse matters, in a forthcoming study of the Aesillas coinage, François de Callataÿ attributes as many as 8 of the same later tetradrachms that Thompson included in her Siderokastro material to the Nea Karvali 1963 hoard. Importantly, only one of the examples attributed to the Nea Karvali hoard by de Callataÿ could possibly be among the 10 tetradrachms from the Nea Karvali hoard today in the Kavala Museum. The overlapping examples of the de Callataÿ/Thompson lists do, however, present an identical profile to the Aesillas issues in the Nea Karvali hoard, where all but one of the 10 examples also come from GROUPS VI and VIII.

So, it seems justified to suspect (1) that a serious mistake has occurred in the gathering of material said to belong to the Siderokastro 1961 hoard, (2) that some coins belonging to the Nea Karvali 1963 hoard have been wrongly attributed to Siderokastro 1961, and (3) that the original contents of Siderokastro actually paralleled the Zlatograd, Strojno, and Southwest Macedonia hoards. After all, if we set aside the now contested Aesillas issues from GROUPS VI and VIII, Siderokastro had (1) Athenian New Style issues down to 106/5 on Mørkholm's dating, (2) a few LEG ΜΑΚΕΔΟΝΩΝ, and (3) numerous Aesillas from the early GROUPS I-III. All of this fits precisely with an original burial date of ca. 90 B.C.

The Aesillas issues in hoards dated to the 70's are different. In the Kerassia 1959 hoard (*IGCH* 653; *RRCH*[36] 283), Roman denarii make their first appearance together with Aesillas issues. The 47 denarii in the Kerassia hoard range from ca. 130 to 78 B.C. on Crawford's dating (*RRC*[37] 386: L. CASSI Q F); and the mid-70's is the likely date of burial. Here, however, the single Aesillas issue comes late in GROUP VI (PL. 17a). If the evidence of one example can be trusted, it follows that the bulk of the AESILLAS coinage, with the possible exception of the CAE PR and the lighter weight, poor style GROUP VIII issues, was produced before ca. 75 B.C.

A similar profile occurs in a second hoard, found in the Bulgarian city of Kjustendil. It reportedly included 5 New Style Athenian tetradrachms, 2 tetradrachms of Thasos, one of ΜΑΚΕΔΟΝΩΝ ΠΡΩΤΗΣ, and 2 of Aesillas

36 *RRCH* = M.H. Crawford, Roman Republican Coin Hoards (London, 1969).

37 *RRC* = M.H. Crawford, Roman Republican Coinage (Cambridge, 1974).

GROUP VI (O68, and O76). On the basis of the Thasian issues, Prokopov dates the burial of the hoard to ca. 70 B.C. *(Pl. 17b, c).*

A third hoard, found at Levka in 1973 (*Coin Hoards* VI, 49) had, according to Prokopov, 21 tetradrachms that can be identified today: 1 New Style Athens from 126/5 on Mørkolm's dating, 1 Byzantine Lysimachus, 3 ΜΑΚΕΔΟΝΩΝ ΠΡΩΤΗΣ, 5 Maroneia, 15 Thasos, including one Thracian imitation, and 1 Aesillas from GROUP I (6A-12). Prokopov agrees with the editors of *Coin Hoards* VI in dating the burial to ca. 75.

Finally, a hoard of some 127 denarii and at least 16 Aesillas tetradrachms appeared in commerce in 1986. No information on the exact location of its discovery has come to light; but since the denarii end abruptly with a concentration of issues from 78 and 77 B.C., and since there is just one further example from 74, the burial date should not be later than 70 B.C. And here, the Aesillas issues are concentrated in GROUPS IV-VI, although two examples from the final GROUP VIII are also reported.[38]

What these hoards suggest is that Aesillas issues continued to circulate in the 70's and were, by the middle of the decade, joined by denarii, with which they were mixed. But unlike the hoards of ca. 90 B.C., the Aesillas tetradrachms of hoards from the 70's are concentrated in in GROUPS IV-VI, with only rare examples of GROUPS I-III and few (or perhaps none, if our reconstructed record is again faulty) from GROUPS VII or VIII. For the concentration of the issues of GROUPS VII and VIII we need to look beyond the 70's to the hoards dating to the 60's and later.

The Nea Karvali 1963 hoard, originally known as the Cavalla hoard (*IGCH* 660; *RRCH* 336), contained a mixture of denarii and Aesillas tetradrachms, of which only a small number are today in the Kavalla Museum. The latest denarius dates from 62 B.C. on Crawford's chronology (*RRC* 416); and the 10 Aesillas examples come from GROUPS V, VI, and VIII. If we add to these the examples attributed to Nea Karvali by de Callataÿ and Siderokastro by Thompson, we get a composite of one example from GROUP I, none from II-IV, one from V, perhaps 18 from VI, and 5 from VIII. Interestingly, the resulting total of 25 tetradrachms is only one more than the 24 attributed to the hoard by Crawford from information provided by I. Varoucha-Christodoulopoulos and T. Hackens.[39]

Another hoard in commerce, reportedly found in 1980 and published by Burnett in *Coin Hoards* VI 139, has been reconstructed to have 91 denarii

---

38 I am indebted to Simon Bendall of A.H. Baldwin & Sons LTD, London, and Charles Hersh for providing photographs and information about this hoard.

39 Crawford, *RRCH* 336. *IGCH* 660 gives the number as ca. 14.

ending with issues of 54 B.C. (*RRC*, 433,1 and 434,2) and 10 Aesillas issues coming from GROUPS V, VI, VII, and VIII.

Similarly, a third hoard, found at Platania in 1959 (*IGCH* 663; *RRCH* 358), includes a mix of bronze coins of Macedonia and Thrace together with two denarii — one from 90 B.C. and one from 49 — and 2 Aesillas, one each from GROUPS VI and VIII *(Pl. 17d, e)*.

Matching the profile of these late hoards is one further Bulgarian find at Blagoevgrad in 1981.[40] This hoard contained a large number of exclusively Aesillas tetradrachms all — as far as Prokopov could determine — coming from GROUPS VI, VII, and VIII and thus reinforcing the growing body of evidence that reflects the existence of a distinct chronological gap between the earlier Aesillas issues of GROUPS I-V and the subsequent issues of GROUPS VI-VIII.

The cumulative force of this increasingly detailed hoard record is clear; and it very closely parallels the organization of the Aesillas type coinage that emerges from the detailed die study of some 1,000 surviving examples. The hoards show (1) that the coinage was introduced ca. 90, but (2) that the issues of that date (GROUPS I-IV) did not remain in circulation for long, being replaced by further emissions struck during the 80's and 70's (GROUPS V-VI), and (3) that, at the end of the 70's or beginning of the 60's, the CAE PR of GROUP VII and the sloppy issues of GROUP VIII appeared and brought the coinage to an end.

But the question remains. How does this numismatic evidence help to clarify Roman policy? What can it tell us about Roman aims in Macedonia and Thrace during the first half of the first century B.C.?

The distribution of known hoards is clearly limited to the river valleys leading north from Macedonia into Thrace. The valley of the Strymon River forms a kind of western boundary and the Hebrus River system an eastern limit south of the Balkan Mountains. During the less than 50 years. — between ca. 90 B.C. and ca. 50 B.C. — that the Aesillas coinage was in circulation and being hoarded, the coinage did not travel outside of this restricted geographical range. When this fact is combined with the hoard evidence, which further indicates that the Aesillas issues themselves had very limited time in circulation — I mean here that the first GROUPS of Aesillas issues struck ca. 90 are only exceptionally found in hoards of the 70's and are not found at all in hoards of the 60's and 50's — it becomes clear that the Aesillas coinage could not have been intended to replace the major coinages circulating in the Eastern Balkan peninsula during the late second and early first centuries B.C. It simply wasn't produced in sufficient volume

40 Blagoevgrad 1981 is listed above, no. 11 with n. 18.

and did not stay in circulation long enough once issued. However, all of these facts: the distribution of hoards, the composition, and the limited volume, make perfect sense if we interpret the Aesillas coinage as a specially produced medium for tribute payments to the Thracian tribes of the region.

Prokopov has proposed that the principal recipients of the Aesillas coinage were the Denteletae, who controlled the upper reaches of the Strymon River valley;[41] but of course, the Denteletae would not have been the only tribe that received, and quickly buried, the Aesillas types. Diodorus, for instance, reports that between 93 and 87, a certain Cotys, king of the Thracians, intervened in the interests of the Romans and detained a certain Euphenes, the son of Excestus, who had declared himself king of the Macedonians and exhorted the populace to revolt against Rome and restore Macedonia's former independence.[42] In return for his timely service, Cotys' reward from the Romans could certainly have included money that the Thracian king subsequently distributed among favored followers who in turn buried the windfall in the territory they controlled. In short, the idea that the Aesillas coinage was intended for payments to the Thracians is supported not only by the geographical distribution of hoards with Aesillas but also by other, more subtle, numismatic and historical evidence.

But why did the Romans do it? Why did they create a special medium for payments to the Thracians? The answer, I believe, must be that they were determined to keep the Via Egnatia safe for the trans-shipment of troops and materials for the war with Mitridates VI, and the familiar, heavy tetradrachm coinage type was the medium demanded by the tribes involved.

It was, then, only in the wake of Sulla's victories in Greece and the subsequent defeat of Mithridates VI that the Romans' own coinage, the denarii, appeared in Macedonia and Thrace, and gradually replaced the older coinages, including the Aesillas issues, that ceased being minted early in the 60's. By the onset of the Roman civil war in 49 B.C., the denarius was the principal silver coinage of the region accepted by Thracian chieftans and Macedonian citizens alike.

---

41 See Prokopov (above, n. 7), pp. 3-11.

42 Diodorus 37.5a. Euphenes reportedly raised a force bent on taking booty, but Excestus warned Sentius, the Roman governor of Macedonia, and asked Cotys to dissuade his son from pursuing his anti-Roman enterprise. After Cotys detained Euphenes for a few days the crisis was averted and Euphenes was ultimately acquitted of charges levelled against him. Chiranky, p. 480, also concludes that Diodorus' Cotys is the most likely candidate to be identified with the Thracian king named Cotys who laid claim to territory belonging to Abdera and forced the matter to arbitration by the Romans (*SIG*[3] 656).

ARCHÉOLOGIE ET NUMISMATIQUE EN ALBANIE: REMARQUES SUR L'ACTIVITÉ MONETAIRE AU IV-II SIECLE

Sh. Gjongecaj

L'archéologie est l'une des branches les plus jeunes de la science historique albanaise. Elle est née après la seconde Guerre mondiale et a parcouru une voie de développement à des rythmes accélérés. L'archéologie albanaise a formé et consolidé sa physionomie pas comme une partie intégrante, proprement dit de l'histoire, mais comme une réalité, comme une science. Le travail des archéologues se caractérise d'efforts sérieux pour une étude plus approfondie d'un certain nombre de problèmes d'importance scientifique et nationale dans l'histoire ancienne de notre pays, à partir de la formation de l'éthnie illyrienne jusqu'a la formation des nationalités albanaises. Notre archéologie a développé et consolidé les études dans de nouveaux domaines, telle que l'épigraphie et la numismatique et elle a crée des liens fructueux interdisciplinaires avec les sciences voisines, telles que l'anthropologie, l'histoire de l'art, la topographie, l'histoire de la langue, et d'autres. L'élévation du niveau qualitatif et quantitatif de toute l'activité s'est traduite également dans l'accroissement du nombre des publications périodiques et monographiques des conférences et des sessions scientifiques.[1]

Avec les résultats fructueux de ses recherches et ses études, grace à la présentation et l'analyse d'un grand nombre d'arguments recueillis lors des fouilles archéologiques, la pensée archéologique albanaise a gagné une priorité totale, reconnue déjà dans les cercles scientifiques du domaine de l'illyrologie et de l'histoire des albanais anciens. L'archéologie albanaise est déjà devenue un facteur connu, apprecié au niveau international.

Dans l'activité des recherches scientifiques, à part les recherches dans le domaine de la préhistoire et dans celui du haut moyen-age albanais, une place particulière convient aux recherches dans le domaine de l'antiquité illyrienne. Citons dans ce sens les fouilles de plusieurs années dans une

---

1 A. Buda, "Les Illyriens du Sud un problème de l'historiographie", *Iliria* 4 (1976) 39-53.

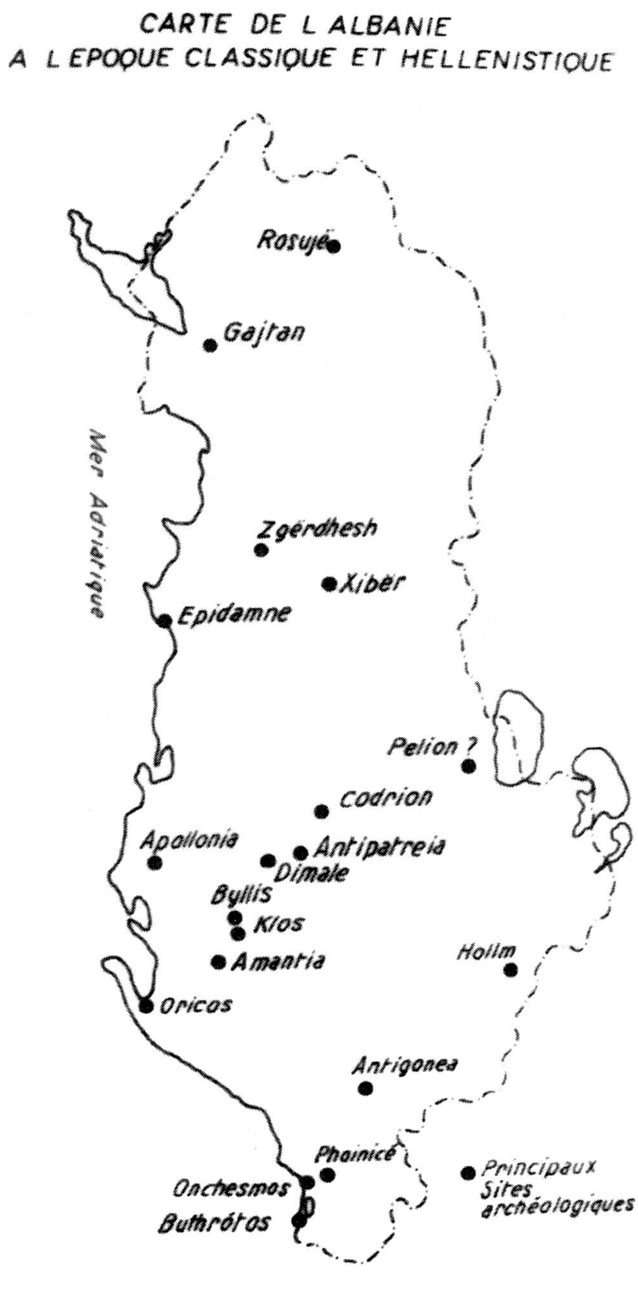

Fig. 1 Map of Albania.

série de villes illyriennes, telles que Butrinto, Antigonea, Cuka e AJtojt, Dimal, Bas Selca, Bylis, Lisis, Zgerdesh, Xibri, Irmaj et d'autres.[2] (voir *Fig. 1*)

Les découvertes faites dans ces villes ont jeté de la lumière sur des aspects du développement économique, social, politique et culturel des illyriens dans l'ordre de l'esclavage. Une attention particulière a été attachée à l'origine de la formation de la ville illyrienne, aux diverses étapes de son développement, aux caractéristiques at aux liens qu'elle a eu avec le monde antique méditerranéen.[3]

Les fouilles effectuées dans les centres citadins illyriens et dans les villes-colonies de la côte, Dyrrachion, Apollonia et Orikos, ainsi que les découvertes d'occasion ont contribué au recueillement d'un riche materiel numismatique, à part les terres cuites, les ornements, les armes et les materiaux de construction.[4] D'où l'origine du cabinet numismatique qui conserve une riche collection qui se distingue non seulement pour le grand nombre des monnaies, mais aussi pour la diversité des émissions. A part les études sur les émissions des monnaies de Dyrrachion et d'Apollonia, on fait également des études sur les émissions des monnaies des cites, des royaumes et des communautés illyriens.[5]

L'objectif de cette communication est de mettre en évidence l'activité monnétaire des ateliers locals plus importants et de tirer quelques conclusions, dans la mesure où cela nous est permis par un traitement unilatéral, le cadre duquel deviendrait plus complet à travers le traitement en général de la circulation monétaire en Illyrie du Sud.

Aujourd'hui la situation a heureusement changé; grâce à la découverte de nombreux trésors monétaires, grâce à leur publication selon des méthodes scientifiques, grâce aussi à des études particuliaires consacrées aux émissions de certains ateliers il est maintenant possible de reconstituer l'histoire de la circulation monétaire dans la période du IV siècle-fin du IIe av.n.è.

Prémière période vers le milieu du IVe siècle -moitié du IIIe siècle avant notre ère.

Cette période coincide avec le début de l'activité monétaire des colonies grecques de Dyrrachion et d'Apollonia. Les monnaies frappées dans les

2 S. Islami, "Naissance et developpement de la vie urbaine en Illyrie", *Iliria* 2 (1972) 7-23.

3 A. Mano, "Le commerce et les artères commerciales en Illyrie du Sud", *Posebna izdanja, Knjiga* 24, 165-173.

4 A. Mano, "Problemi della colonizazzione ellenica nell'Illiria meridionale", in *Modes de contacts et processus de transformation dans les sociétés anciennes. Actes du Colloque de Cortone, 1981, Pisa* (Rome 1983) 227-238.

5 H. Ceka, *Questions de numismatique illyrienne* (Tirana 1972).

ateliers de Dyrrachion et d'Apollonia durant cette période jettent de la lumière, avant tout, sur le développement et l'épanouissement économique de ces villes dans diverses étapes de leur vie. Dans ce sens leur mot est d'un important poids. Elles nous fournissent des données d'une grande valeur sur les rapports commerciaux de Dyrrachion et d'Apollonia avec les régions illyriennes et les autres peuples des Balkans et du bassin de la Méditerrannée et sur le niveau de l'intensité qu'on atteint ces liens économiques dans diverses périodes.

Le marché d'Apollonia, de Dyrrachion et des territoires illyriens tout au tour est dominé au début par les statères du type corinthien de Dyrrachion et d'Apollonia (le type Pegase/la tête d'Athena avec la casque corinthienne et l'ethnique ΔΥΡ, ΔΥΡΡΑΧΙΝΩΝ et ΑΠΟΛ). Leur frappe aurait commencé au moment de l'expédition de Timoleon en 344.[6] Pour le choix des symboles de ces types l'atelier monétaire de Dyrrachion s'en tient aux traditions héritées corinthiennes et il équipe les statères des symboles figurés connus, pegase et Athena.

Les deuxiemes statères autonomes frappés par Dyrrachion et Apollonia ont le même poids; elles ont comme symbole la vache allaitant son veau et le motif floral de même que les statères frappés dans l'atelier de Corcyra avec lequel il existait non seulement des liens du sang et de paternité mais aussi des interêts réciproques, ce qui oblige les deux parties de continuer la coopération dans le domaine économique.[7]

Les statères autonomes en argent de Dyrrachion portaient initialement la première lettre de la ville Δ, tandis que plus tard, vers la fin du IVe siècle lorsque avec l'épanouissement et l'elargissement plus poussé des relations de commerce dans une bonne partie du monde antique, sa monnaie parvient à avoir un bon cours dans le marché antique, sur le revers de la monnaie apparait l'ethnique réduite ΔΥΡ. L'éthnique est accompagné d'ordinaire par une massue, principale arme de Héracles, le fondateur de la ville. Ces monnaies sont frappées en grandes quantités et sous diverses variantes qui portent souvent sur le revers diveres images symboliques.

Ces statères en argent plus anciens, frappés dans l'atelier de Dyrrhachion et d'Apollonia, tout comme ceux de Corcyra suivent le système monnétaire d'Egine. Leur poids normal varie de 10,40-11,40 gr.

Les statères d'Apollonia n'ont pas, du point de vue stylistique, de différence marquante par rapport aux statères du même type de Dyrra-

---

6 C.M. Kraay, *Archaic and Classical Greek Coinage* (London 1976) 126-129.

7 A. Maier, "Die Silberpragung von Apollonia und Dyrrachion" *Numismatische Zeitschrift* 1 (1908) 1-33, voir surtout H. Ceka, *Probleme te Numismatikes ilire* (Tirana 1968) avec un catalogue des monnaies.

chion; la seule signe qui permet de les distinguer des statères de Dyrrachion l'ethnique ΑΠ ou ΑΠΟΛ et le remplacement de la massue, l'attribut de Heracles, par l'arc, attribut d'Apollon. Les tridrachmes d'Apollonia, par rapport à ceux de Dyrrachion sont très rares, mais aussi très pauvres en ce qui concerne leurs variantes. La cité d'Apollonia a maintenu, durant toute sa vie de ville libre, des liens étroits avec Dyrrachion, relations qui, durant les prémiers siècles de leur vie, avaient plutôt le caracrère d'une dépendance économique et politique. Leur grande ressemblance stylistique fait croire que les statères d'Apollonia ont été modelés par le même maître que celui de Dyrrachion.

La pauvreté de l'émission des statères d'Apollonia par rapport à celle de Dyrrachion est expliquée par le fait que le statère d'Apollonia n'était pas en état de concourir celle de Dyrrachion, par conséquent l'atelier d'Apollonia a très vite cessé leur émission.

Il y a toujours eu des discussions sur le début de l'émission des statères de Dyrrachion et d'Apollonia. H.Ceka qui s'est occupé de leur étude les date aux années 430-350.[8] Il est certain que ces dates sont trop hautes.

Le seul trésor qui peut jeter de la lumière sur leur date est celui de Kreshpan, (à 30 km au sud-est d'Apollonia). Il est composé de 206 pièces de monnaies d'argent et principalement de statères, didrachmes et drachmes du type corinthien (Corcyre 18 statères, 8 drachmes, Dyrrachion 91 statères, 49 drachmes, Apollonia un statère et le roi Monounios 39 statères).[9]

Dans l'ensemble, la principale place revient au trésor de Dyrrachion avec 68% et ensuite à celui de Monounios avec 18%, suivi par Corcyre 12,6%. Ce trésor est le premier de ce genre, il comporte des statères frappés par le roi illyrien Monounios(mentionné par Trogu Prol 24), statères frappés avec les mêmes symboles et lemême poids que ceux de Dyrrachion. Ils diffèrent de ceux-ci uniquement par l'emploi de l'ethnique ΒΑΣΙΛΕΩΣ ΜΟΝΟΥΝΙΟΥ.

L'analyse typologique et stylistique des émissions de ces ateliers, l'analyse historique aussi de ce trésor rejète l'idée avancée sur la date du début de l'émission des statères de Dyrrachion et d'Apollonia. La présence dans ce trésor des monnaies du roi Monounios, la période de la domination duquel s'étend entre les années 290-270 avant notre ère est très significa-

---

8 B.V. Head, *Catalogue of Greek Coins. Corinth, Colonies of Coritnth, etc.* (London 1989), A. Maier, *art. cit.*, 12; H. Ceka, *Probleme te Numismatikes ilire* (Tirana 1968) 15-19; *SNG Evelpidis* (Louvain-Belgique 1975) pl. CXLVII.

9 N. Ceka, "Die Personalichkeit des illyrischen Konigs Monounius auf de Basis von archaologischen Daten", *Iliria* 2 (1989) 41-46; a donné un premier apercue. Sh. Gjongecaj donnera un publication intégrale dernièrement dans Iliria.

tive. Il est difficile de penser que les statères de Dyrrachion et d'Apollonia soient frappés au delà du IVe siècle avant notre ère, et plus juste après les frappes de type corinthien Pegas-Athina.

Il n'y a pas dans le trésor de Kreshpan aucune pièce de drachme d'Apollonia et de Dyrrachion. Il parait que vers le premier quart du IIIe siècle, l'atelier de Dyrrachion et d'Apollonia frappe les drachmes avec les mêmes symboles que les statères.

La transformation profonde qu'a connue la structure économique et sociale de l'Illyrie du Sud par suite des transformations qui on créé une perspective convenante à la circulation et la distribution des monnaies en profondeur, a poussé Apollonia et Dyrrachion tenir compte des demandes du marché en uniques monétaires de valeurs inférieures; ont vu ainsi le jour le drachme en argent et le démidrachme qui gardent les mêmes emblèmes symboliques.

Les drachmes de Dyrrachion et d'Apollonia diffèrent des statères et des drachmes de la même période de Corcyre, portant les mêmes emblemes par le droit et le revers, les noms des magistrats, fonctionnaires chargés de l'emission des drachmes et du controle de toute l'activité monétaire. L'unification totale typologique et stylistique et le poids égal des drachmes d'Apollonia et de Dyrrachion fait penser à une coopération monétaire au début de leur activité monétaire qui est liée à lémission des statères et des drachmes d'argent.

Grâce à cette coopération les drachmes d'Apollonia sont présentes, de paire avec les drachmes de Dyrrachion jusqu'aux coins les plus reculés des Balkans. Pourtant, aussi bien dans les régions illyriennes que dans les autres zones des Balkans du nord, les drachmes d'Apollonia, par rapport à celles de Dyrrachion, sont moins nombreuses; c'est un indice significatif de la superiorité de Dyrrachion dans ses relations commerciales avec les régions, mais aussi de son pouvoir économique par rapport à Apollonia.[10] Il y a jusqu'à présent 440 diverses émissions de drachmes connues pour Dyrrachion et seulement 130 emissions pour Apollonia, un rapport de 3,5 à 1 environ.[11]

---

10 B. Mitrea, "Monodele oraserol Dyrrachium si Apolonia in Moldavia", *Studi si Cercetari de Numismatica* 2(1958) 27-90, "Alte drachme din Dyrrachion descoperite in Moldave si Drumu Ler de Pâtrundere la est de Carpati. Tezaurul de la Grogesti", *Studi si Cercetari de Numismatica* (1991) 21-37. G.Poenaru-Bordea, "Circulation de monnaies d'Apollonie et de Dyrrachion en Dacie préromaine et dans la region du bas Danube", in *L'Adriatico tra Mediterraneo et penisnula balcanica nell'antichità*, Tarente (1983) 221. M. Torbagyi, "Trésor de monnaies de Dyrrachion, d'une localité inconnue de Hongrie", *Numismatica Kozlony* 88-89 (1989-1990) 3-12.

11 H. Ceka, *Questions de numismatique illyrienne* (Tirana 1972).

Quant aux émissions en argent, aussi bien pour les statères que pour les drachmes, Dyrrachion avait une supériorité quantitative marquante par rapport à Apollonia;[12] cette cité égalise Dyrrachion dans le domaine des monnaies en bronze, portant l'ethnique d'Apollonia inscrite en complet ΑΠΟΛΛΩΝΟΣ ou ΑΠΟΛΛΩΝΙΑΤΑΝ.

Les séries des bronzes de Dyrrachion et d'Apollonia commencent dès la fin du IVe siècle.[13]

Parallèlement à la mise en circulation des drachmes l'atelier de Dyrrachion et de paire avec lui l'atelier d'Apollonia aussi, pour répondre aux besoins du marché intérieur ont intensifié le monnayage de bronze. L'émission des monnaies en bronze était devenue une necessité dans les conditions des relations commerciales avec l'autre monde héllènique où l'émission des monnaies en bronze avait déjà commencé ainsi qu'avec les centres illyriens autour d'eux.

L'atelier de Dyrrachion a frappé 9 types de monnaies en bronze parmi lesquels le principal était Héracles-ses armes, Zeus-Trépied, Hélios-la proue de bateau. Les noms des magistrats qu'on lit sur la longue série des drachmes coincident presque toujours et sont identiques aux noms du revers des bronzes de Dyrrachion.

Cela signifie que tous les bronzes portant des noms de magistrats sont frappés en même temps que les drachmes.

Tandis que de Dyrrachion, on ne connait que 9 divers types de monnaies en bronze, Apollonia nous a offert presque le double et en plus, avec une richesse d'émissions qui laissent beaucoup en arrière Dyrrachion. Cette grande différenciation ne peut être expliquée que par le développement innégal économique et social de hinterlands respectifs des deux cités.

Chez la majorité des tribus illyriennes de l'arrière pays autour de Dyrrachion et en profondeur du pays au cours des IV-IIIe siècle les relations commerciales étaient realisées principalement à travers des échanges en nature, tandis que les chefs lieux économiques continuaient d'être dans la phase embryonale du développement en cité. Dans ces conditions elles n'acceptent en échange que la monnaie d'argent. Dans de telles circonstances, l'atelier de Dyrrachion était obligé de limiter l'émission des monnaies de bronze principalement pour l'emploi intérieur et dans une certaine mesure pour le commerce avec les zones au sud du Shkumbin, où par suite de l'activité d'une série d'autres ateliers puissants,

---

12 B. Mitrea, "Monodele oraserol Dyrrachium si apolonia in Moldavia", *Studi si Cercetari de Numismatica* 2 (1958) 93 signale un trésor de 800 drachmes de Dyrrachion et un d'Apollonia.

13 O. Picard, Sh. Gjonjecaj "Remarques sur la politique monétaire d'Apollonia au IIIe siècle", à paraitre dans *Iliria* 2 (1996).

avec Apollonia à leur tête, les monnnaies de bronze de Dyrrachion ne pouvaient pas pretendre une grande pénétration dans leurs marchés.

Au sud de la rivière de Shkumbin, dans les avant-terres derrière Apollonia, les conditions pour le développement du commerce de détail et par conséquent pour jeter sur le marché des monnaies de bronze, étaient crées dès le début de la période héllenique. Il y a dans ce bassin une série de cités épanouies, dont quelques unes, telle que Orikum, Bylis, Amantia et Olympas avaient crée aussi, au IIIe siècle des ateliers monétaires autonomes.[14]

Avec le commencement de l'activité monnétaire des ateliers des cités illyriennes (la moitié du IIIe siècle avant notre ère) commence une nouvelle période qui se poursuit jusqu' à la fin du IIe siècle avant notre ère.

Dans les circonstances de la mise sur pied de plusieurs ateliers monétaires, l'atélier d'Apollonia, centre économique le plus fort de tout le bassin, a bien sur mis en circulation des quantités beaucoup plus grandes de monnaies de bronze que Dyrrachion, voire même plus que l'état d'Epire.

La période entre la moitié du IIe siècle -la fin du IIe siècle avant notre ère peut être considerée comme le point culminant de développement numismatique en Illyrie du sud. A part des drachmes en argent et les monnaies en bronze d'Apollonia et de Dyrrachion circulent aussi les monnaies de bronze frappées par les cités illyriennes. On voit commencer leur activité monnetaire les cités illyriennes de bassin de la Vjosa, du golfe de Vlora, telle Amantia, Olympas et Orikum. Plus au nord, ce sont les cités de Skodra et Lis,[15] tandis que vers le sud un important rôle a été joué par la monnaie d'Epire.[16]

Le plus grand nombre des monnaies des cités illyriennes répondent à la typologie des monnaies de bronze d'Apollonia et de Dyrrachion. Dans ce groupe de cités, ile st à remarquer Orikum qui suit entièrement le système monétaire d'Apollonia, tandis qu'Amantia, Byllis et Olympas gardent leur typologie parallèlement aux influences épirotes et apolloniennes. Dans l'atelier monétaire de Scodra se fait sentir surtout l'influence de Dyrrachion.

---

14 H. Ceka, *Questions de numismatique illyrienne* (Tirana 1972), Sh. Gjonjecaj, "Le monnayage d'Amantia", *Iliria* 7-8(1978); C. Patsch, *Das Sandschak rat in Albanien* (Viene 1904) col 113-114 à donné un tableau de monnayage de Bylis.

15 S. Islami, "Le monnayage de Skodra, Lissus et Genthios", *Iliria* 2 (1972) 396-399.

16 P.R. Franke, *Die antiken Munzen von Epirus* (Wiesbaden 1961); Sh. Gjongecaj, "La circulation des monnaies de l'Epire dans les centres illyriens", in *L'Illyrie méridionale et l'Epire dans l'antiquité , Actes du Colloque International de Clermont-Ferrand, 22-25 octobre 1986* (1987) 223-226.

Independamment de ces influences, l'autonomie des cités illyriennes se fait sentir, non seulement dans l'emploi des legendes indépendantes mais aussi dans l'emploi des symboles (tels que les symboles du serpent, de la casque illyrienne, de la torche etc).[17]

C'est à cette période que remontent aussi 3 trésors de monnaies de bronze découverts à Apollonia et dans la région autour d'elle, ce qui témoigne de la puissance de la monnaie de bronze d'Apollonia dans la circulation monnétaire de l'époque.

Le trésor d'Apollonia 1964 est composé de 1158 pièces de monnaies, dont 981 pièces d'Apollonia bronzes moyens Apollon-Obelisque, 163 grands bronzes Artemis-Trépied, 1 Dionysos-corne d'abondance, 2 pièces Autel/Nymphaion-lyre, 3 pièces Athena-foudre.

A part les monnaies frappées dans l'atelier d'Apollonia, dans ce trésor il y a aussi des monnaies d'Ambracie (deux pièces) et d'Orik (neuf pièces).

L'autre trésor découvert toujours à Apollonia, en 1977, est composé de 102 pièces, toutes frappées en Apollonia, dont 24 pièces grands bronzes Artemis-trépied, 67 pièces bronzes moyens Apollon-obelisque et 11 pièces Dionysos-corne d'abondance.

Le troisième trésor est découvert à Cakran, à quelques kilomètres d'Apollonia. Il est composé de 2352 pièces, dont 2340 frappées dans l'atelier d'Apollonia (1630 du type Apollon-Obelisque, 549 Artemis-trépied, 160 Dionysos-corne d'abondance, une pièce Autel Nymphaion). Parmis les monnaies frappées en dehors de cet atelier il y a une pièce du Koinon Epirote du type Artemis-point de flèche, 9 pièces d'Orik Apollon - Obelisque, une seule pièce de Dyrrachion du type Hélios-la proue de bateau, une pièce de Scotoussa (Thessalie).[18]

Dans ces trésors il n'ya pas de monnaies frappées par les cités illyriennes d'Amantia, Bylis et Olympas qui se trouvent pas loin d'Apollonia. Leur absence doit être éxpliquée par le fait qu'elles sont frappées principalement pour leur marché intérieur.[19]

La situation est différente dans l'hinterland de Dyrrachion où il n'y a qu'un seul trésor, mais très significatif. Il est decouvert à Lleshan, à proximité d'Elbasan, où l'influence de Dyrrachion est très grande. Le trésor est composé de 2758 pièces, dont 2700 sont des monnaies de bronze, frappées à Dyrrachion, de type Zeus-trépied, en nom de magistrats.

---

17 H.Ceka, "Apropos de certaines questions de l'histoire illyriens à la lumière des données numismatiques", *Iliria* 6 (1976) 289-293.

18 Le publication integral de ces trésors se prepare par O. Picard et Sh. Gjongecaj.

19 Sh. Gjongecaj, "Le circulation de monnaies étrangères à l'Illyrie du Sud au cours des siècles VI-I av. J. Ch", *Iliria* 1 (1986).

Il y a également dans ce trésor des drachmes de Dyrrachion et d'Apollonia. D'Apollonia il y a 10 drachmes et une demi-drachme tandis que de Dyrrachion il y 2 drachmes, 4 demi-drachmes. Elles sont très usées et quelques unes subarates. Il y a aussi dans ce trésor un dénier romain daté par Crawford à l'an 61 avant notre ère, frappé par M. PISO MF FRUGI à Rome (Craw. 418). Il est à souligner le fait qu'il n'y a aucune monnaie de bronze d'Apollonia dans ce trésor. Les drachmes reviennent à la troisième période de leur frappe (après les années 168 avant notre ère).

On n'a pas l'intension d'analyser en détail ces trésors, puisque l'étude sur leur contenu se poursuit et on espère donc avoir de nouvelles données sur la date de frappe des monnaies de bronze; il compte pourtant mettre en évidence les zones claires de la circulation de la monnaie de Dyrrachion et d'Apollonia et leur influence en Illyrie du sud.

Au nord de Shkumbin, un rôle principal a été joué par la monnaie de Dyrrachion; la grande influence économique de cette cité se revèle dans la circulation intense de ces monnaies. La cité illyrienne de Scodra place dans la prémière monnaie la tête de Zeus et le trépied; cette monnaie a le même poids et la même mesure que la monnaie de Dyrrachion.

Tandis qu'au sud du Shkumbin se fait beaucoup sentir l'influence de la ville d'Apollonia ce qui se traduit non seulement dans les trésors que nous avons mentionnés ci-dessus, mais aussi dans les trouvailles numismatiques effectuées durant les fouilles, dans les centres illyriens au sud du Shkumbin.

Les trésors confirment de manière très nette qu'Apollonia et Dyrrachion ont une politique des monnayages de bronze totalement différente d'une cité, une politique parallèle pour la frappe de l'argent.

La principale place dans la circulation monnétaire en Illyrie du sud convient aux monnaies locales, surtout à celles de Dyrrachion et d'Apollonia.

Tandis que les monnaies frappées par les cités illyriennes d'Amantias, Bylis, Olympas, Orikos, Scodra, Lissus conservent mieux le caractère local.

Dans cette brève analyse il ne faut pas laisser de côté la monnaie épirote, surtout celle de Koinon, dont la zone de circulation est limitée dans la zône d'Epire et dans les cités à proximité de cette zône, telle que Amantia et Olympas.[20]

Mais ils ne sont pas exclus les cas où cette monnaie va vers le nord jusquà Elbasan et vers l'est jusqu'à Kamenica de Korca.

L'examen du matériel numismatique montre que dans les relations

---

20 B. Dautaj, "La forteresse de Mavrove et son identification avec la cité illyrienne Olympe", *Iliria* 1 (1981) 57-91.

économiques avec les cités illyriennes du bassin du la Vjosa l'Epire utilisait plutôt la monnaie de bronze, surtout celle du type Zeus-foudre, Artemis-fer de lanche, Diane-trépied, tandis qu'avec Apollonia l'argent Zeus-aigle.

Les fouilles faites dans la cité épirote d'Antigoné ont révelé 650 pièces de monnaies, dont 500 pièces environ remontent à la période du Koinon épirote et une très petite quantité à Apollonia et aux villes illyriennes, voisines d'Amantia, Bylis et Orikos, ce qui montre qu'Apollonia n'a pas eu d'influence dans cette zone.[21]

Dans cette communication on ne s'est pas arreté sur la circulation des monnaies étrangères, ce qui est presenté dans une étude particulière dans la revue Illiria 1, 1986.

Il résulte que la monnaie étrangère n'est jamais parvenue à satisfaire tous les besoins que dictait l'échange avec les centres citadins illyriens et elle n'a pas joué un rôle aussi important que celui de la monnaie locale, surtout aux IIIe et la fin du IIe siècle avant notre ère. Le second siècle se caractèrise par une expansion monétaire en dehors de l'Illyrie.Les III-la fin du IIe siècle avant notre ère constituent donc la période de la plus grande circulation de la monnaie, expression du developpement intense dans cette période de la vie économique, politique et sociale dans toute l'Illyrie du Sud.

21 Dh. Budina, "Antigonée d'Epire", *Iliria* 6 (1976) 327-346.

A BRONZE DIE FROM SOUNION

Peter G. Kalligas

The ancient Athenian state attached great importance to its coinage, a fact testified by the long series of silver coins which survive from the 6th century B.C. onwards. At the same time, the argentiferous region of Laurion on the S.E. tip of Attica, which provided metal for the coins, was an important part of the state.

Although numismatic studies, especially on Athenian coinage, have a long tradition scant attention has been paid to the mining and processing of Laurion silver. It is only recently, during the last few decades, that studies have begun to appear focusing in detail on the Laurion mines, on the places and methods of processing the metals, and on the social organization of the mines and of the workshops. This new departure is due, in large part, to the ground-breaking work of the late Constantinos Conophagos[1] and of my colleague Evangelos Kakavoyiannis.[2]

Although many aspects of ancient mining and the working of silver have now been understood as a result of such research, little is known about the technique of minting, about the tools and instruments employed by the ancient minters, or about the administrative organization of the ancient Athenian mints. For this reason, if for no other, the identification of a hitherto unidentified bronze die found many years ago in the shrine of Poseidon at Sounion[3] and kept today in the National Archaeological Museum at Athens (Inv. no. A.14926, Pl. 18a) could, I believe, throw light on the obscurity that still surrounds specific aspects of Athenian coinage.

Following preliminary digs by the German scholar W. Dőrpfeld,[4] the

---

1 C. Conophagos, Κάμινοι τήξεως καί τεχνική τῆς τηξεως των ἀργυρούχων etc. Πρακτυκά τῆς Ἀκαδημίας Αθηνῶν 49 (1974) 262-299 (with French resume); C. Conophagos, Τό αρχαίο Λαύριο και η Ελληνική τεχνική παραγωγής του αργύρου (Athens 1980).

2 E. Kakavoyiannis, *The Ancient Mines of Lavreotiki* (Athens 1988).

3 V. Stais, Ἀνασκαφαὶ ἐν Σουνίῳ, ΠΑΕ 1907, 103.

4 W. Dörpfeld, "Der Tempel von Sunion", *AM* 9 (1884) 324f.

two important neighbouring shrines of Poseidon and of Athena at Sounion were excavated more extensively between the years 1897 and 1912 by the ephor of antiquities Valerios Stais with the help of the architect Anastasios Orlandos. The results were published in a series of articles by the excavator and the finds were transferred to the National Museum.[5] These early excavations, however, were inconclusive, leaving many problems unresolved, problems which until recently had not been systematically studied. It is only lately that the Archaeological Society has returned to Sounion to recommence excavations.[6]

In 1907 V. Stais noted a small pit cut into the rock at the SE edge of the shrine of Poseidon, just outside the polygonal retaining wall and at a short distance from the classical temple.[7] This pit proved to be a "bothros" and contained a large number of discarded offerings. These included:

- around 100 small Geometric and Protocorinthian vases.
- around 50 faience scarabs.
- seals, egyptianized faience figurines, clay plaques, a bronze pendant representing the Syrian war-god Reshef, bronze arrow heads.
- and finally as the excavator himself noted: "... a bronze punch and other bronze tools for use in building".[8]

The excavator illustrated these finds in the final report, but did not describe them in any detail.[9] Nor, unfortunately, were these finds recorded in detail in the inventories of the National Museum. Instead they were listed according to the pictures in the publication. Moreover, many of the finds remained unindexed and without an inventory number. Clearly this important group of votive offerings still awaits a final publication. From the evidence gained, however, from the partial study of some of the offerings, and from the conclusions reached by the excavator, the deposit must have been buried prior to the Persian destruction of the shrine in 480 B.C., and the offerings have been dated to the 7th and 6th centuries.[10]

A survey of the condition of the bronze finds from Sounion during 1984-5 (while I headed the Collection of Bronzes at the National Museum) gave me the opportunity of undertaking a detailed study of the bronze

---

5 V. Stais, a) Ἀνασκαφαί ἐν Σουνίῳ, AE 1900, 113-150; b) Σουνίου ἀνασκαφαί, AE 1917, 168-213.

6 Ἔργον 1994, 27-31.

7 Stais (supra n. 5b) 194ff, pl. 4.

8 Stais (supra n. 3) 103.

9 Stais (supra n. 5b) 195, fig. 7.

10 Stais (supra n. 5b) 196.

punch.[11] It consists of a small intact cast bronze tool, 0.14 m. in length. It is oblong with a rectangular cross section, and has in the middle an oblong hole (0.02 × 0.008 m.) for what was almost certainly a wooden handle. The diameter of the tool gradually decreases from the middle to the edges which are vertically cut, thus creating a small rectangular area at each end (0.008 m. on the sides) *(Pl. 18a)*.

The fields of the two ends are similarly engraved with the simple decoration of four sunken triangles formed by four radiating axes, which do not converge at the centre. The area at one end (A) is badly worn and the relief cannot be clearly distinguished, while the area at the other end (B) is in good condition. At the end (B) it is possible to infer precisely how the surface relief was produced (most likely with a small chisel, when the metal was cold) *(Pl. 18b)*.

The engraved ends of the bronze tool were undoubtedly used for imprinting their relief surfaces. One end (A) was used first, and after its deterioration the tool was turned around. The second end (B) was still in good condition when the use of the tool ceased. It should be noted that neither end of the tool showed any signs of being worn by hammer blows. Nor did the tool show any sign of direct contact with other metal, either bronze or iron.

A study of the impressions made by the ends of the tool *(Pl. 18c)* indicate that they are identical with the emblematic-heraldic reverse of the earliest Athenian coins, known as the "Wappenműnzen".[12] An inspection of the tool from Sounion enables its certain identification as a punch (anc. στιγεύς) for the production of similar coins, probably drachmas, judging from the small dimensions of the engraved square.

This comparatively rare group of early Athenian coins, the Wappenműnzen, has been thoroughly studied, but question marks still remain concerning the method and purpose of their production.[13]

Firstly, in regard to the method of production, the absence of punches with types and the lack of written sources or iconographic evidence have lead scholars to deduce information from a close examination of the coins themselves as well as from a study of later dies.

A study of the coins suggests that the flan, while still hot, was placed between two engraved metal punches, an upper and a lower punch, and with a strong blow to the upper punch it was possible to achieve a

11 I would like to thank the head of the Vase Collection of the National Museum, Dr Ios Zervoudakis, for her help.

12 C.M. Kraay, *Archaic and Classical Greek Coins* (London 1976) nos 161-174, pl. 9.

13 Cf. M. Oeconomides, "Les 'Wappenmünzen' de la Collection G. Empédocles", *QTNAC* 16 (1987) 25-28.

simultaneous impression from both dies onto the flan. The lower punch, which carried the obverse type, the main side, was fastened into a fixed base (the akmon) and was called the "ακμονίσκος", while the upper, with the reverse type, was movable and was known as the "χαρακτήρ". These descriptive names are mentioned in an official document of the Athenian state, that of the accounts of the treasurers of the goddess Athena on the Acropolis for the year 398/7 B.C.,[14] where offerings and objects listed include: "αλαβαστοθήκη ξυλίνη άστατος (;) εν ηι οι χαρακτήρες καί ακμονίσκοι εισίν, εθ' ων τος χρυσός [στατηρες] έκοπτον, σεσήμανται τηι δημοσίαι σφραγίδι" (IG. II^2, 1408). This reference shows that at least by the end of the 5th century both punches, upper and lower, could be kept in a box and that the lower one could be removed from its heavy stable base. This allows us to infer that the base for the striking of coins, the "akmon", was not of metal but was probably made of wood. This was in contrast to the "akmon" of the blacksmiths, which certainly was of metal, since on it the hot metal was hammered, as is shown in the well known scene on the Attic black-figure amphora of ca. 510 B.C. now in Boston (Museum of Fine Arts).[15]

The "charakter" die, however, must have had a wooden cap, as can be deduced from the Sounion punch, which does not show traces of striking. The hammering must have been inflicted on the wooden cap, while the lower part of the punch with the engraved surface was left uncovered. Similar conclusions can be reached from the study of a bronze die with an engraved owl found in Egypt and now in the Athens Numismatic Museum.[16] This was used to produce Egyptian imitations of Athenian tetradrachms and J. Svoronos has correctly suggested that it was an upper punch.[17] The existence of a wooden cap would allow the user of the Sounion punch to reverse the tool after the face of the first die had been worn and use the second face.

A wooden handle passed through the centre of the tool, as is indicated by the existing hole. This horizontal axis allowed the movable punch to be held in position securely with both hands when it was struck. The responsibility for successfully striking the flan was, I believe, the work of

14 IG II^2, 1408 (=EM 7815+7816+7811) and 1409 (=EM 7817); SEG 32 (1982) 157; G. Dontas, *AE* 1955, 1-21 (esp. p. 13, no. 9).

15 *CVA* Boston, Museum of Fine Arts 1 (1973) pl. 37, 2 (neck amphora).

16 Numismatic Museum, Athens inv. 1904/5, L'21.

17 J.N. Svoronos, Σφραγὶς Αθηναϊκου Τετραδράχμου, in *Corolla Numismatica* (Oxford 1906) 285-295; C. Conophagos, E. Badecca, and C. Tsaimou, ΠΑΑ 51 (1975) 377-8, trans into French in *Nomismatika Chronika* 4 (1976). Tsaimou (AE 1980, 128-130) later returned to the original position of Svoronos.

the specialist minter, while the necessary blow was given by the assistant, as is depicted on the above mentioned black-figure scene of the blacksmith's workshop. A similar position and pose for the minter and his assistant shown on the picture of a coin workshop in the well known fresco of the Erotes in the House of the Vettii in Pompeii.[18] There an erote-artist holds the upper punch on the "akmon" with both hands extended, while the erote-assistant holds the hammer raised and is ready to strike.

I consider this pattern of "artist with assistant" to be more plausible than the suggestion that it was the artist alone who struck the punch, while keeping it stable with his other hand.[19] We must therefore conclude that the existence of a minter and his assistant is suggested by the archaic punch from Sounion, while recognising that the evolution of minting practices over the next centuries possibly brought about some changes and differences in the organization of mint workshops. The finding place of the punch, Sounion, also raises a number of questions concerning the minting of the first Athenian coins, the Wappenmünzen. The depositing of the punch at the archaic sanctuary of Poseidon at Sounion suggests that the person who deposited the punch was connected with sixth century Sounion. But was this placing of the punch in the shrine meant as a dedication, or was it for the purpose of safe-keeping the object? It is perhaps more natural to conclude that the first explanation is true, but the above mentioned evidence from the Athenian Acropolis prevents us from ruling out the second theory. If, however, it was a personal dedication, then this tool for minting coins is to be linked with a private minter or the owner of a mint workshop. On the other hand, if the punch was deposited there for safe-keeping, then it must denote some form of communal organization by which the state sought to place the minting tools in a secure and inviolable place, such as the shrine of a god. Unfortunately, the tool was found in a deposit among objects that had been disregarded at some earlier period and the tool's original position in the shrine is not known. The early date, however, of the objects, their type, as well as comparisons with other cases, suggest that it is more likely that they were originally offerings from the area of the altar, thus reinforcing the possibility of a personal dedication. The tentative outcome of these considerations is that this tool for minting coins was first in the hands of individuals in the Sounion region.

---

18 Naples, Museo Archeologico Nazionale. Cf. D. Cooper, *Coins and Minting* (Shire Album 1983) 3.

19 Cf. Z.H. Klawans, *An Outline of Ancient Greek Coins* (Wisconsin 1964).

We know from numismatic history that the Wappenmünzen were made exclusively of silver and can be dated to the years of the Peisistratid tyranny, in the second half of the 6th century B.C.[20] It is also known that in these years the exploitation of the argentiferous layers of Laurion was resumed. The reforms of Solon (Arist. *Ath. Pol.*, 10) established a context for the later use of Laurion silver (though the metal had been known since prehistoric times).[21]

Students of the Wappenmünzen have for many years now inquired into the possibility that this 6th century Athenian coinage, which has a regional character in terms of circulation, might be connected with the state, with religious events such as the Panathenaia festival, or with noble families and tribes.[22]

The extraction and processing of the silver ores surely demand the organization of the relevant workshops "in situ", as we know from the 4th century examples. Perhaps the discovery of a 6th century punch at Sounion is evidence that even during this early period the minting of coins was conducted in the neighbourhood of Sounion and not within the city of Athens. It may be that the first silver coins were minted at workshops located in the Laurion and then later brought to the city. It is also possible that since in the archaic period the minter-artist worked close to the source of the precious metal at the Laurion workshops, it would have been natural for him to offer at some occasion his working tools to the god of that region, to Poseidon Sounieus.

In a series of articles J. Svoronos has already attempted to establish the links between the Sounion shrine and the silver coinage via the worship of the Dioskouroi, and of the Stephanophoros hero.[23] He argued that in the classical period the silver used for minting as well as the minting tools (dies, punches) were stored in "Building Δ" of the enclosure of the Sanctuary of Poseidon. This attribution, however, must now be considered erroneous, since the buidling has been identified as a battlement for catapults dating to the years of the Chremonidian War (267-262 B.C.).[24]

20 Kraay (supra n. 12) nos 161-174, pl. 9.

21 N.H. Gale and Z.A. Stos-Gale, "Cycladic Lead and Silver Metallurgy", BSA 76 (1981) 169-221.

22 For earlier dates in older textbooks cf. C. Seltman, *Greek Coins* (London 1955) 43ff.

23 J.N. Svoronos, "Laurion - L'atélier monétaire des Athéniens dit du Stéphanéphoros", JIAN 17 (1915) 53-70; also JIAN 18 (1916-17) 109-130.

24 Tower "D" = J.H. Young, "An Epigram at Sounion", *Studies presented to D.M. Robinson*, II (St. Louis 1953) 353-7; H.F. Mussche, "Note sur les fortifications de Sounion", *BCH* 88 (1964) 423ff; J.A. Dengate, Observations on the Sounion Fortifications, *AJA* 71 (1967) 185; Catapults: V. Stais, *AE* 1900, 136; now Nat. Museum, Athens inv. Br. 12414 a-b; D. Baatz, "Teile hellenistischer Geschütze aus Griechenland", *AA* 1979, 68-75.

Despite Svorono's misattribution, his suggestion of early ties between the Sounion shrine and Athenian coinage deserve reconsideration.

The basic question, however, arises as to who was in charge of the minting and distribution of the first Athenian coins: individuals, or the state? The organization of the State in regard to these matters is known in the classical period when Laurion was public land which was rented by the State to individuals for the mining of silver. Individuals constructed the workshops and conducted the mining. From ca. 400 B.C. onwards there was a special building in the city, known as the "Mint", which was situated in the area of the ancient Agora close to the Panathenaic Way.[25] It was there that bronze coins were minted. The consistency and regularity of these issues suggests continuous state supervision and control.

Is it possible that in the archaic period the State was not yet responsible for coinage? Perhaps the whole procedure of minting silver coins during the 6th century was conducted in the Laurion in workshops which were still in the hands of individuals? Can the subsequent change, when coinage passed under state control, be attributed to the reforms instituted by Cleisthenes (508 B.C.), which were followed by the more intensive exploitation of the Laurion mines and the production of a larger number of coins in the era of Themistocles at the beginning of the 5th century B.C.?

We are not yet in a position to give final answers to the complex questions which are raised by the newly identified bronze die from Sounion but a reconsideration of the archaeological facts may lead to a better understanding of the historical sequence.

---

25 J.M. Camp, *The Athenian Agora* (London 1986) 128-135.

EPILOGUE

M. Oeconomides

L'organisation d'un symposium qui avait comme sujet les rapports entre numismatique et archéologie était pour moi, qui j'ai consacré une grande partie de ma vie scientifique à identifier des monnaies de fouilles, une bonne occasion d'évoque les collaborations que j'ai eues avec mes collègues grecs et de tous les pays.

Chaque rapport qui se trouve dans ces Actes montre combien la recherche numismatique est brillante aujourd'hui; une constatation qui me fait grand plaisir.

Je remercie chaleureusement les organisateurs de cette rencontre, ainsi que les éditeurs de ce volume, dont je connais tout le travail que cet édition leur a demandé.

Il devrait y avoir entre ses rapports, ceci d'un grand savant et un très bon ami, Martin Jessop Price, que la maladie nous a enlevé ἄωρος comme disaient les inscriptions antiques.

Mais nos travaux prouvent que, par delà la vie de chacun, notre entreprise commune d'exploration de la civilisation grecque doit continuer.

Mando Oeconomides

LIST OF FIGURES

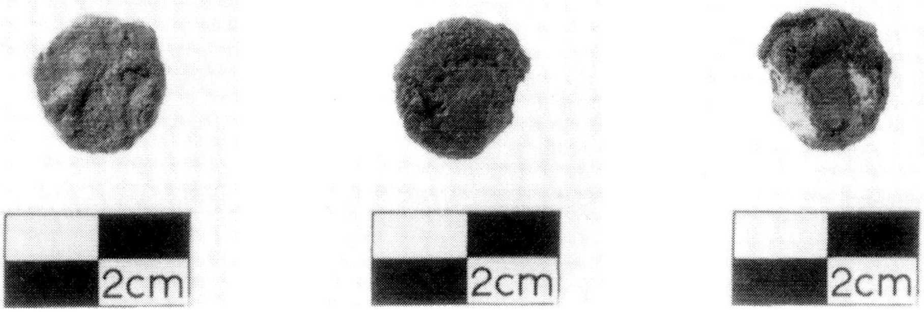

a *b* *c*

d

Pl. 1: a, Coin BE-1040, reverse (two owls on thunderbolt). b, Coin of Demetrios Poliorketes (ΣA-377), obverse. c, Coin of Demetrios Poliorketes (SA-377), reverse. d, Pit with Archaistic herm head in Roman stoa.

Pl. 2: Coins from burnt stratum in Roman stoa, obverses. First row: ***ΒΓ΄-221***, ***ΒΓ΄-222*** (Constantine I or son); ***ΒΓ΄-223*** (*Valentinian I or colleague*). *Second row:* ***ΒΓ΄-217***, ***ΒΓ΄218*** (Theodosius I); ***ΒΓ΄-219*** (*Valentinian* II *or colleague*); ***ΒΓ΄-229*** (*Valentinian* II); ***ΒΓ΄-230*** (*Arcadius*). *Third row:* ***ΒΓ΄-220***, ***ΒΓ΄-228*** (*4th century*).

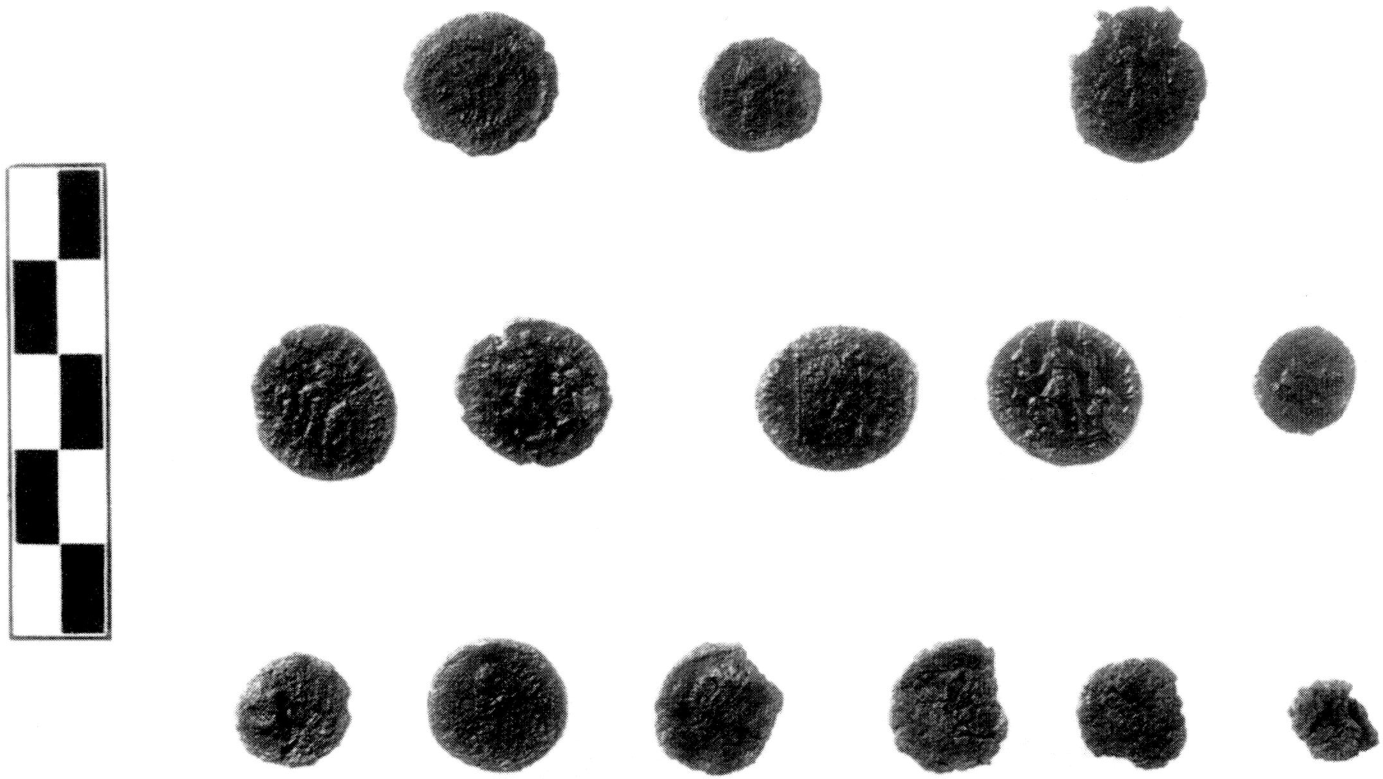

Pl. 3: Coins from burnt stratum in Roman stoa, reverses.

a

b

Pl. 4: a, Coins from pit with herm head, obverses. Upper row: ΒΓ′-199 (Valens); ΒΓ′-205 (4th century). Lower row: ΒΓ′-200 (Gratian or colleague); ΒΓ′-201, ΒΓ′-203 (Valentinian II); ΒΓ′-202 (Valentinian or colleague); ΒΓ′-204 (Arcadius). b, Coins from pit herm head, reverses.

a

b

c

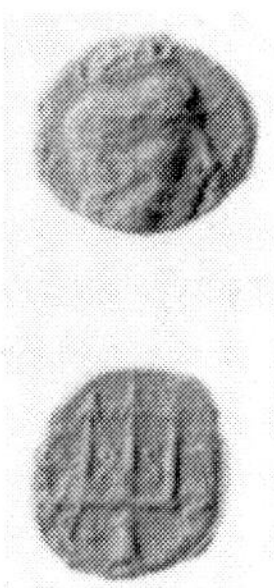

d

e

f

Pl. 5: a, Topiros: Buste de Géta à dr. / Empereur en costume militaire poussant du pied un prisonnier ***ΟΥΛΠΙΑΣ ΤΟΠΕΙΡΟΥ*** *(Nég. EFA, 2838, 7). b, Topiros: Tête de Caracalla à dr. / Héraclès assis à g., sur un rocher recouvert de la léonté* ***ΟΥΛΠΙΑΣ ΤΟΠΙΡΟΥ*** *(Nég. EFA, 2619, 16).c, Amphipolis: Tête d'Héraclès à dr. / sanglier et massue* ***ΑΜΦΙΠΟ ΛΙΤΩΝ*** *(Nég. EFA R2838, 11). d, Néapolis: Tête de la Parthénos à dr. / Trident* ***ΝΕΑ ΠΟΛ*** *(Nég. EFA R2619, 14). e, Bronze de Kese (Ibérie) (Nég. EFA L6085, 26). f, Royaume du Bosphore Cimmérien (254/5 ap. J.-C.): Tête de Rhescuporis V à dr.* ***ΡΗΣΚΟΥΠΟΡΙ ΒΑΣΙΛΕΩΣ*** */ Tête de l'Empereur à dr. NF (Nég. EFA E2619, 9). Photos enlarged.*

a

b

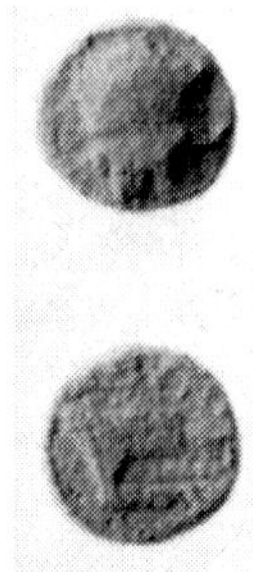

c

d

e

f

g

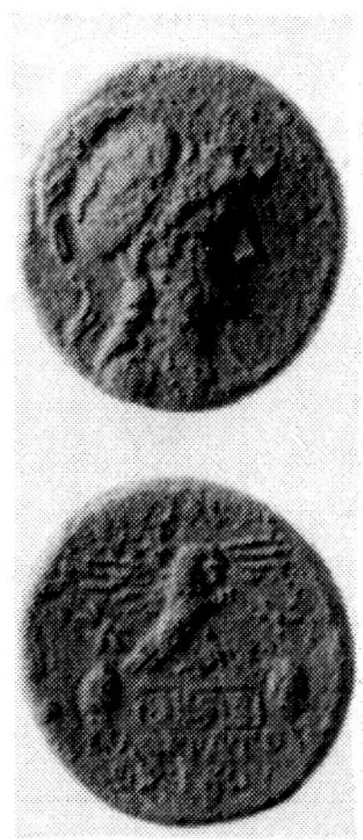

h

Pl. 6: a, Tarse: Tête de la cité à dr. / Pyré de Sandon. b, Alexandrie d'Egypte: Tétradrachme de Maximin. Buste de l'Empereur à dr. / Eiréné debout à g. (Nég. EFA L6089, 20a). c, Amyntas II (c. 394/3): Tête juvénile à dr. / Protomé de loup à dr. ***AMYNT*** *(Nég. EFA R2619, 14). d, Athènes: tétradrachme fourré (406/5) (Nég. EFA L6085, 17). e, Alexandrie de Troade (253-260): Buste de Valérien à dr. / Cheval paissant COL AVG TRO (Nég. EFA L6086, 18a). f, Alexandrie de Troade (253-260): Buste de la cité à dr. CO ALEX/ Apollon à g. devant un autel; un cyprè derrière lui COL AV TRO (Nég. EFA L6086, 21a). g, Apamée de Phrygie: Buste d'Hadrien à dr. / Buste à dr.* ***ΝΑΚΡΑ ΣΙΤΩΝ*** *(Nég. EFA R2619, 14). h, Nakrasa: Tête d'Athéna à dr. / Aigle à dr. au-dessus du Méandre, entre les bonnets des Dioscures* ***ΑΠΑ ΜΕΩΝ*** *(Nég. EFA R2619, 7). Photos enlarged.*

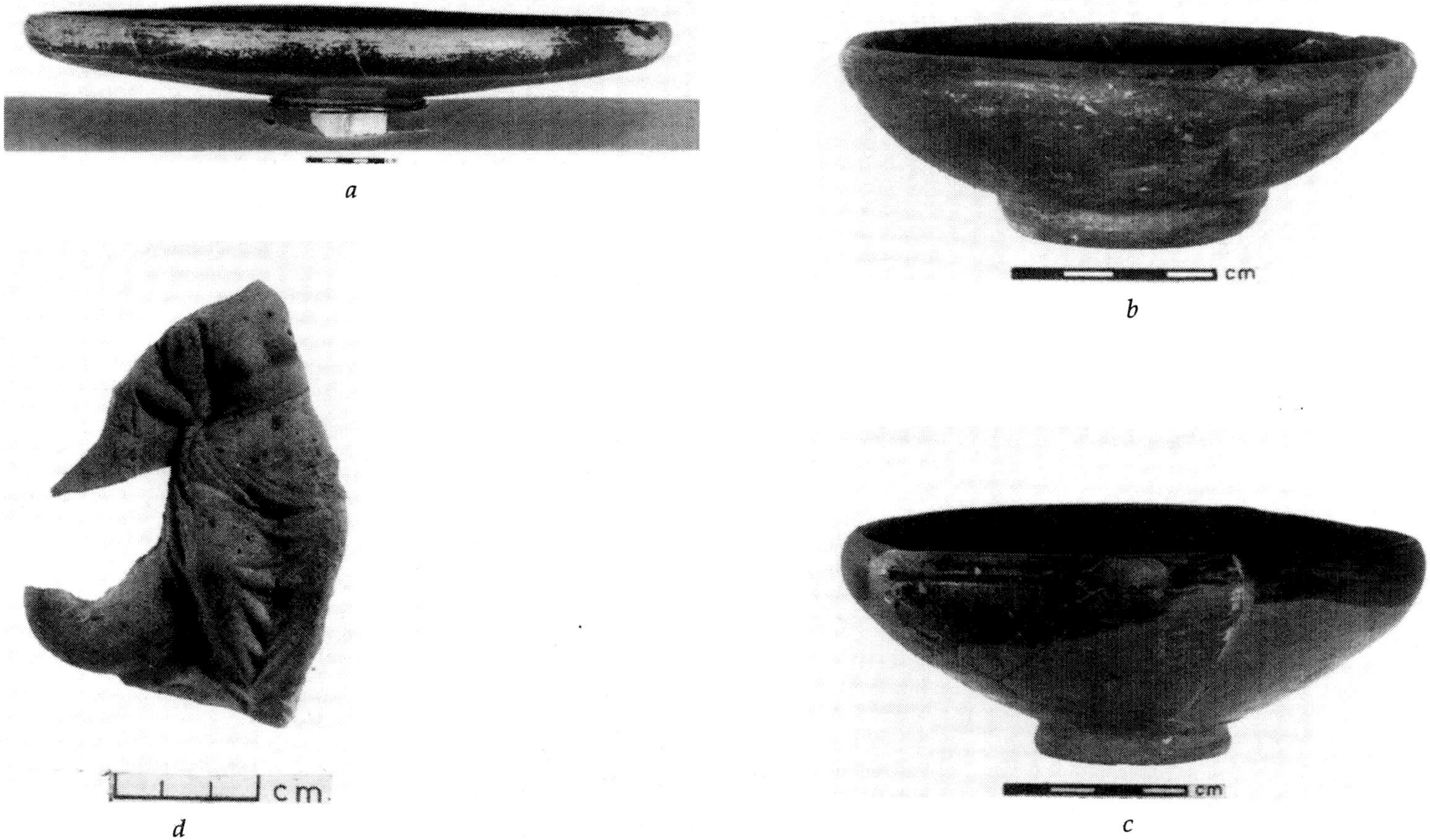

Pl. 7: a, Eastern Sigillata A ware plate. b-c, Two bowls of local colour-coated ware. d, Terracotta statuette of female on dolphin; Ht. 9.2 cm.

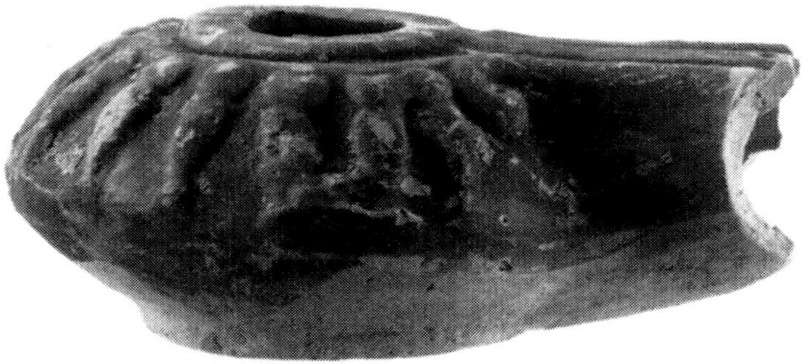

a

b

d

e

c

Pl. 8: a, Red slip lamp; length: 7.4cm. b, Rhodian stamped handle. c, Rhodian stamped handle. d-e, Seal impressions.

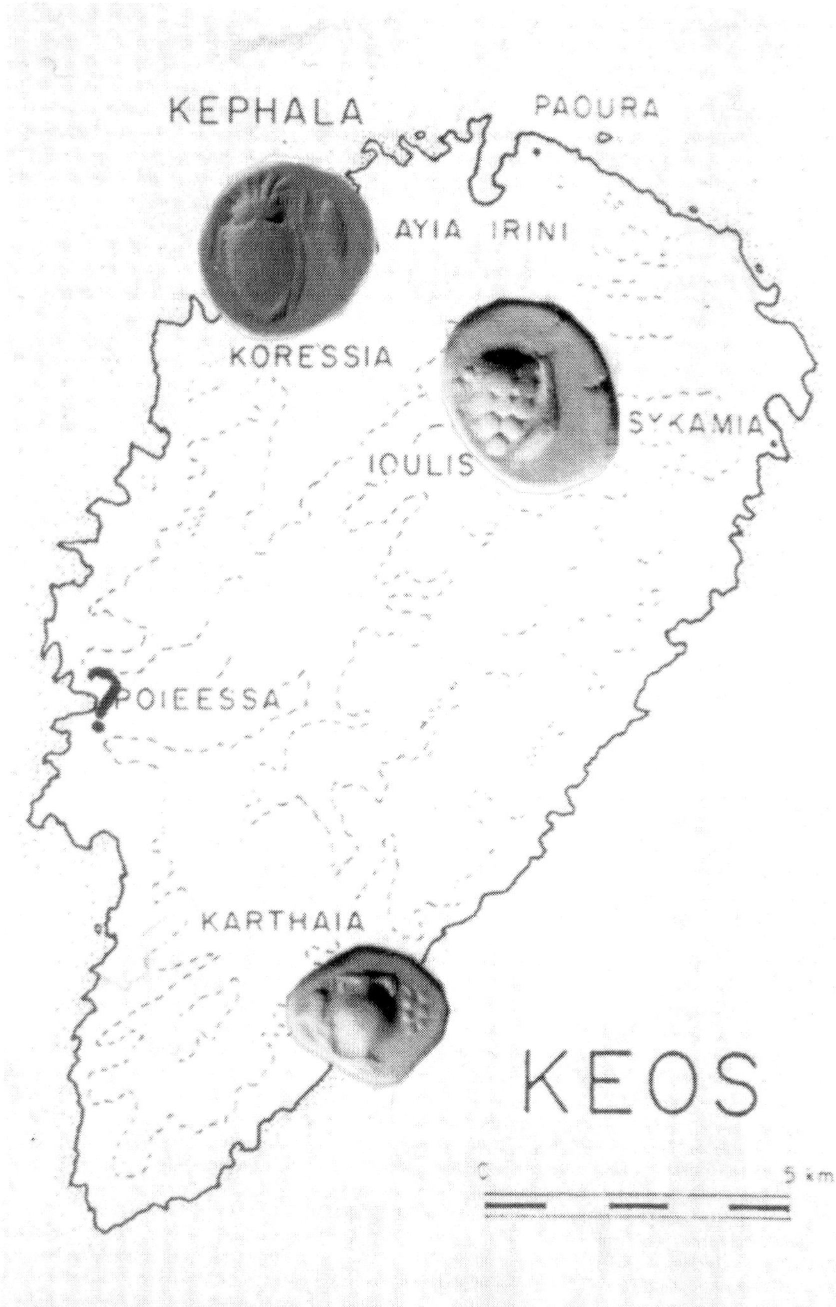

Pl. 9: *Τα νομισματοκοπεία της Κέας.*

a

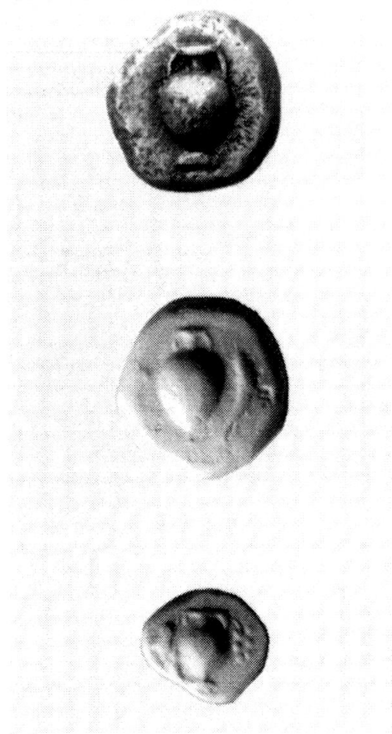

b

c

Pl. 10: *a*, *Κορησία*. *b*, *Καρθαία*. *c*, *Ιουλίς*.

a

b

Pl. 11: a, Syracuse ca. 410-370 BC; Gulbenkian Col; 42.12g.
b, Syracuse ca. 395 BC; Gulbenkian Col; 41.91g.

a

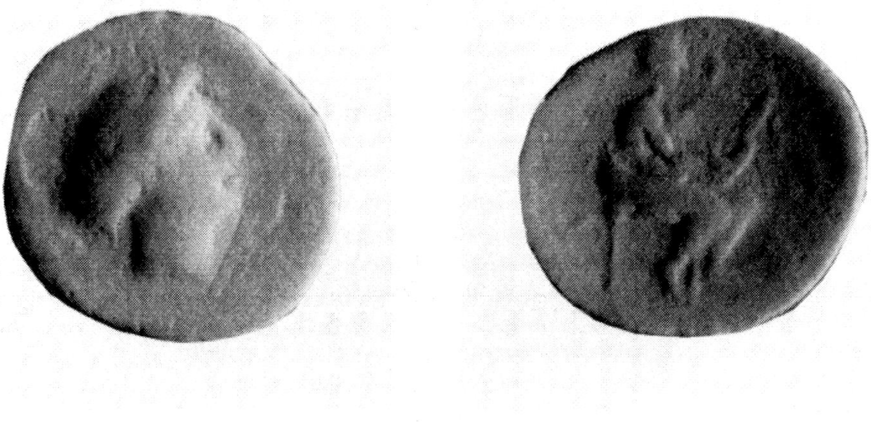

b

Pl. 12: a, Trikka, 4th century BC; Private Col. (cf. cover). Diam 1.2cm.
b, Trikka (?), 4th century BC; Berlin. Photo enlarged.

a

b

Pl. 13: a-b, Larisa Inv. 86/101. Detail of calyx krater by Painter of Munich 2335.

Pl. 14: Coins of poleis in the Achaian League. Photo enlarged.

Pl. 15: a, Uncertain; Santorin Hoard; London. b, Caria ?; Cyclades Hoard; London. c, Caria or Lycia ?; Cyclades Hoard; London. d, Caria; Santorin Hoard; London. e, Uncertain; Santorin Hoard; London. f, Lycia?; Santorin Hoard; London. Photos enlarged.

a

b

c

d

e

f

Pl. 16: Reconstructing the circulation of Roman coinage in first century BC Macedonia.

***a**, SW Macedonia 1981 Hd. (Above, Hd. no. 4) = A. Burnett,* Coin Hoards *VII (1986), 133, no. 25 16.61. **b**, Macedonia? 1980 Hd. (Above, Hd. no. 13) = A. Burnett,* Coin Hoards *VII (1986), 139, no. 93. **c**, R. Witschonke Coll. ex. J. Hirst Coll. = Macedonia 1986? Hd. (Above, Hd. no. 10) 15.84. **d**, Plovdiv, Mus. of History 2788 = Zlatograd 1967 Hd. (Above, Hd. no. 3;* IGCH *969). **e**, Gadoury, Monte Carlo Auction (13-15 Oct. 1980), no. 199 16.70. **f**, Jambol, Mus. of History = Strojno 1961 Hd. (Above, Hd. no. 2;* IGCH *924) = E. Schönert-Geiss,* Griechisches Münzprägung von Maroneia, Schriften zur Geschichte und Kultur der Antike *26 (Berlin, 1987), 106, no. 195.*

a

b

c

d

e

Plate 17

***a**, Athens, Numismatic Coll. = Kerassia 1959? Hd. (Above, Hd. no. 7;* IGCH *653) = I. Varoucha-Christodoulopouloou,* ADelt, Chronika *17 (1961/2), pl. 2, 5.* ***b**, Kjustendil, Mus of History, = Kjustendil? Hd. (Above, Hd. no. 16).* ***c**. Kjustendil, Mus of History, = Kjustendil? Hd. (Above, Hd. no. 16) [Enlarged].* ***d**, Athens, Numismatic Coll. = Platania 1959 Hd. (Above, Hd. no. 15;* IGCH *663).* ***e**, Athens, Numismatic Coll. = Platania 1959 Hd. (Above, Hd. no. 15;* IGCH *663).*

a

c

b

Pl. 18: a, Die found at Sounion (Athens NM A.14926), scale 1:1; b, Detail of end (B), scale 1:1; c, Die impression, scale 1:1.